VASTARIEN

A LITERARY JOURNAL

Volume Five, Issue Two

Jon Padgett, Editor-in-Chief

Paula Ashe, Associate Editor

Daniel Braum, Associate Editor

Alex Jennings, Associate Editor

GRIMSCRIBE PRESS

New Orleans, Louisiana

Cover art by David Bowman

Cover design by Anna Trueman

Published by
Grimscribe Press
New Orleans, LA
USA

grimscribepress.com

ACKNOWLEDGMENTS

Thanks to all our benefactors, particularly Robert Ankney, James Michael Baker, Lambrineas D. Epameinondas, Darren Fisher, Matthew Henshaw, JT Moniteau, Adam Rains, Tyson Sereda, and Webberly Rattenkraft.

ART BY BRIAN THUMMLER

Tenebrous Ramblings

by Romana Lockwood

I have seen much in the history of our little town.

I stood below the gallows constructed for the coterie of priests who took up arms against Town Hall, gallows consisting of four crosses with a hawthorn-rubbed noose thrown over each arm. I saw the holy men dragged down Old Wilson Road to their fates. I stared into the eyes (and he into mine) of Father Darmott, the priest whose neck somehow defied the hanging rope, who laughed a hoarse and recalcitrant laugh even as his cohorts swung like pendula, spinning and colliding with him and with one another, eyes and tongues sprung, throats stretched like the saltwater taffy they sold for a nickel down at Nan's Confections on Clark.

I have stood among neighbors whose toilets spouted great gouts of blood when Father Darmott returned shamed and caponized to his pulpit and resumed, despite his written and blood-signed oath, his damaging testimonies.

I saw coffins tipped onto the town green so that their demised inhabitants might answer for their posthumously discovered crimes, the rollicking insults done to their flesh and, readers, I myself wielded the flaying lash against the cadaver of Miss Constance Cobbs, whose crimes against me included Shooing my Cat with Rudeness, Harboring a Ghoul, and Backtalk.

I have seen the General Store, now a Toyota Dealership, ransacked, its wares spilt, despoiled, micturated upon, and befouled, for the issuance of a coupon they subsequently refused to honor, dubiously and inconsistently citing a printing error, a general misreading, and sabotage. I saw its owner, an important man in the town, driven out and forced to thank for sparing his life those who wielded the manure forks and cattle-prods. I saw the store taken over by William Jefferson Lord, who first wrote of the chicanery in a letter to the Gazette, and who brought the store within months to financial ruin when his credulousness collided with the rapacity of his vendors.

I have seen cankers grow on the pulled-down lip of the moon. I have seen the stone that chortles, the pond that leaps from its crater. I have seen the hatchet blade go soft at the utterance of a syllable, the bullet turned with a three-fingered gesture to black water before it reaches its target, the actor's soliloquy bowdlerized by the will of an offended warlock even as it was spake.

So, I've been around.

But, reader, there are occurrences of which I will not speak, for to share them with you would not only put myself in danger, but, having drawn you into my circle, would potentially harm you as well. The town does not want you to know. But I do.

Readers, let me use the remainder of my allotted space to convey my deepest apology for my last column. Once I completed it, still suffering the aftereffects, I sent it off to my editors, expecting them to reject it, perhaps replacing it with an earlier column, or something from their files, perhaps the prosaic reminiscences of one of my contemporaries, the kind who earnestly discuss vapid books in library colloquies, share stultifying casserole recipes couched in uninteresting family lore, or make inane gardening analogies as a way of coping with life's insults. The fact that they ran my shameful column unedited suggests to me that they're not paying attention. But my aim is not to place the blame on them.

When Evasive James heard tell of the column—in my addlepated state, I had forgotten, or perhaps didn't care, that to name Evasive James is to summon Evasive James—he came to me, as he does, as an unseasonable dawn frost, then as a shadow where no light was thrown, then as a spasm in certain muscles that caused me to convulse in such a way that I managed to dislocate my shoulder. The triad of young EMTs arrived quickly and were solicitous, kind, and forgiving, even as I cursed at them and attempted, without much in the way of efficacy, to repel them physically. Once they had performed their ministrations, which were painful yet productive, and I had convinced them a trip to the hospital was unnecessary, and they were packing up to leave, all of them turned to me with their eyes rolled up to red-veined whites and chanted the Censure Chant as first uttered by Green Edward, the famed devotee of Horace vier Wunden, who split to form his own debased (and widely discredited) faction of the Kindhearted Order of Blue-Striped Jackals.

One of their number was incapacitated by the spell of Evasive James, and so I was forced to suffer their presence for another half hour before I could do the Dance of Penitence, which, I was more than aware, risked further injury and the return of other EMTs. Also, any further manipulation of EMTs or any rescue personnel could lead to a certain exposure. So, my dance was impassioned, but cautious. Whether my dance was accepted—well, that I shall have to wait until tonight's dreams to know.

And in the event that my dance was not accepted, a very real possibility, I'm afraid, then this shall be my final column. In either case, I want you to know that I am indeed sorry. Your forgiveness or lack thereof will not affect my fate, but I ask it nonetheless. I said some nasty things in there, and I don't know that my state of accidental unmedication is an excuse—to me, it sounds like a further reason to condemn me.

In the meantime, I am planning for the future whether or not I have one. I am casting about to find a live-in carer to see that I take my medication, that I eat properly, that I don't leave a stove burner going and burn down the place, that I tend properly to my toilet. One dislikes incursions on one's independence and one's privacy, but I have always prided myself on knowing what is right for me and acting upon it, despite everything.

If the next column is Fanny Carmichael's Classic Casseroles and Family Squabbles Resolved to the Satisfaction of All Parties, you shall know my fate. It is my dearest hope that in that case at least some of you will believe that an injustice has been done. I must go. Evasive James wants a little of my time, and I'm loath to refuse him.

ART BY BRIAN THUMMLER

Little Lamb, Who Made Thee

LC von Hessen

Before every long weekend with Uncle Norton and Aunt Miri, the Metzger children were firmly reminded by their parents to Be Good. Jessie in particular was admonished to Be Nice even though any sudden thwack to the skull from an airborne Power Ranger in the Metzger household could be traced back to the sticky fingers of six-year-old Seth. True to form, he'd been squirming and writhing like a worm on a hook during the three-hour drive to the town of Brookhaven. Jessie sighed as the family sedan pulled into the driveway, tugged at the hem of the pastel dress she'd been instructed to wear.

Brookhaven was a nondescript suburb only notable for an obscure serial killer who had lived there in the early 1900s, almost a century ago, when it was still all farmland. Nowadays this rather embarrassing fact was only attested to by a few corroded placards bolted into trees by the roadside where his victims' bodies were found and which Jessie always tried in vain to read through the car window. Among the Metzger children's ancestors on their mother's side was one of the town's elders, their grandfather's grandfather, whom Jessie only knew from a brown-and-white photograph of an old man with a drooping beard like the wispy fake spiderwebs trotted out on Halloween: he stood before the camera wielding a large handheld hook and a soft, knowing smile outside of a peeling clapboard bungalow.

For as long as she could remember, Jessie had had to spend one long weekend a year with her aunt and uncle in Brookhaven while her parents went on vacation at a rented cabin on the lake. Among her increasing hoard of grown-up knowledge was the suspicion that Seth must have been conceived on one of these trips, especially after her discovery of a book in her mother's nightstand called *How Can We Light a Fire When the Kids are Driving Us Crazy?* Yeah, her parents went to the lake so they could totally Do It.

Jessie had never been to this lake house herself. It was located in a town that did not, as far as she knew, include any famous murders in its history. Perhaps there were drowned people drifting about on the bottom of the lake, puffing up like sad balloons as their flesh was nipped away by fish, but this was a Not Nice notion she didn't tell Seth or her parents.

Uncle Norton stood on the front step, hands on hips, with Aunt Miri trailing behind. Her gait was always slow and cautious owing to her pronounced limp. This was a staged greeting, just for show since they entered their home through the garage. The front door was for deliveries, salespeople, and guests.

Uncle Norton was bald and very tall, as though his hair had been singed off by the sun. His skin, especially on his exposed crown, was deep pink with pale brown spots like the potted meat in a tin of Spam. His smooth, dry lower lip jutted from a beard of grey-streaked white. He had the same dark round eyes as Jessie's mother, pressed into the face like buttons.

Uncle Norton, the eldest of six, was already off at college when Jessie's mom was born. To Jessie, he had always been an Old Man.

He scooped up Seth, who sprang out of the sedan with coiled six-year-old energy, and spun him around as he laugh-screamed. He then turned to Jessie and, without warning, briefly lifted her up by the armpits a couple of feet off the ground, even though she was too old and tall for that now and it was physically uncomfortable and strangely embarrassing. She was 11 years old and wore a training bra. She was going to *middle school* next year. She wasn't a baby anymore and didn't want to be treated like one. Yet big, loud men brought out an innate shyness in herself that she was increasingly coming to resent.

"Jessica!" Aunt Miri cried in her craggy old-lady voice.

"It's Jessie . . ." she muttered into her sleeve.

Aunt Miri with her anachronistic brown-black beehive hairdo that Jessie had known for years was a wig. Aunt Miri who sheathed her lanky frame in long, billowing skirts nipped in at the waist and guarded her sharp collarbone with a string of dull pink pearls. Aunt Miri whose face—with its lavender-white flesh, beady wet eyes, aquiline nose, and narrow but sharply-curved upper lip that closed on squarish front teeth—gave an overall impression of some overgrown species of rodentia.

Jessie had once drawn a picture of Aunt Miri as a kind of human-stork hybrid, balanced on a single skinny leg and *caw-caw*ing like a crow, which had made her mother stifle a laugh before instructing Jessie never to show it to anyone else. *Be Nice.*

Say please *and* thank you. *At the dinner table, don't just grab things and get up whenever you like, the way you do at home; it must be* please pass the butter *and* may I be excused (which Jessie would never ask, because it would have been utterly humiliating to be told *no, you may not*). And a further instruction: *just eat whatever they have, or you'll hurt their feelings.*

Last year, instead of stocking her preferred drink, Sprite, Aunt Miri had managed to procure some local off-brand called Swerve that was distressingly neon, like the canned play-goo Seth would try to smear in Jessie's hair when she wasn't looking. "We'll just have to pretend it's Sprite," her mom had whispered while shutting the refrigerator door.

Jessie was what the adults liked to call a Picky Eater, favoring pizza, pasta, and hamburgers (with *no* pickles and *no* onions). She remembered a family visit to the Brookhaven Country Club when she was about Seth's age: the adults had ordered her a burger without asking what she wanted, and the burger meat was charred and blackened like it had been smeared in furnace ash before being wedged inside the over-toasted bun and she ate it grudgingly, silently, while staring out the window at distant golf carts whizzing around the green and tasting nothing but the char on her tongue. Visiting her aunt and uncle had somehow managed to ruin the pleasure of a simple hamburger.

Jessie eased herself into a creaking wicker chair in the living room next to Seth, who was bouncing up and down in his own to make it squeal and groan for maximum irritation. Why did little children like repetitive noises so much? Jessie sighed, sat in silence, and observed.

Under her feet was a wide white rug that may or may not have been the flayed pelt of some shaggy-haired beast: she was reminded, disconcertingly, of a giant Pekingese dog. Reader's Digest Condensed Books packed the low-slung bookshelves with sun-faded spines and a frosted glass bowl of Werther's Original hard candies sat untouched on the coffee table: mandatory fixtures of old people's homes, along with the fusty smell permeating throughout. Meanwhile the adults exchanged pleasantries, though it was mostly her aunt and uncle who spoke, and of them mostly Miri: about some distant relation who Went Astray in the '60s, or a recent surgical procedure endured by one of their fellow old-people friends, or an approving remark about President Bush that made Jessie's mom briskly change the subject. Jessie shifted in her seat and considered that the thin fabric of her dress meant the wicker was going to leave weird crisscross prints on her butt.

After unloading the luggage into Jessie and Seth's respective guest rooms, the adults gathered in the driveway for an extended goodbye. Jessie peered through the front door's window at the four of them, at Mom's taut smile, at Mom's hand clasping Dad's behind her back so tightly the knuckles were strained yellow-white. They were eager to get away. Maybe this time a drowned body would wash up at the lake house and then they'd have a story.

"Hey, Slugger!" Uncle Norton boomed, referring to Seth, whose nickname this wasn't. "Wanna go play catch in the yard?"

Seth agreed with an eager grin and off they went through the sliding glass door. Aunt Miri trailed them with her eyes.

"'Snips and snails,'" she said fondly. "Oh, how the time flies! Now, Jessica, wouldn't you like to help me in the kitchen?"

"Oh, no thank you. I'm okay," said Jessie. Aunt Miri's creased brow told her several beats later that this was one of those trick adult questions to which one was invariably supposed to say *yes*. But Jessie knew nothing of cooking—dinner wasn't even for a few hours: what could take so long?—and the kitchen had that peculiarly unappetizing '70s aesthetic of picnic remnants that had been left in the sun for hours, everything from orange to yellow to green tinted an earthy brown as if dusted with dumpster grime.

Evading her aunt's disappointment, Jessie decided to explore the eclectic geography of the house. Beneath its high, steep-angled ceiling inset with rows of broad skylights, its massive stone fireplace, and its rotary fans with fuzz caught on the blades, it appeared cobbled together from several disparate house fragments that had come together in an uneasy truce. Jessie also lived in a house in the suburbs, but its rooms were smaller and more tightly packed; and though she rarely thought about money beyond what she could buy with her allowance, she was starting to understand that Uncle Norton and Aunt Miri were better-off financially than her own parents.

Jessie's aunt and uncle had raised four sons, all long since grown and scattered around the country: one in Manhattan who worked at a law firm, one in California whose job had something to do with computers, one in Florida who was an oil company exec or an entrepreneur or didn't he maybe join the Marines, one in Chicago whose job took place in an office and was therefore very boring? Relics of the sons' existence were spread about the house, especially in their former bedrooms: a row of sports trophies topped by gold plastic men flexing and diving, a cloth banner from someplace called "Coed Naked," a paperback copy of *The Official Preppy Handbook*, a grinning WWII bomber model dangling lopsided from the ceiling on marionette strings. She was occupying Hunter's old room—or was it Tucker's?: every shirt in his closet was identical, all polo shirts, except for a single red-and-black-checked flannel for hunting or fishing. She didn't dare look in Uncle Norton's closet but knew its contents must be roughly the same. The absent brothers gazed down at her from fading photos in the halls with shaggy mullets and acne-pitted cheeks, challenging her with their confident smiles.

Jessie stepped into a small, somewhat cramped room, which would probably be described as *cozy*. The only room in this house of men with a notably feminine touch, it was outfitted all in cream-and-pink, chintz, and gingham, like the furniture in a dollhouse. A set of heavy cream-colored stationery with tidy pink trim was neatly laid out on a writing desk in the corner. This brought to mind another Norton-and-Miri-specific instruction: to always write thank-you notes for any and every gift they gave, any $5 bill tucked into a Hallmark card or floppy hair bow she wouldn't ever wear, or *they will never gift you anything again*, her mother had told her with an insistence Jessie was beginning to recognize as discomfort. She did not linger in this room.

Across the hall was Uncle Norton's study, where she and Seth were Not To Go. Yet the door was already open a gap: Jessie peeked at bars of afternoon light filtering in through the picture windows at the back, recoiled from the heady, exotic scent of lingering cigar smoke. She could hear Uncle Norton and Seth out in the backyard.

"Now *growl* like a big ol' grizzly bear!" said Uncle Norton.

"*Gurrrr!*"

"Now *roar* like a *lion!*"

"Rrrrrr-*owerrr!*"

Jessie turned a corner and found the door to the downstairs level, each downward step further muffling the backyard shouting and roaring and Aunt Miri's solitary humming in the kitchen.

This room was called The Den—*Like a den of thieves? Or a bear's den? Gurrrr!* Jessie thought, rolling her eyes—though it was really just a basement with the cement floor obscured by pale shag carpet. Vertical panels of dark wood covered the walls, bedecked with purple-tinged photos of unfamiliar people Jessie assumed were more relatives. A pool table sat in the center of the room, concealed by a tarp. Against one wall was a mirror-backed bar with a handful of Naugahyde-upholstered stools; against the other, a locked rack of rifles and a mounted pair of antlers. The Den was clearly a boys' room, reserved for boys' secrets.

And perhaps more secrets lay around the corner in the small, narrow room at the back of The Den that Jessie had never noticed before. Poking her head inside, she saw, partly obscured by stacked plastic bins and cardboard file boxes, an antique china cabinet that dominated most of the wall. Jessie squeezed in to get a better look and found herself glared at by the dusty yellow eyes of a stuffed owl.

Instead of glasses and dishware like the one in the dining room, this china cabinet was inexplicably stocked with bizarre marvels. She peered through the glass at the rows of cramped contents: the gaping maw of a taxidermy fish with a set of comically vampiric fangs. A limp marionette in the shape of a masked clown. A rusting metal hook like a long-ago farmer might use. A grimacing Japanese devil mask with upward-tilted eyelids that made it look eerily apologetic. On the top shelf, a baby alligator, or was it a—what was it called—a caiman? A portion of preserved organ in a jar with a faint label written in an ornate hand.

"Funny, isn't it?" said Aunt Miri. Jessie started: the carpet had muffled her steps. She lay a cold hand on Jessie's shoulder. "It belonged to Norton's grandfather—no, excuse me, it was his great-grandfather. They called it a *Wunderkammer* back in the Old Country." She pronounced the strange word as *one*-dur *cam*-mur. "It sure is a funny old thing."

Jessie didn't want to be seen as overly weird and morbid to her aunt, which would surely qualify as Not Nice and subject her to extra scrutiny, so she poked about at some old photos in an open cardboard box, looking for something else to talk about. One curling photo near the top depicted a younger Aunt Miri, long before she was anyone's aunt and was simply Miri, gently smiling in front of an unfamiliar porch in a cardigan and saddle shoes, hands loosely clutching the bars of a bicycle, one leg slung over the seat. On the back, someone had written in blocky letters: *Happy birthday, Miss Miriam! Sweet 16 and never been kissed!* and a date. But doing the math in her head—

"I thought you were younger than Uncle Norton," said Jessie.

This turned out to be one of those minefield remarks that set adults off over so little.

"Oh, no! No, no! *Shhh!*" said Aunt Miri, lowering her voice as though danger was near. "The man must be older. The man must be taller. The man must be *more*." She finished with a smile intimating that this was a secret just between girls.

What man? Jessie thought. *And* why?

She was briefly reassured by reminding herself that she was only *technically* related to this woman, not by blood; yet now she was alone with her, in The Den, under orders to Be Good. The confusion and unease must have shown in Jessie's face.

"You know, I always wanted a girl," Aunt Miri mused. "Of course, I wouldn't trade my precious boys for the moon. But a girl. A little girl." Her tone assumed the girl would remain little forever.

From a drawer of the cabinet, she pulled out an old hardback book with its spine obscured by several layers of dry, peeling reparative tape.

"I don't suppose your mother ever read you this story." The tone was slightly accusatory while the words were ostensibly neutral, a trait Jessie, who did not yet know the term *Midwest nice*, was increasingly learning to notice.

Aunt Miri cracked the book open in her bony arms and began to read aloud.

"'One day, a brave little boy packed up his meager belongings and set out from the home of his family. "I will go forth and seek my fortune!" said he. And so he wandered in the woods all alone: oh, he wandered so far, he lost his way! And he despaired of ever seeing his mama and papa again.

"'And just when that little boy was about to cry, he came across a little lamb separated from its flock. And he bade the lamb to follow him in his journey.

"'So, they walked and walked and walked and walked, the little lamb and the brave little boy, for so long, so very, very long! But when they had walked for a very, very, very long time, they found themselves nearly out of food. The little boy ate the very last of the bread in his pack. And all the leaves and berries of the woods were poison and would make his tummy very sick.

"'So, the little lamb said to the boy: "Dear boy! Eat my leg all up!"'" She made the lamb talk in a squeaky-squawky voice that Jessie supposed was meant to sound like a child's. "'"Nourish yourself from my body, little boy!" And the little lamb nipped open its cute little vein. "Drink my blood and slake your thirst!" said the lamb. So, the brave little boy drank of the lamb's blood, and ate of its flesh, and became strong again.

"'And so they kept walking the earth together, the lamb and the brave little boy; and whenever there was a need, the little lamb gave of itself so that the little boy might live and grow strong. That little lamb promised to follow the boy wherever he may roam in the wide, wide world. And even though, over many years, the lamb shed its wool and its flesh for the boy, and it hurt the lamb so much to walk and speak at all, the lamb did not complain, for it was happy only to serve the little boy.

"'After many years of wandering, that brave little boy grew into a brave young man. By then, the little lamb's body was twisted and wasted away, and it could no longer walk or speak any more words. And by then, the little boy grown to manhood had taken a beautiful bride and forgotten the lamb. But the lamb was still inside him forever and always. And the lamb remembered.'" She closed the book and smiled with triumph. "Now, Jessica, what did you think of *that*?"

"Um. It was okay." Jessie looked down at her shoes.

In fact, she thought it was pretty weird. The lamb was probably some kind of religious allegory, except her parents weren't very religious and she only went to church on holidays. She figured this was an oddly gory version of a Sunday School fable for babies, like the *Jesus Made Me* board book Aunt Miri had sent Seth when he was a literal infant, and she chafed at being treated like a baby.

"It's a *beautiful* story. You'll understand when you're older." Aunt Miri looked quite smug. "And what's more, it's all true, every bit. I know because that little lamb is right here." And she reached up to the cabinet's highest shelf, lifted a dusty bell jar, and took down the lamb.

At least Jessie *thought* it was a lamb once she got over the initial shock. What Aunt Miri held was not fluffy and woolly but skinny and skinned, piebald and desiccated, bony legs crumpled and splayed awkwardly beneath its torso like the ominous cramped angles of a swastika. Long rows of tiny, jagged teeth were permanently bared in a joyless grin parting its shellacked pink-red under-skin below a pair of hard-staring black lidless eyes in perfectly round sockets. Its ghastly appearance asserted an existence of constant agony and pain, a driving urge to share that interminable suffering with she who dared look upon it.

Once Jessie had gotten a good look, Aunt Miri placed the taxidermized creature—*the Lamb*—back on the shelf.

"Now remember: that little lamb will follow wherever ye may roam." A profound darkness had crept into her grin and crows' feet. And then, as if the channel had switched: "Oh, it's about time to set the table! Jessica, dear, won't you come help me?"

Jessie nodded. She just wanted to be away from *that thing.*

The glistening of its eye as the lights of The Den were switched off, its remnants of ears tracking every soft creak of the stairs under their feet, Aunt Miri's careful hobble. *Wherever ye may roam . . .*

She wished the door to the basement locked from the outside.

A series of forced screams out in the yard filtered into the kitchen all too clearly, fraying Jessie's weathered nerves. One was a little boy's shriek—*eeeeeeh!*—while the other was more of a bellow—*aaaaarrrh!*

"C'mon, Slugger, *scream!* You can do better than that!"

"*Eeeeeeeeeeeeh!!!*"

"Yeah, c'mon! Scream with me!"

Her eyes drifted over dangling wall-mounted steak knives, a set of ceramic jars printed with cartoon mushrooms, a huge pot on the stove with contents that shared the same compost-heap coloring as the rest of the kitchen, as though they had been infected.

The sliding door opened as Seth and Uncle Norton tromped inside.

"Boy, am I bushed!" said Uncle Norton. "Got dinner ready yet, Mimsy?"

Jessie wanted to laugh at that totally stupid nickname. She smothered the beginnings of a giggle in her palm before her inner tension could expand it into a hysterical cackle, which would Not be Nice at all.

"We were having a screaming contest!" Seth announced. "Uncle Norton says I *won!*" He bared his gap-toothed gums.

An unwelcome flash in Jessie's mind of the red lipless gums of the lamb. Grinning, downstairs, waiting.

She sat in the dining room before a serving of pot roast slopped into a bowl rimmed with brown-green flowers. A fist tightened around her stomach from the inside and compressed the last of her appetite. The meat bobbing in the bowl had been cooked until it was soggy and tasteless and grey as wet wood, something only old people did. She spooned at her broth and waterlogged carrots and potatoes as her ears were unpleasantly tickled by the fizzing contents of a glass of leftover Swerve.

"Heck, you got kids with green hair these days and now you got green soda pop, too!" said Uncle Norton with a chuckle. "Y'know, your Aunt Miri here used to work at the soda fountain. You kids have McDonald's, and that's what we had, way back when." He grinned, revealing slivers of grey meat caught between his yellowing old-man teeth.

"I must've asked this gal out a hundred times before she said yes. And before ya know it, she was wearing my ring." His beefy paw dropped over Aunt Miri's thin pale hand possessively and gave it a couple of pats. Jessie realized for the first time that Aunt Miri took a noticeable backseat in conversation when it was just her and Uncle Norton and no other adults.

She wondered throughout the meal if Aunt Miri would allude to what had happened in The Den, but the evil eye, the sharky grin, the double-edged phrase, never came.

Jessie tried to eat, of course: it would look suspicious if she didn't. She dredged up a square of meat. Started chewing. Considered that meat was muscle in her mouth. A red swath of flesh. Felt it flexing against her teeth, down her throat. As though it would attach to her stomach like a leech to make itself strong and bloody again. Her guts clenched inside the pastel dress.

Jessie considered that she should finally work up the nerve to ask to *be excused*, should pretend to be tired and go to bed early—but then she would be alone in the house, alone with the lamb. And she felt a flush of shame because little kids were afraid of this sort of thing, and here she was, 11 years old, almost in middle school.

She remembered a couple of years ago when she was reading a book on Ancient Egypt and had flinched at a photo of an unwrapped mummy: the eyeless sockets, missing nose, screaming jaw, skin shriveled to leather. The corpse appeared to have died in sheer anguish, preserved in that state for eternity, perhaps even as a warning. She had known, rationally, that it was just a dead person, and that's what dead skin did when it got very dry over many years, and it used to be a regular, living person just like herself once upon a time, *but—*

But it was too human for comfort, and altogether not human enough.

After dinner, back in the living room's wicker chair, Jessie tucked her feet under herself to avoid touching the rug. She stared with glazed eyes at the old four-legged TV showing decades-old programs in B&W featuring people who dressed like Aunt Miri and were occasionally drowned out by the laughter and applause of a bodiless crowd. Seth, wedged between his aunt and uncle on the couch, eventually proclaimed it was *booooориiiiing* and fake-snored, at which Uncle Norton laughed, really more of a guffaw, while Aunt Miri gave her nephew's knee an affectionate squeeze. At home, Jessie knew, he would've been gently chided by their parents for rudeness.

Jessie ended up going to bed a bit earlier than usual anyway: "Gotta get your strength up for tomorrow!" said her aunt with a big cheesy wink. Wide awake under the covers, she stared up at the ceiling with its texture of pilled cotton: why, she thought, did people start *counting sheep* to fall asleep? Because they looked like clouds and could safely float away from the waking world?

Her thoughts drifted to the lake house, the dead people under the water, the dead lamb rising from the water, the eyes with no lids like eclipsed twin suns, and since it was already dead it could never be killed again. Should she slip out of bed, try locking the door? But this would never work. The lamb had lived in this house for decades. The lamb knew everything. The air ducts, the cracks in the walls, the gaps in the floorboards. Teeth chattering behind glass, pushing open the door with cramped limbs, and . . .

On a hilltop under a sunny sky, a smiling baby animal batted its lashes, capering bow-legged on its back hooves, strips of its own skin peeled back and dangling from its waist like a hula skirt, playing fiddle with its own plucked femur grinding against its own outstretched tendons clutched taut in one hoof. *Ma-a-a-a-ah*, it sang to Jessie, a dry stammering bleat meaning *FEEEEEED—*

Jessie woke up around noon, after the others had finished an early lunch: surprisingly, no one had woken her. In the living room, Seth bounced in his seat watching a cable access children's show featuring a lamb-shaped puppet with no eyes. Aunt Miri was at the kitchen table, reading a copy of the *Brookhaven Bugle*'s Life & Style section with the headline: "Generation 'Y': The Next Greatest Generation?"

No, we totally suck, she thought, despite being only vaguely aware of what the first Greatest Generation was. This sarcastic remark brought her a moment of relief, rooting her back in a world outside of Brookhaven and her aunt and uncle's house and its secrets in The Den. Doodling absurd in-jokes in the margins of her worksheets, to her teachers' exasperation. Giggling at the Tampax-sponsored pamphlet about menstruation doled out to the girls of Mrs. Trout's 5th-grade class. Covertly watching *Total Request Live* after school and considering which Backstreet Boy she would pick. Staring covetously at the studded vinyl wrist cuffs for big kids in stores at the mall with intimidating jagged-font signage out front.

Aunt Miri glanced up from the paper and frowned. "What happened to your pretty little dress?"

"I like my jeans . . ." She sounded meek and scared. Looking outside herself at this scared little girl, she felt nauseous.

"Well, I suppose you can borrow one of my little ol' dresses for today," said Aunt Miri.

Jessie said nothing. It was Not Nice to protest.

She was served a late solitary lunch of leftover pot roast. It might as well have been the same bowl from yesterday, replenishing itself on the dining room table forever. Jessie dipped her spoon into pools of grease, a bland, earthy taste ground into mush between her molars as a chirpy woman's voice emerged from a puppet's cloth lips on TV.

After lunch she was corralled into the backyard for what was described as *a family game from the Old Country!* Uncle Norton played a tape-recording of some old-fashioned fiddle music while the four of them stood in a circle in the grass, penned in by the high picket fence.

"Now clap along!" he said

The "game," as far as Jessie could tell, was a type of square dance, like she'd had to learn in gym class last semester, but its movements were paired with nonsense lyrics. The boys, for instance, were to chant *higamous hogamous!*, after which the ladies would respond with *hogamous higamous!* After some interminable amount of time, the lyrics shifted to some other nonsense, apparently at Uncle Norton's whim.

The starched white dress borrowed from Aunt Miri, which still smelled of musty old lady despite being from her aunt's own childhood, was too tight under the arms and around the chest, and Jessie couldn't be as boisterous as the game apparently demanded even if she'd wanted to. After sleeping so long, she was still so tired. Her body slipped into a dull trance, backed by the growing drone of crickets and cicadas. How long had they been out there? Had they really spent hours dancing and laughing and clapping and hopping and spinning?

Aunt Miri was on the verge of tears. Her breathing was hard, ragged. Sweat swamped her pale forehead and the armpits of her dress.

"Christ, Mimsy, would it kill you to smile?!" said Uncle Norton.

"I'm okay," she said weakly. "I'm fine." She forced her thin lips back over big square front teeth nestled in frosting-colored gums. The next exhausted hop flipped her skirt up almost to the knee.

Jessie noticed, for the first time, that Aunt Miri had a wooden leg.

Why hadn't she known before? Was this one of those family secrets that everyone was just expected to pick up by unspoken familial osmosis, like why Cousin Bruce had to get married when he was 16, or what was wrong with Aunt Tilly, who was almost 40 but still lived with her parents, spoke with strange intonations, and spent all her time collecting garage-sale Barbie dolls that nobody was allowed to touch?

But Aunt Miri had two real legs in that old photo from The Den. The leg and the wig, an artificial Miri cobbled together over decades, controlled from the inside by a little rat or a little bird or a little—

Jessie's head was full of slurry. She needed to go lie down.

With a turn of the ankle, the stars came to collect her. She barely felt the impact of the grass.

Jessie opened her eyes in the dollhouse room, all cream and pink. Standing above her was a tall skinny lamb in a dress, also cream and pink. The lamb clapped its front hooves together and grinned so wide its lips shriveled back and tugged the skin all the way over its head to leave the skull and its muscles bare and glistening. Pink and white and red.

Jessie looked down at her body on the carpet. A fresh band-aid was stuck on the inside of her elbow and a line of surgical tape on her calf, concealing the pulse of a terrible ache. The hem of the white dress was dotted with red.

I had an accident, she thought, *when I passed out in the yard.*

The doorframe of the dollhouse room was blocked by a giant slab of potted meat in a polo shirt and khakis. A row of yellow teeth gleamed through its mask of white hair like a set of old piano keys. Its hands rested on the shoulders of a little boy. Red ribbons leaked through the gaps in his grin, trailing down his chin, staining his sticky fingers.

Everyone is smiling, she thought.

The lamb-lady pressed a cold hoof to her cheek.

You're a big girl now, Jessica, said the lamb.

Over the next decade or two, Jessica Metzger will grow tall, but not as tall as Seth, hunching a little so that her spine starts to curve. She will inspect her face for crow's feet and marionette lines. She will trace the sharpness of bones beneath flesh, of cheeks and hips and ribcage. A meek smile at cocksure voices, a gentle assent to her husband, a docile nod at the tugging hands of her children. She will walk slowly and delicately to conceal her increasing limp. And she will quietly advise her only daughter to always, always Be Nice.

Ghost Woman in Worm World

Amelia Gorman

"In short, if all the matter in the universe except the nematodes were swept away, our world would still be dimly recognizable, and if, as disembodied spirits, we could then investigate it, we should find its mountains, hills, vales, rivers, lakes, and oceans represented by a film of nematodes."
Nathan Cobb, "Nematodes and their Relationships", 1914

There is nothing here to smell, but it smells
like petrichor in this world of round worm
divulging the old familiar. She tells
herself (well, the ghost of herself) the firm
earth and heavy trees are still there as much
as memory keeps anything intact.
With no one left to remember, worms touch
worms to remember for us. This contact
represents shapes of spectral trees and dogs,
that field of grasses with a fat old cow
eating, separated by rotting logs
from the garden. Her ghost eyes which are now
just worms focus till a specific face
crawls by, she loved and knew before this place.

Into the White

Steve Rasnic Tem

THE METEOROLOGIST PREDICTED snow. This time of year, the meteorologist was usually right.

When he was a small boy, and the snow depths were legendary, his father would watch the rising accumulations of white from their front window, now and then repeating, "well, we needed the moisture," until the snow stopped, and he pulled his snow suit and boots on, and went out into the silence to shovel and scrape and take back their small world. His mother, who hated the snow, muttered from the kitchen, "I hope he doesn't have a heart attack." Even as a child he understood the risk was significant.

His father didn't have the heart attack, but both his mother and father died in their sleep one winter while he was in college, their bellies full of pills and wine. They did not leave a note. That home full of questions and empty of answers was the house he lived in now. He'd always imagined he would one day marry and have children, but reality let him down. He had been and still was, alone.

He had a college friend, a woman, who loved him, but not the way he loved her. Every week they exchanged messages on the internet, and every other year they visited one or the other's home. He imagined more but understood the danger of imagining someone else's thoughts and feelings. He would not risk that ration of love they shared.

Sometimes they reached out over the phone, but the phone calls always felt strained and left him yearning for more, so eventually they dropped that method of communication. They still sent their messages back and forth, intimate acquaintances on opposite poles of the world. She was not the solution to his life.

The last few years had seen increasing amounts of snow. It filled the shallow places as if they did not exist. It erased the roofs until only the walls were visible. Some months the snow lasted so long he could not remember what lay beneath it. At least he could still wade to his mailbox, and for the rare occasions his groceries could not be delivered he kept a well-stocked pantry.

He stopped looking outside his window. He knew he would see little more than white, little more than trees and posts rising from the white, little more than houses half-buried in white as far as he could see. He sometimes heard the echoes of children playing, and if he searched for them from his windows, he might see a few distant dots coming together, falling apart, gliding over the snow as if on wings.

He did not mind, not looking out. It gave him more time for reading, consuming the books which fed his imagination. He read until he fell asleep in his chair, then when he woke up again, he read some more.

He wasn't aware it was still snowing. A fine white mist suffused the air. Over the next few days, it grew thicker, heavier, and when he finally rose from his chair and gazed outside, he could not see the distant line of trees, and he could not see the fields in front of those trees, and he could not see past the road separating his land from those fields. He could not see the road itself. By nightfall, the icy air was full of flakes the size of his head, as if reality were disintegrating to disclose the unimaginable whiteness beyond.

He'd been awake too long, and now he was experiencing the consequences. At some point what had been an adding to had become a taking away.

The next morning the world outside his windows was completely white, soundless, and vaguely threatening. He slipped on his father's shabby old snowsuit and battered boots and walked outside.

The snow was deep, but his boots barely sank in. He knew there would be no mail delivery today, and not likely for any subsequent days. He wanted to know if there were other people in the world, or anything at all to see, and so he began walking.

In a world of all white, he couldn't say in which direction he was traveling. In a world which was all white he couldn't tell if any progress was being made.

He heard ice rattling and snow cracking, the distant explosions of collapse. In a world without obstruction, sound travelled far. When it finally arrived it was amplified, and painful.

The sky was so intense it became a dream scorched into his now. Smoldering shadows moved through the mist like memory. The clarity left him snow-blind. It became a burden to see. The snow continued to fall, the flakes becoming embers behind his eyes.

This was the world without pretense. This was the world as it was, with everything humans imagined removed.

Occasionally he came across pools of melt lying on top of the snow. Staring into those pools made them shimmer.

The white air was a perfect screen to receive his memories, an endless chronicle of yearnings, couplings and uncouplings, searches for solutions never found. He had run out of ideas. If he could have interrogated his parents, he felt sure they would tell him his birth had been a tragic accident. His had been a long journey and approaching the end he had outpaced his capacity for joy.

A mass exodus of animals crossed his path. Other than the steady crunch of his own footsteps, their hoofbeats, paws, and claws created the first sounds he had heard in days. He felt an overwhelming urge to follow them into extinction, but they were too swift for him, and soon disappeared into the mist.

He wasn't sure where he was relative to the world he had known. He had forgotten much of it. He knew there were streets far beneath him, road signs and intersections, bridges perhaps, on and off ramps, superhighways. But here in the world of white, he had to make his own way. He had to create his own path forward.

His boots hit something solid, and he tumbled off his feet. He crawled around and found it: a brightly painted piece of wood. Digging further, he uncovered pieces of a merry-go-round beneath the snow, brightly painted horses, the riders mannequins the size of children.

Further along he discovered upright posts protruding from the snow, burnt and broken trees looking like shattered bones wedged into the snow, like the bones of dinosaurs, like the bones of ancient cities.

A sudden wind came up. The world moved by him so fast it whistled. His snowsuit began to shred. The emptiness washed over him, embedding itself in his flesh. He saw blood upon the snow.

Ahead of him the sky began to tear. He thought at first it was the Northern Lights, but he came to believe it was something quite different.

NO LONGER REMOTELY HUMAN: METAMORPHOSIS IN THE HORROR OF JUNJI ITO

Aleco Julius

THROUGHOUT HIS RENOWNED career in manga, Junji Ito has disturbed his readers with visceral tales of body horror and psychological dread. His characters often experience transformations, the product of inner demons that manifest themselves in physically monstrous qualities. Sometimes, however, social pressures work to compress characters' psyches to the point of collapse, whereupon mutation commences. Volume 7 of *The Horror World of Junji Ito* series, published in 1997, contains a story called "Slug Girl," a prime example of how this process occurs in Ito's storytelling. Soon after its publication, a story called "The Snail" appeared as a chapter in the work *Uzumaki,* a series which originally ran from 1998-1999. In that particular tale, an unusual young man is subject to peer aggressions that catalyze a disturbing metamorphosis. Each protagonist is a student set amidst the turmoil of adolescence, and each suffers a uniquely gastropodal horror.

From the very first panel of "Slug Girl," Yuuko's affliction is discredited before it even has a chance to show itself. As the titular girl, she is labeled "lazy,"[1] and by her supposed friend, no less, who is the story's narrator.

[1] Ito, "Slug Girl."

Though it seems Yuuko has developed a speech impediment, this condition's association with laziness is tenuous. Her friend notes that Yuuko was once known for being talkative, but something has apparently changed. The narrator's unfair assumption is the first in a succession of subtle attacks on Yuuko's character, which quickly escalate throughout the early part of the tale. It is true that at first the narrator shows signs of concern for her friend, yet ultimately Yuuko's condition progresses beyond the point at which she can attend school in good health. Ito's haunting panel, showing her vacant desk, sets the tone for the emotional abandonment that is to come.

After some time, the narrating friend, whose name is revealed as Rie, pays a visit to Yuuko's home to check on her. Here is where the troubling gastropodal intimations begin. Yuuko's parents are in the back courtyard, violently fighting a slug infestation. Yuuko's father is seen stomping on the slugs, their gelatinous bodies flattened into two-dimensional outlines. Demonstratively destroying the creatures, his disgust will soon smoothly shift unto his daughter. Mother affectionately guides Rie to Yuuko's room, but once there, the pair is concerned to see Yuuko in bed with a facemask, Ito's trademark sweat beads excreting from her brow. Covering her face with her hands and unable to enunciate words, Rie offers what she might consider supportive solace. She says, "The doctor had only mentioned that your mental health is weak."[2]

This statement is key, because it illuminates Yuuko's real problem: the prejudice and intolerance she has endured for being herself. Whether it be mental illness or a learning disability, the unfair qualifications of laziness and mental weakness directed toward Yuuko have erupted forth horror from within her. The changes in Yuuko would not be readily accepted by society, which values and encourages the "cheerful" and "chatty"[3] personality she heretofore exemplified. In a memory flashback, the reader learns that Yuuko was once, as a child, tormented with a slug by a classmate. She was essentially traumatized, for she subsequently never set foot in her family's slug-infested yard. Her terror never really left her— not just that of the offending creature but of being the target of her peers.

In *The Body Keeps the Score,* psychiatrist Bessel Van Der Kolk outlines the ways in which trauma can manifest itself in various physiological ways, especially if not treated or if ignored by the individual. He explains that

---

[2] Ibid.

[3] Ibid.

trauma can sap energy and motivation, as well as lead to "headaches, muscle aches, problems with your bowels or sexual functions," while including "irrational behaviors."[4] Alienation from peer groups, most especially during adolescence, is a trauma that Junji Ito explores with Yuuko (as well as with Katayama of "The Snail," but more on him later). The day after her initial visit, Rie is met with a revolting incomprehensibility: Yuuko's tongue has metamorphosed into a slimy, undulating slug.

How does best friend Rie react? By literally running away, never to return for another visit. Abandoned by her best friend and met with revulsion instead of compassion by her own mother, Yuuko resorts to self-mutilation, a common coping mechanism of adolescent alienation and anxiety. However, slicing off the horrid appendage is to no avail, as it keeps growing back. Her father's take-charge attitude is coupled with hostility. He yells at his timid wife every chance he gets, clamoring for her to do this or do that in his blind focus to nullify the slug. This may at first seem like parental devotion and care. However, tellingly, the parents do not try to actually understand what is happening with Yuuko. Rather, they endeavor to eliminate her affliction at all costs, even if that means possibly hurting their daughter in the process. After failed attempts to kill the buccal parasite, including a salt bath, the regenerating gastropod still lives. Yuuko's body has dissolved, save her head, which now acts as a protective shell, and she in essence becomes a snail. Tragically, social pressure to fit the mold has rendered her into a shell of her potential self. Yuuko's weary gaze in the last panel directly confronts readers, perhaps a challenge to consider someone like Yuuko in our own lives.

In "The Snail," an adolescent boy experiences cruel rejection by his peers, only to endure the emergence of his pain by way of physical transformation. Katayama, as he is called, develops these molluscan traits in response to his classmates' antagonism. As the story opens, students forlornly stare out the window during a torrential morning downpour. A student creaks open the door and reveals himself drenched not only rainwater, but in a viscous substance as well, as the careful detail in Ito's artwork suggests. Katayama only comes to school when it rains it seems, and straightaway his classmates start into their verbal assaults, targeting his slowness and apparent malaise. The teacher joins in the belligerence, admonishing Katayama for being late and also for not using an umbrella. According to an article in

[4] Van Der Kolk, *The Body Keeps the Score,* 235.

ComiXology by Noah Berlatsky, Katayama's entrance scene is akin to a kind of birth, a "fertile source of horror" that emanates the "claustrophobic intimacy of a primal scene."[5]

Katayama's primary bully, Tsumura, uses the former's poor volleyball skills in gym class as the perfect opportunity to perform in front of his followers in malice. Katayama sees it coming, as an extreme closeup of his agitated face suggests. Tsumura, in a revealing moment, rebukes the antagonized boy for pleading with him in a familiar tone to stop the harassment, yelling, "Don't talk to me like we're friends!"[6] The insinuation of latent homoerotic anxieties continues as the bully cruelly strips Katayama naked and drags his body into the crowded hallway for all to see. Thus violated, his tormentor laughs, "Get a good look!"[7] The dehumanization of Katayama in this scene signals Ito's shift into body horror fiction, as a noticeable spiral appears on Katayama's exposed back.

The features of snail anatomy continue to develop as the rains subsist. As the spiral becomes a tumorous exterior growth, and Katayama's sliminess thickens, the classroom teacher only calls more attention to his deformity. Other characteristics forcibly emerge as Katayama becomes more socially isolated. He becomes not only marginalized but maligned into an outcast. In an essay called "Creating the False Self," therapist Harville Hendrix concludes that traits not part of one's original nature "are forged out of pain and become part of an assumed identity" that "helps [one] maneuver in a complex and sometimes hostile world."[8] Katayama's full ostracization becomes finalized when he is confined to an outdoor pen, bulbous shell and tentacled eyes fully formed. He had escaped through the classroom window, vertically gliding on the side of the school building until violently knocked off with a broom. The group of students now a veritable mob, the organized expulsion of Katayama symbolizes their total and utter rejection.

Two girls somewhat sympathetic to Katayama, noticing that he has not emerged from his shell since the rain ended, splash water on his snail body. When his long eye appendages sprout forth, however, they run away screaming in revulsion. This is not unlike Rie's reaction in "Slug Girl." Soon thereafter, the bully Tsumura himself begins to transform. Once he is

---

[5] Berlatsky, "Fecund Snails."

[6] Ito, *Uzumaki,* 240.

[7] Ibid., 241.

[8] Zweig and Abrams, *Meeting the Shadow,* 51.

entirely transformed and also imprisoned in the pen, the two snails turn out to be attracted to each other. One of the girls' comments, "Tsumura was such a bully. How ironic."[9] The class teacher reminds everyone that snails are hermaphrodites, as the two come together and apparently mate. Berlatsky writes, "There's a weird tenderness in the rapprochement between the two boy-snails, as they rest face to face with their phallic eyes intertwining."[10]

Digging their way to escape, the two snails leave behind a slimy trail which is followed by the teacher and the two girls. Discovering a nest of eggs, the teacher remarks: "It's clear these two boys are no longer remotely human."[11] Certainly, each boy had subsumed within himself deep-rooted wounds that they managed in opposing ways. In Katayama's alienation and Tsumura's aggression, societal expectations are transgressed. The teacher violently stomps on the eggs and shrieks, "It's disgusting, it's unnatural!"[12] Recall that in "Slug Girl," Yuuko's father stomps on snails as his method of non-acceptance, a representative act of his inability to connect with his daughter and his refusal to acknowledge the changes in her life. In his article "Rejection and Betrayal," psychologist Robert M. Stein notes that when young people suffer these title experiences, "the more human personal relationship [will be] missing or inadequate"[13] in their lives. What is key is the concept that in the presence and aftermath of abuse, one's very humanity is compromised. With these stories, Ito demonstrates how the stripping away of his characters' capability to feel human yields to bodily corruption, an intensifying malignancy dense with suppressed shame.

One of the most troubling aspects of these stories is the parental rejection of Yuuko and Katayama. The reader is given a peek at the attitude of Yuuko's father when we first meet him in the yard, where he stomps away at the unwanted infiltrators. Exhausted by his violence, he commands his wife to bring him salt. Significantly, salt is also his suggested solution for curing Yuuko. Indeed, his approach is to fix his daughter, not heal her. He eventually eradicates her body in an outright rejection of undesirable characteristics, as it dissolves in a heavy salt bath while the head remains to serve as gastropod shell.

---

[9] Ito, *Uzumaki,* 261.
[10] Berlatsky, "Fecund Snails."
[11] Ito, *Uzumaki,* 264.
[12] Ibid., 265.
[13] Zweig and Abrams, *Meeting the Shadow,* 52.

In Katayama's case, his parents call the school to inform his teachers that he has not come home for several days. This is understandable, apparently, for one teacher comments, "How could he go home looking like that?"[14] Ito's dark humor notwithstanding, the school asks Katayama's parents to come and collect him. However, once the father sees Katayama's new form, he exclaims, "That can't be our son!"[15] The horrified parents immediately go home in a quintessential example of parental refusal to acknowledge their child's identity. Now abandoned by his own mother and father, Katayama is a true pariah to all of society. While Yuuko is last seen pitifully gazing out atop a courtyard tree branch, Katayama and his new snail partner Tsumura are never seen again.

In 2020, Ito published a graphic adaptation of Osamu Dazai's 1948 novel *No Longer Human*, a work generally considered to be highly autobiographical. In Dazai's novel, the opening line to the protagonist's first-person narrative is, "Mine has been a life of much shame."[16] This statement, which Ito also uses as the beginning of his narrator's chronicle, serves as the nucleus of protagonist Oba Yozo's narrative. Ito's illustration of this quote is a panel of black ink, the text within a white egg-shaped figure, an indication that his shame is the point at which the rest of his life experience is birthed. In the first part of the novel, Yozo recounts the story of his early childhood, during which he suffers abuse and mistreatment at the hands of his classmates, his family, and their servants before learning to mask his dejection. The connection between Yozo's early life and the plights of the young characters in his manga work is not difficult to see.

Early in the novel, Yozo repeatedly but vaguely alludes to an unutterable "crime"[17] perpetrated against him by the servants, though the impression that he was sexually abused can be surmised. Ito, however, rather clearly represents these heinous acts in his adaptation. Yozo's confusion results in "painful wounds" that "unlike the scars from the lashing a man might give, cut inwards very deep, like an internal hemorrhage, bring intense discomfort."[18] While there is no real suggestion that his manga characters suffered similar sexual abuse, Ito's work is demonstrably concerned with the ways in which trauma can claim an individual's inner experience and transform it

---

[14] Ito, *Uzumaki,* 250.
[15] Ibid., 251.
[16] Dazai, *No Longer Human,* 21.
[17] Ibid., 38.
[18] Ibid., 48.

into something monstrous. In turn, their view of the outside world is paradoxically distorted through a lens of trauma while simultaneously opening a clear window into the horror of the cruelty of human beings. One such character in *No Longer Human* is the social outcast Takeichi, who, suffering from physical disability and possessing a uniquely cynical worldview, is "scorned by all."[19]

The main way Yozo manages his childhood distress it to become a "clown,"[20] whereby he outwardly pretends happiness and silliness in order to disguise his inner turmoil. He is able to skillfully fool all his friends and family, but Takeichi sees through him. Yozo, after making his schoolmates uproariously laugh at a tumble he takes in gym class, is confronted by Takeichi. He tells Yozo: "You did it on purpose."[21] This phrase haunts Yozo throughout the rest of the narrative, especially in the nightmarish and hallucinatory episodes of Ito's adaptation. The fact that an outsider is able to look so clearly into his psyche is an idea too much for Yozo to bear. His solution is to befriend Takeichi, who proves to have a visionary sense of reality's bleakness.

One day, Takeichi brings Yozo a self-portrait by Van Gogh, which he declares to be a picture of a "ghost."[22] Some artists, Yozo comes to realize, are the kinds of people "whose dread of human beings is so morbid that they reach a point where they yearn to see with their own eyes monsters of ever more horrible shapes."[23] Ito develops this theme throughout the adaptation, as Yozo becomes a visual artist whose chief goal is to represent the monstrousness of humanity. His influences are Van Gogh, Munch, Goya, and Modigliani, artists whose works often portray psychological pain. It can be easily imagined that Ito himself identifies with this vision. In the novel, Yozo goes on to reflect that the great artists did not "hide their interest even in things which were nauseatingly ugly, but soaked themselves in the pleasure of depicting them."[24]

Eventually, Yozo's fear of intimacy grows as the two boys become closer, and because of this he perpetuates a cruelty unto Takeichi. In Ito's graphic version of the story, Yozo has an attractive cousin, and he makes

---

[19] Ito, *No Longer Human,* 43.
[20] Ibid., 51.
[21] Ibid., 49.
[22] Ibid., 58.
[23] Ibid., 60.
[24] Dazai, *No Longer Human,* 55.

Takeichi falsely believe that she admires him. When she shows her disgust toward Takeichi and vehemently rejects him, he kills himself. As an adult, Yozo himself attempts suicide by drowning with his lover, though he survives while she dies. On the morning of their suicidal act, Yozo reflects that his lover, like he, "seemed to be weary beyond endurance of the task of being a human being."[25] Some scholars have recognized Dazai's novel as a sort of literary suicide note, as the writer and his lover ended their own lives by drowning shortly after he finished the book.

An oft-cited influence of Junji Ito is writer Edogawa Rampo, whose collection *Japanese Tales of Mystery and Imagination* contains early stories of the grotesque and the perverse. The 1929 story "The Caterpillar" is one such example. The title itself is a precursor to the Ito manga titles discussed herein. The Rampo story revolves around a soldier who suffers terrible wounds in battle, resulting in amputation of all four limbs as well as an extremely disfigured face. Rampo writes, "In this monstrous face, however, there were still set two bright, round eyes like those of an innocent child."[26] In this way, the conflict between inner innocence and outer monstrosity is a thematic precursor to Ito as well. His wife is his caretaker, and although she seems to care for him at first, she gradually begins to torment him with little acts of teasing and then cruelty. The mutilated man ultimately escapes the house one night, gliding along on his belly before disappearing into a well in the ground.

Another notable tale that might be considered early body horror is that of Gregor Samsa. The famous opening line of Franz Kafka's novella *The Metamorphosis* sees the protagonist waking up transformed into a monstrous vermin, often imagined and depicted as a giant insect. Gregor's job as a salesman is strenuous, offering little respite from the tedious repetition of tiresome traveling. In other words, he is exhausted by the expectations of being an ordinary human in society. Intent on not leaving his bedroom in his insectoid form, Gregor's manager comes to the house to elicit him out. The manager says through the door: "I am dumbfounded, dumbfounded. I believed you to be a quiet, reasonable person, and now you suddenly seem intent on flaunting bizarre moods."[27] When Gregor is finally seen, his mother swoons and his father attempts to push him back into the bedroom.

---

[25] Ibid., 86.

[26] Rampo, *Japanese Tales*, 89.

[27] Kafka, *The Metamorphosis*, 128.

In a video analysis, one YouTube critic likens Yuuko of "Slug Girl" to Gregor Samsa, whose metamorphosis is a "desperate cry for help of someone who tries to express their struggles with depression and social anxiety in a time when mental illness literacy was practically non-existent."[28] This reading of the absurd tale complements the eventual abandonment of Gregor by his family. He dies alone, bereft of his humanity.

In an article titled "Black illumination," horror scholar Eugene Thacker writes that Junji Ito stories often take a "simple idea, which is then methodically inverted and perverted, until what results is a terrifying, mesmerizing, philosophical parable about the limits of being human."[29] The natural anxieties that plague the human being in the world, in Ito's stories, are exacerbated by the societal pressures around them. Osamu Dazai's protagonist asserts that society is nothing more than the collective struggles between individuals. As we see in Ito's work, these struggles can result in traumatic psychological distortion. Near the end of his graphic adaptation of *No Longer Human,* there is a metatextual twist when the author Dazai himself appears and meets his protagonist, Yozo. They seem to be virtually the same person, as Ito commingles perspective and dialogue. "For both of us," says Dazai to Yozo, "it's hard to keep acting out our comedy."[30]

---

[28] YouTube, "Junji Ito's Slug Girl."
[29] Thacker, "Black Illumination."
[30] Ito, *No Longer Human,* 568.

BIBLIOGRAPHY

Berlatsky, Noah. "Fecund Snails." ComiXology. Rpt in. The Hooded Utilitarian. 31 Oct. 2011, https://www.hoodedutilitarian.com/2011/10/fecund-snails/.

Dazai, Osamu. *No Longer Human.* Translated by Donald Keene. New York: New Directions, 1958.

Ito, Junji. *No Longer Human.* San Francisco: Viz Media, 2017.

—. "Slug Girl." https://imgur.com/gallery/HLC93ZP.

—. *Uzumaki.* San Francisco: Viz Media, 2010.

"Junji Ito's Slug Girl & the Horror of Being Different." *YouTube,* uploaded by RagnarRox, 15 March 2020, https://www.youtube.com/watch?v=d3iM8Xus8UE.

Kafka, Franz. *The Metamorphosis, In the Penal Colony, and Other Stories.* Translated by Joachim Neugroschel. New York: Simon & Schuster, 1993.

Rampo, Edogawa. *Japanese Tales of Mystery and Imagination.* Translated by James B. Harris. Rutland: Tuttle, 2012.

Thacker, Eugene. "Black Illumination." *The Japan Times,* 30 Jan. 2016, https://www.japantimes.co.jp/culture/2016/01/30/books/black-illumination-unhuman-world-junji-ito/.

Van Der Kolk, Bessel. *The Body Keeps the Score: Brain, Mind, and Body in the Healing of Trauma.* New York: Penguin, 2014.

Zweig, Connie and Jeremiah Abrams, editors. *Meeting the Shadow: The Hidden Power of the Dark Side of Human Nature.* New York: Penguin, 1991.

The Outer Thread

Venezia Castro

We walk on the outer thread of a spider's web.

It is a narrow street of houses darkened with time, older than Germany or the telephone. The silken ground glistens and sticks to the soles of our shoes. It rained not long ago.

I can see, further down the road, the steeple of a church peeking through the silhouettes of the trees. We drag our feet in that direction. The rest will become clearer as we go.

I try not to think of the mistakes that brought me here and, instead, focus on the tiny fingers wrapped around my forearm. Soft and clammy fingers. Nails dig into my skin, but I can hardly feel them. I wish for a greater pain that would keep me grounded and distracted, but the child is too weak, and my skin is numb from the cold.

Out of the corner of my eye, I catch a red glow and stop short in front of one of the houses, only a few meters before the end of the road where the chapel stands. The child stops too and clings tighter to my arm. She senses something is about to happen. I feel her trembling next to me.

The house we face now is not too different from its neighbors, tall and oddly symmetrical, topped with turrets on each side and built with stone dense and precious. An earthquake would not make it shake. The place looks lifeless; all the windows are dark except for this one beacon: a small oval lit with bright red light, a mockingly seductive eye beckoning from what could only be the attic.

"We must go in," I tell the child, but neither of us move for a while. We pretend to be waiting for something as the house seems to be waiting for us.

The child takes the first step, braver in her anxiety to get home, and I follow her through the unlocked door.

We are now closer to the center of the web. The diagonal thread is a hall where the air is silvery and heavy with the smell of dust and humidity and cigarette tar. The child lets out a small cough, sticking her tongue out, and cowers behind me. She seems afraid that the noise will wake something up, but the house remains undisturbed and inviting.

"It's okay," I whisper as I pat the blonde head that rests against my thigh. She nods and I feel her relax just enough to keep going.

We do not see any doors or any more windows, there is just the hall that stretches for longer than would seem possible. We walk along it for unbearable minutes, careful not to touch anything on our way since surely, everything here means to keep us trapped. The walls and empty picture frames, the carpet, and the rotten wood furniture; everything is covered in the same gummy substance that glistens in the low light of my phone screen.

Finally, we come upon a flight of stairs. Although the top is still too dark to see where they lead, I know there is no other way. The child looks at me questioningly, unable to find the words to refuse, to beg for us to leave the house, or to ask what we will find upstairs. It does not matter. I have promised to take her home and so, when I force myself to smile and begin to climb up the steps, she follows me. Her legs are short, and I have to hold her hand to help her up. She is smart, I can tell. She has not been badly spoiled. I can see in her a bit of myself when I was her age: a dumb bravery, the knowledge that comfort has a price-tag. We both want to go home and because of that we find the strength to move forward, hand in hand, towards the center of the web.

The thread grows thinner. It happens sometimes; there is no reason to worry, I know it will not break. It just makes the stairs grow narrow and I have to duck slightly to avoid hitting my head on the low ceiling. The child begins to cry quietly next to me. I hear her sniffle and once she uses our hands intertwined to wipe at her face, but she does not stop walking.

"It will be fine. We are almost there," I say and squeeze her fingers. Hers is the hand of a baby, and I try to picture her standing under a light summer rain, with her palms facing up towards the sky, trying and failing to catch the drops. She looks nothing like me. Her eyes are the gray of rain clouds.

When I was her age, I would have given anything for eyes that were the color of morning. I longed for bright blue but would have settled for stormy.

Dark eyes, however, are better for catching the light at night. I see the door at the top of the stairs before the child does, blinded by tears as she is. I know this because she does not stir until we are just a step away from it. The metal door is carefully—lovingly—woven, thick, and heavy, but waiting ajar at the exact point where two threads of the web meet. Red light seeps through the crack from the other side. It will not be difficult to push our way in.

I check my phone for signal one last time before I put it in my pocket, let go of the child's hand, and rest my palms against the door. I wince when I touch it. It is still warm. Fine threads of glue stretch and snap, one by one, as the door opens.

Each time is slightly different from the last. The road would bend one way or the other; the stairs would go up or down; and there would usually be more rooms, more doors. Tonight seems too easy. Too rushed. Too eager. The metal door swings open as soon as I touch it.

The child has stopped crying but only because she is now too afraid to think about her mother and the life she used to have. Survival is the only thing her body craves now. I want to tell her that I too chased a rabbit down a hole once, but now I have forgotten the life I used to have, and I rarely cry. Our stories will not end the same way, and there is no point in repeating that I will get her home safe. I feel, however, that we both are just as scared, and there is warmth in that knowledge.

My hands are shaking when I wipe the gum off them on my jeans. I cannot get rid of the stickiness, but the child does not seem to mind. She grabs my hand once more, only feeling safe in our togetherness and she lets me guide her into the red attic, at the center of the web, where it nests.

It never gets better. Every time I see this place, I want to be sick. There is a smell, very faint but always there, that is painfully sweet, a pink smell, a smell that has been used to conceal something deeper still. The fake scent of cherries in a sick-man's mouth. It makes my eyes water as they try to adjust to the light that floods the room. It comes from a single bulb hanging from the ceiling, a small red sun. Slowly, the shapes of the room make themselves known.

There is a bed in one corner, only large enough for one adult. The bedsheets, the lightest shade of blue, are rumpled. Above the bed there is a small silver crucifix. A variety of toys litter the wooden floor: naked Barbie dolls and marbles in many sizes and coloring pencils with dull tips. Among them, candy wrappers are scattered around, the evidence of unkempt living. There is only one window, the small one we saw from outside. It shows nothing now. The world beyond the house is empty once you are inside. The walls are mostly covered in large mirrors and small pictures, which makes the room appear larger and maze-like. The mirrors are frameless; the pictures are polaroids.

Fine threads of silk hang from the ceiling like garlands, drawing patterns across the room. Wisps of it hover over the bed and drift around the floor. They part like curtains as we step in. They are not meant to catch anything. I can picture it leaving them behind in its excitement, crawling up the walls and waiting, almost unable to contain itself. I know it watched us walking outside and its fangs began to leak. Now the floor is slippery poison. It heard us climbing up the stairs. It sees us. It waits. It is impatient.

The child throws her arms around me, terrified. She cannot move any further. She buries her face in my stomach. I hug her back and pat her head and tell her that everything will be fine, but I am shaking just as much as her and I know she does not believe me.

"You have to be brave. You cannot go back. Now you have to be brave."

We hear it unfurl. Its legs crack when it extends them, one by one, in the dark. The sound echoes around the room, so it is impossible to tell where exactly it is coming from. It feels like it is coming from everywhere at once. Massive as it is, it makes the floorboards tremble when it moves.

The sharp stench of urine suddenly fills up the room. The stream is thick and loud. I feel the warmth of it splashing around my shoes, sliding down my calves from our legs tangled up. I try to remind myself that she is just a child, a baby in diapers not too long ago, that she is one of the youngest ones so far and that she has never been as afraid as she is right now. I cannot blame her, but still a wave of annoyance and disgust fills me up. She is weak. Her hair between my fingers is too thin. She is holding on to me as hard as she can and yet, it would take hardly any strength at all to push her away.

She is lucky not to see it when it lumbers out from one of the dark corners of the attic.

It is white and bulbous. The color and texture of fat, except for a few pink bristles that grow sparsely on its back. Its body reflects the red light in a way that makes it look like raw meat, wet to the touch; an overgrown organ or a tumor about to burst. The only sharp angles on its body are its legs, the top of them raised above a head that is all eyes. It stares at us with red hunger.

I have seen it grow larger with the years. It was always massive but now it is grotesque. Pale, almost transparent, hairless, and slow, it reminds me more of a maggot than a spider. Its kind ages terribly, and it is getting old. Older and greedier, more insatiable, and more hateful. Time has erased the threat of consequences. It no longer cares about anything but being satisfied.

Its stinger brushes the floor excitedly.

I feel the child tense up against me. She knows it is here and lifts up her head just enough to peek through her half opened eyelids. When she sees it, all her bravery dissolves. She begins to wail, to babble incoherently. She yells for her mother, asks me to take her away, to take her home. I promised. I promised I would keep her safe.

I pry her away from me. Her chubby arms do not offer much resistance, but she bites down on my shirt like a crazed animal to keep me from pushing her off. She claws her way back to me, wrapping herself around my waist in desperation. She clutches at my clothes and tries to hold me. I have to pull her hair, so thin it comes off in clusters when I tug at it, to keep her away. I shove her to the floor and step back before she has time to get up.

It reaches her in one swift movement, traps her down its long pale leg. It is dripping poison and wet silk all over her small frame. From it comes a feeble whimper. She knows it is over. Her fingers slide over the floor and cling to nothing. I can barely hear her anymore. Instead, the sound of its exhilarated breathing fills up the room; it's heavy panting. It wants me gone so it can begin. I look away.

I want it to see me before I leave, to remember I am to be thanked for the pleasures of tonight. "You will like this one," I manage to say when I finally find my voice. "She has the smallest hands," I whisper before leaving the room and closing the door behind me.

I want to run downstairs, but I force myself to walk. I feel dirty. My hands are wet with tears and spit, and I stink of urine and sweat. As I make my way out, I fantasize about tearing off my clothes and lighting them up in a fire that would burn the whole house down. The ashes would fall down like rain and the sky would be the color of my eyes.

The fresh air outside lifts my spirits back up. The night is lovely, and I can see a few stars, almost like a "thank you" gift. It is happy, I can tell. The road does not stick to my feet anymore. The light on the window of the attic has been turned off.

On the outer threads, life is mostly quiet. Living is pleasantly predictable, all needs always within reach. All I have to do is keep it happy, keep it spinning, keep a secret.

I marvel at my own good luck. I am happy, impossibly happy. As long as I am out of that house, I am perfectly content. The rest is nothing but a chore, easily put out of mind.

Another day I get to live on this road of huge houses with trees and a chapel that was not built up on top of ancient ruins smeared with blood. I walk safely at night with eyes that were made to get lost in the dark and look up at the steeples that are centuries old, and every building looks lifeless, but they are all covered in vines, spun from the belly of art and industry, beautifully knitted with the same silk that makes flags and fine dresses.

I dreamt of these days. When the chasing of rabbits was a hunt for food, I told myself that one day I would get to be idle in a town with snowfalls. Now I have made it. And for what price? To me, no price at all.

I take the long way home. I pull out my phone from my pocket and put on my earbuds. I play a song that reminds me of television heroines and golden chandeliers. I shake off the strands of blonde hair still stuck to my fingers.

A shame, really. This one had the loveliest hands.

Time is Like a Spider, Love Like a Dream

Michelle Muenzler

The clock.

Ticks in the corner—tick tick, tick tick. My scalp itches in tandem, like a little nit gnawing at my skull. Or a hundred little nits. A thousand.

Our love is running out. With every tick, another grain dives for the forest of the carpet, rejoicing as it breaches. I've lost cats in that carpet. Hamsters. Boyfriends, girlfriends. At least a dozen dimes.

So much lost in so little time.

Oh, wretched time...

I grab your hand from the bed, next to mine. Hold fast. Time is always fleeing. Fleeting.

Our time is—

—a bus. Gross and yellow and covered in graffiti, its tires worn slick. We're speeding down the road, one of us driving, but I'm not sure which. There is no steering wheel.

More potholes than road dissect our path. The road splits. Like a scalpel, shears the bus in two. I've still got your hand, but we're further apart now.

The road splits again.

And again.

Our fingertips shred against the wind. Against each other. I can't hold on.
Another pothole, and ahead the road scissors wide, aiming for—

-—the sun. It's a bosom pressing against the corset-banded sky. Straining. Squeezing. Plum purple and ready to pop.
Spiders. The sun is made of spiders. Hundreds, thousands, millions of them rupturing the sky.
They spill into sweet air. Whisk like silk.
Have I told you before, how love is like a spider? Many-faceted and multitudinous, its eyes? I will tell you this if I see your face again. Your beautiful face.
With your screaming mouth and your so wide eyes.
How beautiful—

—an egg. Sizzling in the pan, fat yolk glaring with its fat yellow eye. Grease hangs in the air. Strands of it dangle from the ceiling.
How to fork in a world of spoon?
My love leaks like a popped balloon, spilling into the sea. I've made you breakfast. Again. Enough to feed the sky, but the instead of sky you give me moon hunched beneath the blankets, feral-mouthed and white.
I don't understand.
I only want to feed you—

—the clock. Back again.
Tick tick. Tick tock.
The inconsolable tick of time.
I want.
You.
I need.
You.
Why are you still screaming?
Why won't you let me into those fat sun-egg-bus eyes?
I spider for you and only for you.
I hunger for—

—time.
More time.

The Bleating Belfry

John Brownlee

IN OUR SHABBY-CHIC neighborhood, crushed between hip bodegas and colorful cafés, there is a little church entombed alive. Hidden from gentrification, a smoke-gray chapel of oolitic limestone and time-blackened glass sucked up by the surrounding architecture. My wife, Eugenia, first spotted the belfry peeking over the neighborhood's slate-roofed canopy like a knob of fossilized bone. She immediately became obsessed with finding it, but wherever the church's entrance was, it defied easy discovery.

Long-lashed, delicate, and fierce, Eugenia's signature talent was her almost preternatural ability to fit in with any crowd. That's how I originally met her, hiding away from a party my roommate was throwing. Mistaking it for the bathroom, many rapped on my door that night, but only Eugenia's playful pecking caught my attention. She tapped in Morse code, which I knew well enough to follow along: *come come come.*

"What is a handsome boy like you doing hiding in here?" she asked in her lilting Andalusian accent when I unlocked the door. "Come and join the frolic!"

I was very shy back then. My instinct was to beg off, but I drew daring from her face. I knocked my response on the open door between us—*if you insist*—and drew a smile from her as she linked her arm in mine. Later, it turned out she'd crashed the party and knew no one there, which only bewitched me more. I've been her slave ever since.

Cloaked in her dark Spanish charm, Eugenia went to the buildings surrounding the belfry to see if our elderly Portuguese-American neighbors knew how it might be reached. Marked by bathtub Marys and São Cristo azulejos, these neighbors traced their families back a half-dozen generations or more to the same old part of the world Eugenia came from. Like everyone, these old widows were charmed by my wife, and invited her in for espresso and *biscoitos.* But despite their impeccable hospitality and loose European kinship, they either couldn't—or wouldn't—tell Eugenia how to reach the church. All they would say was that it was not abandoned. Service was still held there.

"It is like they try to keep me from it!" she said, stamping her tiny foot. "They make like it's bad luck to talk about. It's right there!"

I smiled at her temper. She was not used to being denied. But this very subject—gentrification—was, ironically, what I was pursuing my doctorate in.

"It's because we're tourists," I explained.

But that just angered Eugenia more. Tourists, for her, were Americans going to Europe—not the other way around.

"No, we live here now! We belong."

"It takes more to belong to a place than just paying rent," I explained. "You need to pay the generational blood price. To sacrifice and suffer there. Until then, we have no right to complain if the neighborhood keeps its secrets from us."

"We live here too," she fumed. "Even if we're not Portuguese, we have just as much right to go to the church as they do."

"Perhaps it's not their church to invite us to," I thought aloud. "Maybe it's not Portuguese, and you're talking to the wrong people. No neighborhood is culturally homogenous, even an old one. We can't just storm in, and immediately understand all that has accumulated here, or the hidden symbioses that have allowed this neighborhood to thrive for almost two centuries."

Eugenia rolled her eyes. "You read too many books about only one thing." And I laughed at her pique, admitting this was true.

In the end, we Googled up a satellite view of the neighborhood. It confirmed there were no hidden alleys leading to the chapel. The most likely entry point was a purple pseudo-Victorian with expansive ground-floor windows that might once have been a funeral parlor. According to a bird's eye view, the chapel was ensconced in its private back garden. But on the multiple occasions when Eugenia knocked on the purple house's front door, no one answered.

One night, Eugenia and I were ambling home from a party at the sociology department when we saw a large man standing under the pseudo-Victorian's porchlight. With an attitude of expectation in his dark frock, he looked like a monk: jolly and pale, with a trestle of burst corpuscles underlying his wine-dark beard.

Behind his bulk, I could see the door to the purple house was open. The candle-lit interior was empty of furniture, revealing bare mahogany floors polished to a high crimson. Another door twin to the first opened out back. And past that, through a saturnine garden thick with catmint, up three luminous steps—the entrance to the elusive chapel!

Always so daring, Eugenia seized the opportunity. With the monk watching us from the porch, she drew me aside for an embrace, whispering:

"It's our chance to finally see! Are you so very tired, my love?"

I was, but I could deny her nothing. I let my forehead touch hers, tapping into her palm: *if you insist.* Her reply was a well-practiced flurry of kisses, spelling out: *come come come.* Then she spun around, skipping lightly up the porch steps.

"Hello! There's a service tonight, yes?"

We were both a bit tipsy from the party—our mouths, in fact, were stained with tannin. But from the way his wet moustaches hung around his mouth like vermillion tassels, it seemed like the monk had been drinking too. Twisting one thoughtfully until it started to drip, he appraised my wife, who stood fearlessly in her dark dancer's clothes beneath his scrutiny. You could tell he was charmed; I may as well have not been there at all.

Finally, he asked:

"Is this your first time?"

"No," Eugenia lied, because it was a rule for her to belong wherever she went. She hooked my arm. "But I brought an initiate."

With a welcoming smile, the monk nodded. He bid us enter.

The house felt cavernously empty as we passed through it to the back garden. There was no furniture, nothing to see except dark corners and candlelight. The only sound as we passed through was the squeaking floorboards. Under our feet, they almost sounded like a rhythmic bleating, coming from the basement. Then we were outside.

Out in the garden, Eugenia slithered up the path toward the chapel as luminously as a milk snake. We could now fully see the exterior. Like many long searched for things, I found the exact contours of the chapel's appearance slightly disappointing. The belfry itself was the most interesting feature, and as I walked arm-in-arm with Eugenia up the path, my eyes were drawn up the tower to where the rusty bell shivered sumptuously with bats and hung frosted against the sky like a blood moon.

Isn't it exciting? Eugenia tapped into my palm.

It *was* exciting; unnervingly so. I never had my wife's thirst for adventure, her compulsive desire to sniff out secrets and go where she was not meant to go. I was not a social chameleon like her, capable of fitting in everywhere and making admirers of everyone. I felt awkward everywhere, and most of all *here*, sneaking into some midnight mass in a secret church in what amounted to a neighbor's backyard. I wasn't even Catholic, for God's sake. Yet I'd always drawn bravery from her beauty, so I swallowed my misgivings. For her, there was nothing I would not do.

Beneath angular voussoirs, an usher met us at the chapel entrance. For a moment, I thought it was the same monk we'd passed at the front door, but they were just near twins. Both, at least, had sampled the sacrament before services: an ursine giant, the usher's beard, too, was wine-dark and wet. Like his fellow, he asked if it was our first time.

"I am an acolyte, of course," Eugenia said, flashing her tannin-stained eyeteeth charmingly. "But I bring a friend for communion."

The monk's bear-like head appraised me with the flashing eyes of a cat. Then he bowed and lead us both into the church by the arm. I tried not to show how much his long nails pinched as he seated us in the first pew to the right of the altar.

"A place of honor for an initiate," he said, his smile fixed upon me. "You're the first to arrive." Then he departed.

Left alone, we surveyed the church. For such a hard-to-accomplish locale, it was dingy and unremarkable. There were none of the cheery trappings I associated with the neighborhood's Roman-Catholic religious streak, supporting my notion that it was not, in fact, a Portuguese church. With just five rows of time-blackened pews facing a simple altar, it almost seemed an anti-church. Like inside the house, all the illumination came from hundreds of haphazardly placed votives, which made the chapel either glaringly bright or impenetrably dark, depending on where you looked. Our eyes had a hard time adjusting to the contrast.

Craning my neck, I could see the vague outline of the bell hanging sixty or so feet above the altar, from which dangled two equally long ropes. I knew nothing about architecture, but it seemed unusual that there would be no ceiling between the bell and the place of service. Did the priest pull the bell himself with those ropes during mass? No, surely not. As many years as we'd lived in the neighborhood, I'd never heard the bell toll once... although sometimes at night the windows at home pulsed in their panes as if something enormous nearby was being rhythmically struck. If the bell rang, it did so silently.

I felt exposed in the front pew. Luckily, Eugenia agreed.

"Let's move," she said. "We are too conspicuous here."

We changed locations, with Eugenia picking the darkest seats in the back row of pews. No one saw. The chapel was still empty. When we were seated, she put her hand in my lap, as mischievous as ever. *The lover's row*, she signaled by squeezing my penis through my slacks.

Despite my drunkenness, I felt myself becoming aroused. Quickly, I removed her hand and held it, tracing the silver rings she wore on every knuckle as I waited for my blasphemous erection to subside. But the blood pumping away from my head only served to leaden me. The scent of hot wax and dust, the unbearable closeness of the many candle flames—all combined into a dreamlike soporific.

With Eugenia squirming giddily beside me, I drifted off...

And awoke like being jostled against a live wire: electrified, teeth chattering.

We were now crushed together, my wife and I. However long I'd slept, all ten pews around us were filled: at least 80 people in all, twice as many as the seats could comfortably hold. The combined body heat should have made the church warmer, but instead the frost formed on my breath. It was as if, beneath their robes, each newly arrived parishioner straddled a block of ice.

I rubbed my eyes. All the parishioners were strange to me. They did not look kin to our neighbors at all. Like holes poked into balls of white bread, their milky faces had a hollow quality to them. Only their mouths were colored. Like us, they must have come from wine drinking. From those open lips, the parishioners' voices joined together in an atonal hum.

"The service is about to start," Eugenia whispered excitedly.

Swallowing my tension, I said nothing.

From the back of the church, there was a bleating.

The humming stopped. We all looked back.

Like a single man split in half, the two monks from earlier walked abreast down the aisle, escorting a calico nanny. With clopping hooves and protuberantly swollen teats, the goat's very presence in such a place was profanely comical. Mounting the altar, it bleated defiantly and dropped a small pile of turds. Eugenia stifled a giggle; many in the congregation snickered. But I felt that same sense of unease that you sometimes feel when a dream begins twisting into a nightmare.

One of the monks forced the goat to kneel. The other took one of the ropes dangling above the altar and wound it around the nanny's hind hooves.

"Rise!" his voice boomed.

With the murmur of fabric and the creak of old wood unbending, the congregation followed his command. Eugenia, almost frantic to stand, was one of the first; I, an outsider, the very last.

With its quivering pollywog pupil, the goat looked straight at me.

"Baaaah!" it shrieked in terror, as it was hauled upside down.

Hand-over-hand, the first monk hoisted it with the second rope, while a rusty pulley squeaked in the belfry above. Though the goat must have weighed at least a hundred pounds, the monk handled the job with sweatless strength, his very back muscles rippling beneath his cassock. Meanwhile, the other monk waved a censer, filling the altar with incense until it resembled a magician's smoking stage.

The goat was very high up now. Craning my head, I could barely see it, thrashing and braying as it entered the lightless recesses of the belfry. Wherever the pulley was attached, it looked like the goat was being hoist into the very bell itself. "Baah!" it screamed one last time, before the shadows swallowed it.

I squeezed out Morse code on Eugenia's hand.

What's happening?

Her eyes alight, a smile frozen on her face, she shook her head.

"Rise!" the monk bellowed again.

The incense parted like curtains. A priest appeared.

From his vestments, he was a cardinal or something similar. But unfamiliar with Catholicism as I was, my mind could not make sense of his appearance. His miter was an alien cathedral, all ibex-horn minarets, and tenth-dimensional apses: a miniature city perched upon a strange god's head. An unfathomable mosaic had been painted on his face: a series of multi-colored panels, each containing a feature — a nose here, an eyeball there — that seemed to shift across his visage, like facets recombining inside a kaleidoscope. Even his robes were bizarre: a single stripe of gold-fluted crimson winding around a dark inner cassock, so that he resembled a man partly peeled like an apple. Like the pale doppelganger of her heart, Eugenia's hand fluttered in mine. And from that, I knew his appearance was alien to her too.

From the chapel's lightless vaultings, the screams of the dangling goat multiplied into a cacophony within the bell. Meanwhile, the cardinal blessed the church, making first a familiar but top-heavy sign of the cross, then a circular multilayered zigzag which gave the impression of triangular superimpositions. It was unidentifiable as a symbol, but familiar somehow, like seeing someone trace a forbidden word in the air.

The dream had well and truly turned. Everything now was making me sick with fear.

The cardinal raised his hands. The whole congregation burst into song. Eugenia sang too, as if she already knew those polyglottal dissonances by heart. Full-throated, eyes unblinking, like her life depended on it. Was she scared too, or just enraptured? I couldn't be sure. Maybe she knew the song, but I doubt it: she was always so good at blending in.

I couldn't even understand the words, but I knew it was imperative for me to at least try. There was a hymnal in the pew in front of me. I picked it up; it was sticky.

As everyone sang around me, I opened the book's soft leather covers. They were moist and peeled apart like sopping layers of skin separating in a gash.

I tried to read what was printed on the open page but couldn't.

Whatever the song, it was printed in a font only a beating heart could read.

As the joke goes, the hymnal wasn't read, but red.

A psalm of plasma in a book of blood.

They began to shake terribly, my hands. But what terrified me more than the abominable book was my sudden awareness of Eugenia's face, which was staring down at the dripping pages. That face, which I had never seen afraid before, and from which I had always borrowed my bravery, was now utterly hollowed in fear—its elfin beauty transformed into something doglike and pitiful.

For both of us, time stopped: a single moment unraveling upon the event horizon of a nightmare We forgot everything except our fear—the painted pontifex, the crimson-lipped congregation, even the goat dangling screamingly above us.

Then the moment broke, and in thick ruby droplets, time again began to shower down upon us.

Baaah!

The nanny bleated one last time as the two monks at the altar madly jerked the rope tied to its hind quarters up and down.

Aaa-aaaa-aaah....

In wet muffled smacks, the goat collided with the bell's wrought-iron sides. I understood now where the shaking of our windowpanes at midnight came from; the very air itself vibrated as the goat's screams were knocked from her body. As her bones audibly snapped above us, blood ran down her body in rivers, dripping gelid clots upon the congregation. Clots which the rest of the parishioners save ourselves raised their open mouths to catch. To sizzle upon blue thrashing tongues as they bleated mockingly into the sky.

And, on the altar, the high priest of this revulsion intoned:

"O quae deliciae."

I felt, rather than heard, my wife gasp. But I was frozen, powerless to make any move except to squeeze her hand tighter in mine.

The singing stopped. The bell stopped striking. We all sat down. Except for the splashing of goat guts around us, the church became utterly silent. And then, in a syrupy-yet-ancient voice, the cardinal asked:

"Do we have an initiate who would join the congregation?"

Like two segments of the same bisected man, the monks turned their yellow eyes to where they thought I was. But we had moved from the front row.

Sensing something amiss, the congregation rumbled around us like a hungry stomach.

The cardinal stepped down from the altar. Exsanguinated robes swirling, he strode down the center aisle, peering searchingly down each row of pews as the two monks stalked up the far sides.

"We know you're here," he called.

Eugenia and I didn't dare exchange glances. We just squeezed hands, utterly alone in this nightmare except for each other. Our only hope was that we could escape detection.

It was not impossible. Covered in a slick coagulation of blood, we looked like revenants... and besides, Eugenia always fit in, no matter where she went. As long as I did not show *my* fear, it was plausible we could escape detection.

Yet as the clergy drew closer, it became clear to me that it was Eugenia who would give us away. Eugenia, who now trembled like a reed. Eugenia, with her jutting tongue and eyes too manic to blink. Eugenia, who had begun to emit a whine on the edge of hearing. Eugenia, whose hand throbbed stochastically in mine, not in our secret code, but in frantic jactitation, like a baby bird about to be crushed to death.

Her eyes sought mine. They were terrified.

As the monks drew even with our row, I stared at that frightened face I loved so much. And once more, I drew my strength from it. I kissed the back of her hand, and tapped into it:

Don't look back.

Then I launched to my feet, and because I knew it was the only way to move her, pushed Eugenia as hard as I could into the aisle as if trying to throw her off of me.

"Here I am!" I shouted, clambering over the back of the pew. "Catch me if you can!"

Which the parishioners easily accomplished, like catching a lamb for the slaughter.

"*Baah!*" they bleated mockingly as they dragged me down the aisle, away from my wife's stricken face.

To the altar, where the monks slammed my head hard against the stone.

And the high priest—whose putrid eyeballs rolled like marbles in their segments of his stained-glass face—flicked open both sides of my jugular with his spiraling thumbnails.

While the two monks guzzled first of my spurting arteries, smacking their bearded lips.

My life dribbled over the altar in rivulets, and the congregation assembled for communion in orderly lines, bleating into my face before they swallowed:

Baah! Baah! Baah!

And I, gasping as my inner voids collapsed into bloodlessness, sang delirious thanks to God...

"O quae deliciae."

Because at least my plan had succeeded. As the congregation drank away my life, my last sight was Eugenia slipping undetected out the back door.

But not before disobeying my final request.

Wilting her face in an instant, she spared a look back.

Eugenia came back in the daylight, body trembling, voice quavering, with two policemen who wearily scoured the chapel for a single drop of blood that could confirm her wild story.

They didn't find it. My congregation is very thorough. We ate all the hymnals; we licked the very floor tiles clean.

One of the officers climbed the ladder up to the belfry to look for a goat carcass around the clapper. But we'd devoured it down to its marrow. All he saw were bats.

And I was among them.

Hanging upside down with my congregation, I watched Eugenia scrabble pleadingly at the officer's lapels, begging him to keep looking. In that moment, I was struck by the unattractiveness of her upturned face, the near loathsomeness. How quickly her beauty faded, once it was given to grief and fright! Is it strange to say I desired her then more than ever?

With the cardinal's permission, I tried to go by our old house, to do to her what she once did to me. To ask her to join the frolic.

But the neighbors believed Eugenia, even if the police did not. A bathtub Mary now stands on our front lawn, and a São Cristo azulejo hangs on the front door. Eugenia had paid the generational blood price, and so our neighbors have loaned her the things that by ancient agreement will keep my congregation away.

But I too am now a local. And I am patient. These cheap knick-knacks might keep me from our old home, but they cannot keep her away from *us*.

I know my wife. Just as she cannot move away, which she should, she will not abandon me to the church forever. Some evening, Eugenia's curiosity and bravery will get the better of her fear. With the proper encouragement, she will once again creep by midnight through the catmint to confirm that which—save my disappearance—might otherwise have only seemed a dream.

And so, every night, as the congregation disperses the belfry and spreads through the neighborhood in search of new parishioners, I linger behind and rhythmically pull the rope. The bell is silent—the rust is too thick, the clapper too worn, for sound to escape—but you can still feel its reverberations from blocks away.

Five short jerks and five long tolls the ancient bell, in a code I know she will feel in the shuddering of her ruined heart: *Come come come.*

Eugenia is brave. Braver than her husband, whose thirst so quickly outgrew his sacrifice. She will answer the call of the bleating bell. '*If you insist*' will come her pulse, splashing the back of my throat in rhythmic jets.

And after, when we are married again in the eyes of our congregation, she will have come to know what it means to truly belong.

JELLYBEAN

John Paul Davies

When I was ten Grandad made me a coffin–
bone-white, six inches long. Cushioned lining
nestled a Dracula in dinner jacket and cape.

Smattering of red about his blanched face
betraying a recent feed, the vampire manikin
rose on thin wires when the lid was unlatched.

All I can remember when I'm shown yours,
ushered by the nurse into a strangely narrow room
where you've been placed on an old school-chair.

A nun lurks with literature confirming your soul.
In the half-raised sash window an alabaster Christ
overlooks the Children's communal plot.

Presented with a phial of holy water,
I sprinkle the lot – ignorant of procedure –
across the toy casket in a broken vertical line,

watching blessed water drip onto overly-bleached tiles.
Only thinking later I should've wetted a finger
to make the cruciform watermark, only thinking later

of liquid cells seeking each other in darkness,
droplets quivering before pooling,
of burgeoning life outsprinting the elements,

the primordial hungering for a simple hug.
Of you, waiting in contained gloom
to rise on thin wires at the lid's opening.

The Bones of Small Mammals

Scott McNee

RICHARD FOUND THE globster his first day on the beach, glistening by a cracked and whitened hunk of driftwood, as if it had crawled there for shelter. He assumed it was a stranded jellyfish, and kept his distance, because even dead he was afraid it could still sting. So, he resumed his scouring, wafting his metal detector over any curious spots that drew his interest. He had plenty of days ahead, and a coastline to fill them.

The divorce had brought him to the sea, to a caravan on the coast, free to indulge himself in childhood memories of coastal holidays. Free from all of Rosemary's complaints, though in truth it was she who had surprised him with the divorce. "Irreconcilable differences." Quite a straightforward admission that they had nothing in common, though a welcome surprise all the same. Sitting in the pier side café, he would look up from his bowl of chowder and appreciate the empty chair across the table.

His new home was dated, but he could always make the time to tear down shabby curtains and weed out the collectible ornaments cultivated by the previous owner. His hypocrisy in this amused him – he was fully intent on decorating the mantelpiece with anything interesting that was scoured up by his new metal detector.

The bleakness of the British coast was always the appeal for him. There would be some crowds in summer, the usual drunken teens, but it was hard to imagine crowds now, with the sky consistently overcast and looking down on beach pebbles scattered among the seaweed like bleached bone. Before the sea wall, an old puppeteer's booth stood stripped of curtains and paint, exposed interior revealing that even Punch, Judy and the baby had long since vacated the town.

There was a sense of privacy here – he told Alan, his eldest, as much over the phone.

'Your mother never cared for it. I always wanted to bring you and your brothers out here.'

'She said it wouldn't be good for us. Besides, I think she preferred travel.' Alan's voice was always hesitant, still a nervous boy in certain ways.

'It's still travel if you stay within the borders,' Richard said, and caught the rising tone in his voice as he considered that none of this was his son's fault. Even as a grandfather, he felt he should protect his children from any drama. After all, he assumed retirees were not typical employers of divorce lawyers. 'And you're always free to visit.'

'Hm,' said Alan, 'at some point.'

Most of the time, patrolling the stark stretch of beach below the pier, he could expect his only company to be the seagulls, their shrieking calls somehow reminiscent of the obscene banter of sailors, louder than any wave. He wondered if he resembled the members of this profane honor guard, another stooped figure picking along the beach, thinning hair like loose feathers. In time he might become a beloved sight, the sort people would nod at from café windows and say, 'there goes the detectorist again'.

On the day he found the globster, there was little to harvest on the beach. The sensor exposed tin cans and rusted flakes of long-decayed fences. This was within expectations – he'd chosen a patient man's hobby. Through the pier's long wooden pillars he glimpsed another treasure hunter leaving the beach, just as unsuccessful. Richard sympathized, but it was better to be alone with the gulls.

As he followed his route back up to the caravan, he passed the globster and stopped. Not a jellyfish then, he supposed, noting the lack of tendrils. The thing looked like a boulder made from the wrong material. He grimaced and went on to the caravan, to a ready meal and the collected stories of Paul Bowles and tried to forget the strange blight on his coast.

No one called that night, and after the boredom set in with the gin, Richard gave some thought to the thing on the beach. He could still work on a computer, despite what his grandchildren claimed, and he soon identified the lump as a globster. Nothing more than carrion, shaped oddly by the flow of tides. He was sure that sort of thing hadn't happened in his youth, but it was a reasonable explanation.

The next day, picking his way down the worn steps to the beach, he resolved to approach the globster properly. Those lines of text glaring from the screen the evening before had wiped any fear of the unknown from his thoughts, and besides, it was ridiculous for a grown man – a retired man! – to shy away from something so banal. The rent flesh of a whale rubbed away into obscurity, at worst collecting others along the way.

Once he was certain that the two boys he could see - atop the pier, leaning on the fence at the defunct arcade and laughing - were not watching him, he cornered the globster in its driftwood shelter.

Just flesh and brine and seaweed, he thought. Pulped together and shivering in the wind. Any identifying features had long since sloughed off and been whipped away into the currents, a fat carcass lashed into shapelessness. He knocked the detector against the driftwood, and the log rocked tentatively, the few remaining branches glancing off the globster's blubber as if repelled. Richard plucked a used tissue from his coat and covered his nose. Had the seaside always held this rank smell? Stench never came through in all those family photos.

He pressed the detector into the driftwood and forced it off balance. The branches sunk into the mass with a squelch, and when he stepped away, the driftwood did not roll back into place, its prongs fixed in the globster's bulk.

'Disgusting,' he said, and laughed. A local character, chattering away to himself.

He had more luck with the metal detector then, a few buried glints to be taken home and washed in the sink – one in particular, with multiple edges, appeared far more interesting than the bottle cap he initially judged it to be on the end of his trowel.

Sea water collected in a divot around his boot, and he straightened up to check the tide. Still safe, still quiet enough not be heard among the calling seabirds. The two boys had descended, now loitering at the other side of the pier pillars. Underage drinkers probably. Well, he thought, as long as they left him alone. Their figures were blotted, impressionistic under the dark overhang. He was about to return to his business when a third shape emerged, slow and stooped.

It looked to be the man from the day before, the other treasure hunter, though even at a distance Richard could tell he carried no equipment. The wrong sort of local character, Richard thought, from the way he sidled up the boys and appeared to engage in conversation.

Richard summoned enough recollection of his years as a disciplinarian to stride forward – before he knew what to say. The taste of salt in his mouth took on a metallic hint as he climbed over thin rises of crushed shell and pebble. Nearing them, he could see water drip from the boards of the pier down between the boys and the stranger. The sudden motion to the image slowed his pace. The sight was unsettling, yes, these boys turned attentive to the mariner-esque figure confronting them. But Richard could not find anything objectively *wrong* about it. The witchfinder attitude was unlikely to endear him to the townsfolk if he mistook a beloved local character for a predator.

He stood there, with his polystyrene bag of sand and relics, waiting for them to notice him – waiting for one of the boys to catch sight of a friendly face. He ventured a surreptitious cough. The sound disappeared amongst the gulls, and his assertiveness with it. He could have misread the situation. Surely he had – the boys did not look uncomfortable.

When he looked back all three were gone.

That night he arranged his successful scavenge – dull and encrusted with sand and seaweed, but his to claim nonetheless. Two little trophies to clean up and display. He ignored the ringing phone – more legal nonsense. Demands for more money, or accusations of invented misbehavior. That could all wait. If she really wanted to talk to him, she could get in her car and drive. When everything was cleaned to his satisfaction, he sat on the caravan's front step with a gin and tonic and looked out over the drystone walls at the faint light on a darkening sea. The phone continued to ring.

It was in the café a few days later that he heard about the boys.

Over an overly salted bowl of minestrone, his gaze drifted from the framed photographs of Punch and Judy shows on the pier to a flicker of movement in the window. At this angle, he could see across the street and through the railings of the sea wall, where a throng of people could be distinguished moving along the beach, loose hats and hair bobbing into view. They appeared to be walking in formation – seagulls scattered up into the air as the line moved forward.

He motioned to the waitress. 'What on earth is going on down there?'

'Couple of boys from the village went missing the other day. Their mum's got everyone combing the area. Well,' she said, indicating her uniform, 'everyone who can afford to.'

'Some sort of kidnapping?' said Richard, startled by how quickly the image of his grandchildren came to mind.

The waitress smoothed her apron. Her expression was strange. 'Most people think they drowned.'

He paid for his soup and endeavored to head down to the beach to investigate. The waitress seemingly forgot him, ear pressed to her phone as soon as her break started. Perhaps the mother left her boys in the care of Punch and Judy, and perhaps they drowned. Perhaps they lay under the globster's squat shimmer. But the silhouette of the beach's other occupant loomed whenever he tried to picture the missing – that stooped scavenger on the other side of the pier.

The search party were far along to the rocks by the time he got to sea level, and it appeared as if the gulls were going that way too, in hope of dropped food or rubbish. Richard rubbed the ache in his knee. He wouldn't be able to catch up to them now. He could call in a tip about the man later. Anonymous – he shouldn't get involved.

The globster was gone, dragged off by the tides that first brought it. Among the splintered remains of the driftwood, he could make out the empty shells of long dead crabs, and even small bones, bundled up like owl pellets. Feeling ridiculous, he glanced up. No owl, of course. Maybe the globster was more carnivorous than internet searches could reveal. A mouse's skull caught the dim sunlight and gleamed, still slicked with traces of the globster's gelatinous hide.

He sent a text to Alan once settled in the caravan with the heat on, asking after his grandchildren, as pleasantly as he could, so not to alarm him. He poured a gin and sat admiring his scavenged goods on the mantel – cleaned and bleached and new again. He regretted not taking before-and-after pictures.

Richard decided not to waste thought on the missing boys. These things were always down to bad parenting, not strangers lurking under rotting piers. He imagined the mother was much like his own Rosemary, too soft to ever discipline or reprimand. God knows how it took them this long to get divorced, the way he saw it. If he hadn't taken control of their sons, Alan onwards, they might have found themselves in the same situation as the incompetent on the shoreline today.

Richard's phone buzzed. The message made no sense, and he read over his own text in the hopes that he could make out a connection to the response.

I don't want you anywhere fucking near them, Alan's reply read.

The door to the caravan shook. 'Mister James! Mister Richard James!'

He could see the shape of them through the blinds, through the shabby, dated drapes. They did not have to shout 'police', but they did so anyway.

'We need to speak to you about an incident, Mister James.' The door handle jarred in its lock.

Richard looked to the mantle. It occurred to him that he should have avoided decorating it with his treasures.

THESE BONES OF CLAY

Dyani Sabin

THE HOUSE AT the top of the hill has a basement that's always open to the public. A man sits in a booth set up by the cellar doors, in an orange ball cap and a tweed sweater. He's reading a newspaper, the morning's edition of *The San Francisco Chronicle*. In front of him is a placard with slightly faded blue letters that reads:

"Visit the Endless Holes! $5 Entrance. All Sales Final."

This place always seemed like a tourist trap. The holes aren't visible from the booth, or the windows, you and some friends had snuck up there one night and got chased off by the desk attendant. Either way, it has to be some kind of prank, endless holes—a total racket. But your desk-mate from Destinsurance took a date here and they couldn't stop talking about it at the office holiday party.

"It's incredible, just holes, right there in the wall—I don't know how they do it!"

Standing alone with your second Aperol spritz and a plate of uneaten, bad, spicy ham hors d'oeuvres, you had rolled your eyes obviously enough that he'd dared you to go take a look, elbowing his date like they knew something you didn't. Assholes.

And here you are, ready to prove that it was a fake and he is a fool. A fool with a girlfriend who will go on fun dates to random attractions, but whatever. You'd prove something. As you stand here, your heart thumps loudly in your chest, as if you are a rabbit staring up at a dog. As if there was something to be afraid of. A hole is a hole, and this is an old house with a gimmick.

The golden-yellow paint on the shingles is chipping in that square way that means it was old enough to have a few lead paint jobs in its lifetime. Now the house sags a little over the booth, age pulling the wood back to the Earth. The paving stones of the sidewalk are sunken into the ground, moss creeping across the edges.

For a tourist trap, you've never seen this place advertise anywhere, but everyone who lives nearby seems to know about it. For a moment you try to remember when you first heard of the holes beneath the house—were you in second grade? The memory slips away.

You walk up the stones to the booth. The man is younger than you expected, maybe in his thirties, but his eyes are weary.

You gesture at the sign. "Are they really endless?"

"Seems like." He shrugs.

"You've never tried to find the end?"

"No." He grabs the bill of his Giants cap, flips the hat up, resettles it on his head. "Folks do. We don't police the holes. But everyone who's gone into one of the holes has stayed."

"Seriously?" You look down at the cellar stairs. They're concrete, the cellar beneath a dim brown, dank shadows in contrast to stripes of sunlight shooting through narrow basement windows.

"Are you going in?" The man asks. He holds out a hand.

You jerk your five-dollar bill away from him. "In a hole?"

"No, to the cellar." His mouth tightens in irritation.

"You want to come with me?"

The look he gives you would curdle yogurt.

You hand him the bill.

"Holes are down the stairs, straight ahead, you can't miss them." He leans back in his booth, completely unconcerned about you now that his task is complete and opens up the newspaper again. The sports section, where the Giants are mentioned below the fold. Typical.

The temperature drops as you walk down, just a few degrees, but enough to notice. The basement seems pretty ordinary if an oddity for California. A very old house, built before World War II and the construction rush. Concrete steps lead to a bare earth floor, copper pipes in the ceiling, the smell of stone and musty air, a slight tang of decomposition. The walls are reinforced with stone, but they're earthen, not poured concrete. You add a handful of decades to your mental estimate of the house's age.

On the far wall, like you've been told, are the holes. Four of them, perfectly square, two feet by two feet wide, in a two-by-two pattern, about a foot of dirt between them. You step closer. Exquisitely square, cut into the dirt, as far back as you can see. The soil is a dark clay with a dank smell that reminds you of nights catching salamanders as a child.

You cannot see the back of the hole.

It has to be painted, a false back. The dirt in the holes shift gradually into darkness, the color deepening until there is a square without light at the far back. You glance between the holes, pull out your phone and turn on the flashlight. More of the hole is illuminated, but the dark square of black at the center remains.

For a second you look back, but the man at the cellar door hasn't made any noise except for the slight rustling of newsprint. You stick an arm into the hole and try to feel for the false back. The air pulses around your fingertips. You lean a shoulder in, head on the outside, straining—nothing.

It can't be real. Endless holes?

You stretch farther and try to remember the first time you heard about the holes.

Second grade. The little girl with the pigtails. You can't remember her name. Constantly runny nose, drew monsters in orange and green crayon, would play pretend horses. One day you were foxes instead, up in a burrow.

"They are endless!" she said, a stamp of her foot as you sat inside the turn of the slide at recess. "They go back and back and there's nothing there."

"No way. Someone had to dig it," you said with all the conviction of a seven-year-old.

She clenched her little fists, the yellow light glowing through the slide and making her into a creature of sun and magic. "The holes go on forever. My mommy left us, she crawled into a hole, and we watched her go and go and then she was gone."

For some reason this made you scream uncontrollably, like she had trapped me there, a rabbit in a fox den. They dragged you out of the slide and your shoes fell off. Little black patent leather things that pinched your feet.

When your mother picked you later, hair half-done and makeup smeared, she kissed your forehead and got you In-n-Out. Sitting in the drive through, she smiled at you in the rear-view mirror. "It's true her mother died unexpectedly, but I am sure it wasn't from crawling into a hole. You shouldn't worry," she'd told you, seven and scared shitless, clutching a paper bag of fries like a lifebuoy, "people don't leave that way."

Now you wonder if that was your friend's last memory of her mother before she'd died, stretching into one of these holes and touching the back. A harmless trip to the sights of the neighborhood. You could prove it right now.

But you don't want to crawl face-first into the dark.

You stick a foot in. They wouldn't be able to hide the back much further than that. Darkness wraps around your leg, the air warm, and again you feel nothing. No resistance. It tugs at you, even. You drag your leg out, panting. Sweat beads at the edge of your collar and temples.

There's no reason to think that if you enter the hole you can't come back out.

And had that been the first time you heard about the holes, anyway? You'd had some knowledge, an argument about holes needing to be dug. That had to come from somewhere. You study the holes. Which one seems the most difficult to dig, the hardest to hide the false back?

Light moves across the basement all day, so in the morning, the light from the cellar door would shine directly into the one on the top left.

It's a little awkward to climb into but the dirt is firm and doesn't crumble. It's just close enough that you feel dirt on both sides of your legs, and you can rise up onto your elbows but no higher. You have to walk using your toes and forearms, scooting back into the dark. Each motion you feel sure you'll hit the back. It takes a little to get used to, but soon the edge of the hole is a full body's length away and you're cocooned in the dark.

"Dude, how deep is this? How did you do this?" Your voice in the hole is small, the earth muffling the noise.

The man at the booth doesn't respond. You close your eyes and pretend it's like playing foxes, dug into your burrow, and preparing to hunt. Her name was Kit, you remember. Little fox. She didn't talk to you after that day. You open your eyes to the dank walls, the smell of fog from the bay and redwoods growing and rotting.

For a moment you panic. You flail against the walls, against the ground, beating it with your hands and feet. Scratching and screaming, clay gets under your fingernails, stains your elbows blue and grey. When you look up, the exit is at least fifteen feet of crawling away. The scratches you left aren't visible, the walls are too dark already.

You could crawl back out, the hole assumed to be endless, go home. But. There's something about this hole. It's cool in here, the air velvety across your skin.

You're three, digging in your backyard, in a pit of dirt up to your shoulder. The sensation of the memory grows as you press an arm to the wall. The clay is smooth on your arms. You dig and dig until your mother picks you up and puts you in a bathtub. She scrubs your arms until the flesh is raw and pink.

She isn't here so you rub your arms on the walls and enjoy the soft, slick muck of the clay. The dirt around you changes in color, softening as you look towards the basement, where a square of brightness sits in your vision. You're deep enough that you can't quite make out the details of the cellar, or the light through the door. You have been scooting for hours.

In your mind, there is someone screaming. A memory. The voice is low and rough. "It didn't have to be like this! It didn't have to end this way!"

Your mother holds your hand, her palm large around yours. She is perfectly still, in an orange sundress, a straw hat on her head. You wear shoes that pinch and a dress with pink lace.

A man is hip-deep in one of the holes, shoving himself backwards, face red. "You've driven me to this, you know! This is on you!" He doesn't quite fit in the hole, his movements awkward, but he gets it, the shuffle, and vanishes.

Your mother smiles as she picks you up and carries you away. The four squares, like gaping eyes, stare at you as you're carried up the cellar doors. The man is still wearing that same orange Giant's hat.

You press your forehead against the clay, sobs wracking your body. Your father. That man was your father. He crawled into one of these holes.

The dark soothes you. It's okay, you think, to be in a hole.

It's easy to scoot backwards. The back has to be there. Or your father's bones.

But if other people crawled in here, wouldn't you find their bodies? You're far enough back that wouldn't you have found someone by now, if it was something people did? Die in here? There's no way to turn around, to look behind you. There's only your feet. You kick off your shoes, using your toes alone to wiggle out of them. It's hard to scoot over them, the heavy heels you wear to feel cute and attractive, but soon they vanish into the dark in front of you.

Free, your feet press against the dirt, learning the contours of the square, the straight edges. There's nothing but the clay, no trace of anything. You touch the ground, spreading your palm across the dirt. It's perfect, unmarred.

There is no reason to think anyone else who crawled in here ever stopped.

You could.

If you wanted.

Light is a memory now, a pinprick that dances in front of your eyes. It's hard to know if what you see is a mirage, or the way light comes, on and off, as sun moves in front, and then away, from the cellar door. You no longer know how long you've been in here.

The hole embraces you. Your rabbit heart suits this place, its patter the only sound other than your breath and the earth eats both without asking if you wanted them.

You curl your toes. Press against your arms and move your body.

Deeper in. If there's an end, you'll find it.

You can always go back.

Postulation

Sophia N. Ashley

To merit a crisis, we stomach a foreign object,
tide our tongue with grace.
my ribs, lodged into a vessel.
the slow river of my vomit, kayaking.

my tutor says: girls who house girls in their mouth permutates.
the skin— directly proportional to a constant miracle.

girlhood is maths worn sideways.
we're conjuring a heated assumption,
& I take the space between your legs for
an accurate premise.

here, I debunk my father in past tense,
unnaming the ashes.
I've lived his name to a grudge.

I intend pinning you down, purposeful as a bullet.
I intend a lettering:
our loins ruptured into ampersand— the way your head meets my thighs in reverse.

we put the warmth to use.
summer, leaking from our sunned flesh.
this season names you after a theorem alive, but for a while.
we catch ourselves trailing its bullets to a logical surrender.

mid-solstice, I dug up our passports.
a sweatless migration unsettling the soil.

I identify as a gash somewhere on the face siphoning your labia region,
to spill a poison that writes our loins in third person pronoun.

your lips on mine reminds me: each wound begins with an opening.
each crisis begins with a mouth.

in the dark, I offer myself as a vista for how women should be perceived.
the gap between a thigh & a thigh is an object going same way into each lively hole.
the ricochet, barking our worths.

your mouth meeting mine is how I learn to spark a flame.
I give off ashes as an aftertaste.
trail how sweat by way of heat landlocks your loin,
rioting to prove our bodies first principle.

Pipes

Alina Măciucă

When the pipes spoke to Cătălina, they fidgeted in their brass stands and sand dripped through the cracks in the walls.

"We saw you talking to her. You carried her groceries to the ninth floor." They jangled and groaned. "You went out of your way."

Plastic boxes of all sizes, filled with food that had traveled by bus from the small mountain town she grew up in, now lined the shelves of her fridge. But she snatched two eggs and cracked them open over her free-cycled frying pan.

An unfortunate and frustrating fate, to be imprisoned in walls. Cement plaques eroded on top of other cement plaques. Together, they built an intended-to-be-perfect, ten stories high parallelepiped. All the blocks had pipes running through their walls. But not all of them ran their mouths on the tenants.

Cătălina crafted a pair of earplugs out of a cotton ball and stuffed them deep inside her ear canal. Still, her bones vibrated to the rhythm of their speech. Even while sleeping, she could predict the pipes' verboseness, skill which had glued two dark circles under her marten like eyes.

"We told on her. You knew she had a lover, right? We told Dan she'd never leave her husband. And we proved it, too."

She dumped her fried eggs on a grease smudged plate, next to three slices of marinated cheese.

"Dan never came unless he called her 'mom'. Can you imagine? Her husband knew everything about the affair. She was in it for the money, and he loved his gambling, so he couldn't really complain, if she took care of his needs, too. Such a promiscuous woman. Of course, you can't empathize with what it feels like to be mocked by someone you love. You can't comprehend something you don't know."

"Was any of this even true?" she scratched the plate with her fork when she dipped a piece of bread in egg yolk.

"So, you hear us. Does it matter? She is dead now. Dan gutted her like you gut a chicken before shoving it into the oven."

Frost crystals thickened her window, splattered in a chaos of angles. To cancel the pipes, Cătălina counted them all while she ate. Two hundred and thirty-four before she gave up.

Last month, the plumber claimed to have replaced the crumbling lead with PVC. That should have fixed it. But the pipes never ceased their gossip.

Pileș of sweaters and jeans adorned the lino covered floor of her studio, much to their dismay.

"Your clothes reek," they said. "And your house is disgraceful. Women like you, few as they are, always end up alone." They never raised their voice. However, she took the condescension and sternness in their tone like a punch to the stomach.

"Do you tell others about me?"

"There is nothing to tell. You lead a boring life."

That evening, she cut dozens of paper sheets into almost perfect tiny squares. She filled them with formulas and definitions, lettering so small you'd need a magnifying glass to read. By sunrise, she had transcribed all the highlighted chapters in her Textile Engineering hardcover to hundreds of minuscule pieces of paper she had stacked on her desk.

"You could spend your time studying instead of looking for so many ways to cheat," her neighbor said. By the yellowish tinge of his fingers, he melted two packs a day, for sure: cigarette after cigarette, eighteen hours straight. "I pity the poor idiots who'll give you a job one day." She pushed the red button that stood out as an ugly canker on the iron panel. As if summoned, the elevator roared into the shaft and started its descent from the top floor.

Onions, celery, potatoes, and chicken boiled together in a pot big enough to feed a family of four for a week—one housewife on second brewed chorba. The women on the second and fourth always stayed home, unless they went shopping for groceries. A few students lived dispersed throughout the block of flats—they always came and went, thus Cătălina never had a precise number. Two seamstresses, one nurse, four schoolteachers and at least twenty-nine other women who had reached the official retirement age had made homes out of the tiny, gray matchboxes they called apartments. That left about twenty doors which she had never seen opening.

Six floors later, she stepped out of the elevator without saying goodbye. "I know about your son," she said.

She wiped the slush off her boots on her free-cycled door mat. Sunbeams speared through her broken shutters and shone little ponds of light on her living room carpet.

Cătălina snowballed her laundry and dumped it in the rattan basket she kept in the kitchen. Because she couldn't figure out what to do next, she swiped the floors and did the dishes, while pondering at the emptiness filling the cement cube, they all lived in when the pipes were too busy to chatter.

Earlier that day, she had won them an undeserved victory. She should have never thought of her neighbor's son.

"You're the only person I know that uses a landline."

"My parents use one, too. So does my uncle. That's the way it's supposed to be."

No boy had ever set foot in that flat before. Not since she had moved in. Maybe her aunt had welcomed boys, men even. None of them had spent enough nights to be remembered.

Cătălina's overall blandness made it impossible for her to class as one of the cool girls. Neither tall, nor short, almost blonde, but not quite. A green scrunchie strangled her ponytail.

She gulped down a mouthful of cocoa liquor. Despite its almost unbearable sweetness, it burned her throat and landed in her stomach like a Molotov in a bankrupt bakery.

"Should I turn the radio on?" she asked. She had wired two sturdy speakers to her radio, as she once thought it would shut the pipes up.

"I won't be able to concentrate with music on."

"Just one song and I'll turn it off". She pressed the red button and love-me-boom- boom tunes melted the icicles with their beat.

His lips felt coarse, his tongue scraped her gums like sandpaper. In a moment of self-forgetfulness, she snorted tangerines and motor oil off his neck.

When she had planned her move, she thought she'd ride him like a wild beast in heat. But she couldn't cancel the transactional vibe attached to every thrust. The pipes must have burst during her transgression, for they said nothing.

Inside her, infinite rows of teeth chattered. They had castrated and muted the boy. He squatted by the door and tied his shoelaces. Didn't even shoot her one glance. Perhaps the blood running down her leg had gushed out of him, not her.

She let the night enwrap her, as she sunk into the couch. Alone felt good.

They roared like war trumpets. “Love is not for you.” For the first time in four days, they talked. “Don’t waste your time on love.”

“You have paid no attention to us at all, have you? I don’t love him.”

“We already told everyone that you do. We had to. They’d think you were easy. No,” they said. “It did not upset us. We felt honored you had us witnessing you becoming a woman, so generous of you to have given us such a gift.”

“You’re welcome.”

“In return, we’re restoring your dignity. You told him about the baby. You argued, he pushed you around. He got scared, you got scared. You plunged a kitchen knife into his stomach.”

“What if there’s no baby?”

“You lose the child. All the spotlights are on you, and you can’t handle it. The authorities harass you with phone calls and paperwork. You’ve been trending on social media for seventy-three exact hours, but a couple on the fifth just admitted to having assisted their elderly neighbor with killing herself, shortly after finding out there’s a will to their name. You are the star of the neighborhood groups. Tired of everything it had brought with it, your body now kills it and then spits it out, mangled.”

“And what if I say no?”

“It has already happened. We have told the tale. It is now their truth.”

“It couldn’t have all happened in one week.”

“Many of your neighbors already stared him down while riding the elevator together. You killed a man. Also, mold got to your pickles. Be sure to dip the lids in boiling water and strain the brine.”

Without even trying, the pipes hit hard. Cătălina, the mythical heroine who matched her pleated skirt with snow boots poked the dragons in the walls with her toy sword and lost the battle with significant casualties: a life she neither owned, nor had the right to, wasted on a petty quarrel.

The next day, she woke up to a persistent knock on her door. In a faint gesture of solidarity, the housewife on second touched Cătălina's arm for a second, and then passed her a bowl of potato salad—huge, pink, wrapped in plastic foil. Behind her, Gabriela, the nurse, and a few of the unnamed students saluted her as a war hero. Outside, snowflakes dropped like Tetris pieces on the semi-frozen branches.

"They're a minor nuisance, the police. But you've won the respect of your fellow neighbors, that's all that matters," the pipes said as soon as she bolted the door.

"What pipes are there that speak?" She pulled a strand of hair out of her scalp and twisted it around her left index finger so hard she thought it might fall off.

"But we are not pipes." They laughed so hard, her aunt's framed needlepoint patches fell to the floor. Windows vibrated, glass shattered. "We are your aunt, Mariana. And Anca, the first worker woman that set foot in this grovel. Ioana, wife to the farmer who owned this plot before, all women to have ever worked this land, their daughters too. We oozed into the earth and when this block sprung—the ugliest flower of all—we climbed up the pipes, little by little, like mold. We listened to everyone argue, argue, argue, argue, and argue with each other. We saw babies coming out, and old men tripping down the stairs, their brains pouring from their old, fragile skulls. Wives cheating, men hitting their women with their fists and their children with leather belts. Some people here have their mattresses stuffed with enough money to buy the entire building with, while others have hung themselves standing on top of a pile of unpaid bills. But you're gonna be a tough nut to crack, first one to ask us who we are."

"I killed him because he wouldn't get me a car. I asked. He refused, so I broke his face with a hammer I had placed on the counter for this very purpose." Her neighbor would believe she could kill a guy for as dinner in a restaurant downtown. She should have never mentioned his son. However, this time, his hatred of her came to her advantage. If she couldn't prove that no one had died, not by her hand, at least, she could weave another story herself. Anything but theirs, even if she needed to spend the next twenty years locked up. Away from the pipes, it didn't stand out as a bad idea.

"Eventually, one of us will find out who you are. For real. The rest will know what one of us knows. You'd better say goodbye to your fans." He stepped out of the elevator once it reached the second floor.

Someone had left a pot of warm stew on her cooking machine and replaced her moldy pickles with edible ones. For the first time, she needed a moment to figure why she fought them, after all.

One morning she checked for a way to tell whether someone had had a miscarriage recently, or if they should expect any symptoms. Another time, she snuck into the technical room, hoping to find him dead or alive.

"Did you really kill him with a hammer?" One kid from the fifth buzzed at her door.

"Take a seat, and I'll share all the juicy details." She removed the chain and opened the door wide.

"You won't kill *me* with a hammer, will you?"

She made the kid take his shoes off and lit him a cigarette. Poured him a glass of cold coke and sliced him a piece of homemade strawberry zephyr cake.

"Only a few of them believe your lies." This time, the pipes raged. Plaster dispersed in hundreds of tiny white pieces when it fell off the walls.

"Then why all the screaming?"

"The child we breastfed grew up to be a snake." The kitchen faucet burst and covered her in cold water. Her sweater sponged it all up.

The myriad of stickers glued to the tiles surrounded her in a dance of death. Encapsulated in her wet clothes, she dashed out of the kitchen. Cold as the river it streamed from, water sprinkled from two of the pipes crossing the living room ceiling. It showered over her couch and over her desk, as if the strongest pump in the world pushed it through. Her soaked socks and slippers only encumbered her, so she dumped them as she rushed to the fuse panel.

On her way to the bedroom, Cătălina stumbled through cables. She slipped on the linoleum and landed on her back, but the cold water numbed the pain.

The pipes had drenched all of her piled up clothes, now an underwater mess. She stood up and raced for the door. Water burst out when she opened it.

"Stop listening to them." She pounded her neighbors' doors with her fists. "Get out, get out of your houses." She shook one doorknob until it rattled free.

When one stay-at-home-mothers opened hers, Cătălina grabbed her arms and pulled her out of her flat. Her untrimmed nails left scratch marks on the woman's forearms.

"Get out, go." She pushed her towards the stairs. The woman sobbed. She wore a velour tracksuit and flannel socks.

Cătălina gripped an older neighbor's flannel shirt. He backed down and shoved her tumbling on the floor.

"Get her some tea," one voice in the crowd said.

"It's because she lost her kid. It screws with your hormones," said another.

"I planned it." She rose to her feet and pointed at someone she didn't even know. "I'm a cold-blooded killer. I did it for the money." She staggered.

"You pushed him because he wanted to hurt you and your baby. You can't kill a fly. What is this nonsense?"

She shoved the stay-at-home-wife into the wall and then grabbed her by the hair in two concise action-movie moves. She expected they'd seize her and bind her hands, push her off the woman, to the floor. They all stood as spectators to a once-in-a-lifetime show.

"Look at me," she said, and eyed the crowd, one by one.

Her legs convulsed at the song of Cătălina bashing her head against the wall. It smudged a heart with the bottom of a pineapple on the wall. Submerged in a sea of strikes and blows, her face eventually caved in. The crowd blinked in unison with the thumping sounds. For a few moments, their hearts found a new rhythm to beat to.

Drenched in water and blood, she dropped the body and stood before them. Water had stopped pouring, and the walls stood quiet. Outside, an icicle smashed to the ground and dozens of pieces glided on the frozen pavement.

Then the railing detached from the concrete stairs and took everyone that leaned on it with it when it fell. Nothing else around them budged, but their block trembled in waves. The flight of stairs broke into two separate pieces, walls crumbled. Dust stuck to Cătălina's clothes. It went up her nostrils, into her lungs. She covered her face with her wet blouse.

She clutched her elderly neighbor's pants. Strange, she would never have expected to cling to life. Pieces of mortar and bricks hit her head. She let go. While sliding on the pile of rubble, her knee twisted to her back after it hit an iron bar.

Her bones started chattering as she swam through the debris. They fidgeted in her flesh. Those bones had many stories to tell. Like the dead upon waking up for the last judgment, they jangled, and they groaned.

Defeated, she let her limbs go numb and floated, as vibration lifted her high in the air. Under the pressure of unseen hands, her knee twisted back into place, and her shriek silenced the voices in her bones.

Click-bait headlines will announce the tragedy of the concrete mastodon crushing its tenants under its frayed bones. On TV screens, yellow ribbons will state the body count. Architects, engineers, and anthropologists alike will debate the city dwellers' need to keep up with the ever-changing standards of living: young families tearing down the walls between the kitchen and the living room. After work, tired men watch the game while their wives cook dinner and video call expatriated cousins, but the missing wall tricks their brains into thinking they spend quality time together.

"That's why everyone on public transport smells like they're working in a burger joint." As expected, the moderator will throw a joke into the mix of platitudes.

Just to secure some screen time, the anthropologist will dump a series of statistics on natality, which correlate to a very common request the interior designer guest receives—expanding the matrimonial bedroom into the kids' room. Nonetheless, they will all agree that you shouldn't really tear down walls in your flat, because it messes with the building's structure.

While the first responders checked for survivors, Cătălina stole a blanket from one of their crates and wrapped it around her shoulders. She took a seat in the back of the 739 that she usually rode to classes. Leaning against the window, she cracked her knuckles and waited for other passengers to hop on. Now, the monolith blocks towering over the boulevard struck a different chord with its thousands of secrets and millions of turns things could take should the tenants unravel them.

Boys, teachers, heartbreaks, and new sneakers—the silken-haired teenager next to her covered it all while on the phone with her friend, and their secrets spread like an airborne disease. Screens flickered all around them. Passengers argued with their spouses and confessed their sympathies to their co-workers in a frenzy of taps. Cătălina eavesdropped. As her eyes rolled from one phone to the next, her bones rumbled—the scapula and clavicles, the metacarpals, the sacrum, and the coccyx—all in unison with the war chant of a thousand ghosts.

Ghosts, Always

David Rees-Thomas

THE SOUND IN the room is a wash of silken static. Dove stares at the windows on the other side, blackness like a thick coat of paint beyond, and nothing between the strangeness of the bed and the darkness triggers any memory.

There is a plaque on the wall suggesting someone famous once stayed here. She's read it twice, but the name doesn't stick. Someone from the sixties?

Sounds, music if she focuses, trapped then expunged, rising again, unable to leave her, and she opens herself to it all. She has a note in her hand, and she knows she's been holding it some time. Dove tries to focus on the words. Her words? She doesn't think so, but...

Remember me. We are ghosts. Always, it reads, and she mouths the words silently, her lips dry and sore.

She places the note on her laptop and stands, feeling the softness of the bed with her hand. The suite is large, luxurious, embellished with the weight of the vintage torn from old TV shows and movies. But Dove prefers quiet lines, the sense that the ambient nature of a space can just recede into itself, completely disappear.

And even then, there are always noises.

Ghosts, she thinks. Always.

There is a record player in the room, but no records. Dove brushes her fingertip against the needle and turns the power on to hear the crackle on her skin. She takes out her phone, ignoring the alerts, and records the sound of herself. She names it, "Skin on Needle," and files it away in her reference folders with the mind to using it later. So many sounds, hoarded, unused.

The door reverberates as someone or something on the other side knocks twice. Dove presses her ear and her hands against the thick wood, holding her breath, hoping it may or may not knock again.

She peeks into the corridor, the light is dim, suffused by a sulfur glow, and the wallpaper reeks of the past, a shabby browning floral pattern. The man stands back from the door initially, then walks past her into the room only after she makes eye contact.

"Good morning," he says.

Dove stares at the windows, the blackness giving no hint as to the veracity of his claim.

He places a tray containing a pot and two cups on a stand near the bed. "Darjeeling," he says. "I think I remember reading somewhere that you like it."

Dove closes the door, and sits on the floor, grabbing a cushion from the bed as she does so, a chill draught against her feet.

He hands her a cup and sits cross-legged opposite her.

"Thank you," she says, and looks at him intently, trying to discern his features, trying to locate the essence of him in her mind, but nothing is stable, and she gives up, content in the end to watch as his face merges with itself. He could be anyone, he could be everyone.

"I was listening to you this morning," he says.

Dove looks away, trying to focus on the floral scent of the tea, to something that feels real.

He laughs awkwardly. "Not to you, not in here, but to your record, the first one you ever released. It's beautiful, every time I listen, I hear something new, it could just be a sound, but it's always so much more than that. It always invokes a memory, an ambient detail."

He nods toward her laptop. "Are you working on something now? I love how you blend the recordings of the daily world, with radios, with voices, with impossible sounds."

Dove stands and walks to the laptop, closing the lid, her back to him. "I, I don't know," she says. "Sometimes I still hear things, and I just need to get them, I need to collect them. But already I feel there is a palatial hauntology collected within me. Nothing I have to say comes from me, I am a collection of the dead." She turns back to him. "As are we all, I guess."

But he's no longer there. Just a room, with blacked out windows, and an open door. And somewhere down the corridor, music, old music, maybe hers.

She returns to the bed, places her hands on the sheets, feeling the weight of all the people who have slept here, all the dead.

Does he work for the hotel? A fan?

Her first album, *Scrapes*, was used as the backdrop to a TV show she never watched, its distilled ambient harshness so quiet at times as to almost become simply breathing. She sits on the floor again, sipping at the cooling tea, unable to remember where all the sounds emanated from, or how she chose which of the recordings ended up in the sampler, then projected onto her musical tableau.

Other people, close to her, and some she only remembers as shades and silhouettes, fill her mind, complete with nagging thoughts of unfinished conversations, uninitiated obligations. Always ghosts, she thinks, always incomplete.

She calls reception, the music growing in the dense air of the room, filtering toward her through the corridors of the hotel as if the sounds somehow picked up other sounds, old sounds, dead sounds, as they collided with the architecture, the textures of the furniture, and the molecular level debris of all that has passed.

The voice on the other side of the phone is already talking as their lines connect, but she can't understand, it's just a stream of words that could be English but could equally be something altogether different.

"Is it me?" she asks. "Are you talking to me?"

The voice pauses, then continues, only slower. "I am the manager," it says, and she thinks it's a man.

And then she hears crying, soft sobs coming down the line, and with this he starts the incantations once more, so many words and so many tears that it seems impossible for it all to emanate from one person.

She looks around with a sharp glance. There is someone else in the room with her, has to be. But the shadows hold no secrets, there is only the dead air and the dense windows. The music changes, and now it's music within music within music, each layer transforming and sliding in and around the rest, and all of it filtered through the decades, and the dead of the room.

"We can't fight forever," says the voice of the manager. "Always ghosts." And then he slides once more until the sound gradually diminishes and dies.

Someone pulls the curtains, and it's not her. She blinks. Asleep? It's unclear. She doesn't remember curtains before, just the impenetrable darkness of the window.

There is sunshine, at least what she remembers as sunshine, and it warms her feet which dangle over the end of the bed, almost as if they don't belong.

The hotel staff stands between the bed and the sunshine, a halo around his head. Is it the same man as earlier, the fan who knew her work?

So many sounds, not just whatever is in her head.

"You like my music," she says as she pulls herself into a sitting position, sliding to the foot of the bed where the sun has created a lighter patch against the heavy dark red of the bedspread.

The staff member moves and looks at Dove with a glance that suggests she's seen many things, and this doesn't surprise her.

"Ah, sorry," says Dove. "I thought you were the other person who works here. He brought me a cup of tea earlier, I think."

"Tea?" says the woman, with a slight hint of an accent, maybe Liverpool.

Dove points at the pot on the floor between two cushions.

The woman looks but doesn't seem to care. "There's only me here, love. Maybe a friend of yours stopped by."

"Only you?"

The woman nods, and steps back into the sunshine, her hand against the glass. "I want to return."

"Return?" Dove stands and steps toward the woman, picking up the teacups and the pot as she does so, placing them back on the tray.

The woman turns to her and takes the tray. "My brother got married. I would have liked to have been there, but..."

"Does he live far away?"

"Of course. They all do in the end. I feel like we've been fracturing since birth, and that although we can sometimes return and touch, it just means we move further away the next time."

Dove takes her recorder out again, eager to get the woman's words and the strange music down.

The woman grasps her hand, staring at the mic, and the moment freezes. She bends down and enunciates with a breathy clarity. "It's hard. Always ghosts. They crowd our minds."

Dove gathers sounds, tapping at the walls, on the furniture, straining to hear any creaks or groans or whispered voices in the old hotel. Where is this hotel? She can't remember checking in, but she knows she was escaping.

The foyer is empty, the world beyond the revolving doors at the front black and empty. All the lights are low, and when she looks at them, she senses they are in the course of dimming. No one is at the reception desk, but she hears a faint scratching sound from a back room. The whole place smells of lavender dropped in a bath, and under that, there is a faint trace of undisturbed dust, mottled damp that crawls into the shapes and structures of the hotel.

"Is anyone there?" she asks, surprised at how muffled her voice sounds, expecting that it would ring out in the empty foyer. "I need some help, I need to leave. I don't know when." She pauses to wait for an answer, and the rustling scrapes and scratches still emanate from the back room.

She thinks she sees something flickering, and it reminds her of an old black and white TV she once saw in a movie.

"Soon," she says, her voice even quieter.

Dove wants to search the room, but when she reaches behind the reception counter to undo the latch for the swing gate, the chattering noises cease, and the flickering dies, the space merely darkness, just like the world beyond the doors.

She runs back to her room, careful not to touch the walls, or the banister on the stairs, extra careful not to look too closely into the dusky corners, the strangeness beyond.

Inside, she is relieved by the warmth and the soft lights. She shuts the door, checking that it's locked, and boots her laptop.

She opens her folders of finished work and works in progress. Dove clicks the most recent piece. She doesn't know it, she can't recall creating it, and when she tries to open it, there is an error message. She stares at the title, and it's meaningless, just a random string of numbers, grammatical marks, and letters. She tries another, the same thing happens, and another.

Folders within folders within folders, deeper and deeper, spiraling in such a way that she can't find the way out anymore. She slides to the floor, overwhelmed by the amount of information, the laptop open on the bed, opening and closing folders all by itself, over and over, the whole room sliding back down into the center of a bleak hole.

Dove comes to, a sticky string of saliva dribbling from her mouth. She sucks it in and wipes her lips with the back of her hand. The musty odor of a dying carpet is thick in her nostrils, and the sounds are distant, as if they are being played at a far off party, music for someone else's benefit, but music she recognizes as her own.

She stands and centers, positioning herself in the middle of the room. "I have no memory of this place," she says to the air, enjoying how the words fill the room with something that isn't in repose. She takes her phone out and records herself saying the same words.

"I have no memory of this place. I have no beginning here, there is nothing left in this hotel except the dying and the recently decayed. Remember me. Those words, words spoken. Words arranged from neat letters on a slip of paper, the paper placed, with delicate precision, in a room, a room I've never known before, a room."

She pauses and takes a quiet breath, already thinking about how she'll cut the sentences, edit, and splice, obfuscate with intention, allowing the wider piece, the actuality of the music to live and search out meaning through other people.

She continues. "I am the manager. I am..." The words don't come, and she places the phone onto the bedside table, leaving it in recording mode. She wants to fill it with the energy of this place she's in, there is so much here, and as she opens her mind to the strange forces of the hotel, she hears it all. Each child's voice scared and lost, each resident who died within the walls, each party where someone always ended up in tears, alone, afraid, forgotten. In this place, she records it all.

She grabs her bag, placing the laptop inside, holding the phone out to every surface, every wall, resting it against every door of the hotel, soaking up the noise, the ambient flutters, and cracks, and whispers, and the other sounds of the dead.

She walks into the foyer, the blackness at the windows receding. The rhythms of life outside the hotel start to penetrate her thoughts. She keeps the recorder running, needing to capture it all, to play it back later, to start to understand.

There's a figure just outside, standing in what looks like early morning rain with no umbrella. She feels she should know him, and perhaps she does. He's waiting for her, and as she takes her last step from the hotel he smiles, and nods toward a car parked further down the driveway.

She holds the phone toward him. "I have music," she says. "New music, music for tears."

He nods, and when she catches up to him, they walk side by side to the car. He is jiggling the car keys in one hand, and she keeps recording.

"It's not just about happiness, is it?" she says. "I mean, it's also about discovery, or maybe it's all about discovery. This otherness, this embrace of the other, even the dead other, that's happiness."

He takes her bag, drops it in the back, and opens the car door for her, still smiling, still listening.

"We are inhabited by dead people," she says. "Their ideas, their words, their manners. Perhaps in some way, we are the dead people."

He nods with a smile and starts driving toward where the sun is peeking above the clouds that dangle on the pine-infused mountainside.

She plays back the recordings and is surprised to hear her own voice in a recording from a few days earlier. "Remember me. We are ghosts. Always."

The Other Sides of Doors

Charlene Elsby

IT WASN'T A tapping, and it wasn't a knocking, but something either in between or altogether new. It wasn't the inquisitive tapping sound one makes when they're trying to figure out if there really is anyone inside or if there isn't. It isn't the knocking sound one makes when they want something from someone whom they already know is inside but don't want to disturb too much. It was the in-between sound in which there wasn't yet any demand included, but neither was it an inquisition, but a simple assertion. *Something exists, and it exists on the other side of that door.*

It was a wooden door, still wooden in color, since no one had thought to paint over it. There were rectangles, three on either side of the center, meant to break up the rectangularity of the door itself, make it something more than a rectangle. Seven rectangles instead, for luck. I could have made do with fewer. There were three sounds. Three sounds is the minimum number of sounds that you need in order to start wondering what type of thing might have done it. One sound isn't enough to merit attention, and two could still be accidental, but three sounds with a measured space in between the first and the second, the second and the third—three sounds is the minimum number of sounds you need to hear so that it doesn't come off as just sounds but instead as a *rhythm*. But not all three sounds are rhythm. Three sounds without rhythm wasn't anything, but three sounds in a meter and it's suddenly clear—there's some*one* on the other side of that door. Someone with a basic understanding of time and how to parse it.

What does it want from me?

From the sounds of it, it might not want anything.

But then why is it here?

The expressive function of sounds is that they're meant to communicate; what they communicate varies but *that* they communicate is always the case—not for the accidental sound or two, but for the rhythmic three. But we've gone over this. It seems that all it wants is to assert that it exists out there. Does it even care that I'm in here? Yes. For otherwise it would not be making sounds at all. It exists. But why does it want me to *know that it does*?

Replace your questions with literal claims. It's advice that I'd give anyone trying to clearly express a viewpoint. When one asks a question, they invite a multitude of answers, but when one makes a literal claim, the answer is already given. You can't rely on your reader to make the assumptions you want them to when you ask an open-ended question. Tell them instead. Tell them what to think. Tell them what you want them to think. But what if I can't? What if there isn't yet any answer? What if there is no literal claim to make?

What does it want from me?

By asking the question, I assume first that it wants something and that whatever it is, I'm capable of providing it, up to and including my own demise, forefront to my consciousness since I heard its non-insistent sounding seconds ago. Perhaps a better question is not what does it want from me, since I may not be involved at all in the resolution of its desires but simply, more simply, quite simply, what does it want?

And is it Madison?

She only came to mind for a moment, and it was much earlier today. She'd have to have traveled so far, if she was where I left her, in order to get here on time for this, and that's only if she'd left at the moment when she came to mind.

But if all that had happened, then surely she wouldn't be merely exerting enough force on my door that the barest of consciousnesses should become just aware of it but not *too* aware, not *too* forcefully aware. For while there are no gradations of consciousness, yet there are differences in attention, intensity, and the longevity of someone's presence within a consciousness.

Had I thought about her more, would she have gotten here earlier?

If I had thought about her harder, would her knocking not be louder?

And I promise she was barely there to think of for a moment, barely long enough to make it out, to go over it again, to sort out the details once more.

The longer it takes, the longer someone is kept waiting, and I'm really not sure how long they can wait or if waiting counts to them at all. Surely someone who comes asserting their existence on the other side of that door this way should know that there will have to be calculations taking place before I can possibly respond appropriately.

How many calculations, and how long does each one take?

Wrong question.

Thoughts are not sounds, and their rhythms are atemporal.

Madison only crossed my mind for a second, and she *crossed* it. She didn't stop, announce herself with the minimum number of rhythms one could get away with and then just wait there, refusing to provide any additional clues as to what or *if* she might want anything.

The kind of being who does not want is indeed the most terrifying. For we want for as long as we live, and not to want is to die. If in fact it doesn't want anything, then it is because it dead, or death, or both, if death must necessarily be dead by definition.

The fact that the past doesn't change doesn't mean we don't want it to. You can't stymy desire by necessity. I didn't want to see Madison again or even to think about her. I only wanted to change how she happened. What I'd wanted was *not her*.

For how long it took, no human could be on the other side of that door and not have tapped again by now, or left, in which case I'd see them. If only I'd thought to look before the sounds drew my attention, then I'd have seen something through the window instead of the damned door which obscures and obscures and obscures.

Madison and I didn't know each other and as it turns out, never would. But the less I knew of her, the worse it was, for as she appeared to consciousness, there was nothing but a shadow to comprehend. *It's not about her.* It was like I was erasing her again.

But the thing about expressions is that there's always someone on the receiving end of them, someone who's going to question what you meant, for it's barely ever the case that you can say all that needs be said in the number of words you have.

In any case, I didn't know her very well at all, and yet it didn't seem to matter. I knew what she needed me to do. She needed me to see her.

She needed me to see her in her chair, eyes closing, and get her out of there.

She needed me to carry her, to call someone, to be someone.

She needed me to make sure that the man in the other corner couldn't get what he wanted from her.

And I don't know if he did.

But I should.

That's what she needed.

It was harsh, but I did it, and it couldn't be undone.

She wasn't angry about it and if she was, she might not even know she should be angry with me in particular. But then why was she here, at the door, if it was her at all, or is she only present to mind and not outside, where I had left her?

Shut it down! Make it stop. Let me out.

But it wouldn't. It was there on the other side of the door, and there was only one of them, after all.

It can't be Madison, because whatever it is, it wants something, and Madison doesn't want anything, because Madison is dead.

I don't think it was my fault.

But the only way to in any way assuage the insatiable desire to change the past is to attempt to bring it into the present, and that means that everyone involved has to be alive. Instead, it was Madison who seemed a little closed off now, dead as she was.

Another sound, this time from the side of the house. There's no way it could be Madison any longer. Another possibility is dead.

So many dead things and not myself among them.

That's what it wanted to announce—that I'm on borrowed time. Death is coming, death is inevitable, and out of everything that exists, there are some things that are dead *so far* and some things that are *dead not yet* and from these two categories, it seemed I fit best into the latter. But everything in that category becomes eventually *dead so far*, while new things become *dead not yet* and as those things approached, it seemed I was edging ever closer to the dead. The more things around me died, it seemed the more I should die too—the empiricist inference from relevant similarities.

Is that what it wants? Recognition? If so, that counts as a desire and whatever it is must be alive in order to have it. But perhaps alive and wanting is not so much better than dead after all.

Instead, it simply asserts itself, like there's nothing to be done about it. It's there. It's there and there's nothing you can do about it now. It's there it's there it's there.

That's what happens to the past as well.

It asserts its existence and wants for nothing.

It is and must be dead.

So why do I need to kill it?

It's odd that it abides by the rules of doors at all, if it's not just some kind of person. We're the ones who agreed that the doors would be the things you'd come in and go out by. I don't remember when we did it—I wasn't there—but if it weren't anything but human, surely it wouldn't be buying in on the scheme.

If that's true, then if I don't open the door, it should go away.

Which is for the best, since I can't open it at all.

Some doors are best closed, for what's on the other sides of them.

And you don't know which ones those are.

Monster Seed

Agwam Kessington

you hear thunderstorms,
i hear the wails of dead infants,
who have been buried on
unfiltered ground.

in my country,
young girls plant children
like monster seeds

they grow up damned
till their tails wither
— even when winter dissolves
& heavens melts into water

the word, *privilege*
will come in crumbs
& it will be the taste
of myth

& the children will beg
to be kissed by affection
but will be handed guns

& we will call it nature,
call it food chain.

Confusion Now Hath Made His Masterpiece

Shawn Phelps

"I've got one for you Johnny," Norman said. "A 55-year-old man released back into the community after a six month stay at the Essondale psych hospital. You'll be shocked to hear his treatment was less than a complete success. Despite the top-notch care, he remains convinced that he's God."

I am a social worker and care for the insane, addicted, and traumatized residents of Vancouver's Downtown Eastside. My supervisor, Norman, is a sadistic potentate with a twisted genius for making those under his authority miserable.

"They want us to take over his case," Norman said. "We discussed him in our morning conference and since you didn't deign to attend, I took the liberty of assigning him to you. Here's his address. His name is Percy Oswald, but all his friends just call him God."

"I want you to make sure he's settling in ok. Maybe ask a few favors while you're there. See if he can do something about the flow of heroin in the neighborhood. Better yet, get the winning numbers for Saturday's lottery. Don't worry; I'll keep on working here even if I win. I'm a committed humanitarian after all." He laughed until tears streamed down his face.

Over the years I had developed a particular loathing for individuals with religious delusions. I had been raised in an evangelical church of the "millions now living will never die" variety. Of course, they did die, just as people always have. My own mother had recently succumbed to cancer. Prayers, weeping, and the gnashing of teeth had done nothing to slow its progress.

My father was left a confused shell by her death, simply going through the motions of living. The congregation rallied behind him. Casseroles were delivered, along with rationalizations as to why her death had been part of the larger Plan. But the philosophical house of cards they constructed could not bear the weight of his grief. I found him one day, hanging from a rafter in the garage.

Since God did not seem particularly inclined to help, I concluded that humanity would have to look after itself. I became a social worker with that end in mind. It was a poor career choice, but it paid the bills.

Percy Oswald had been assigned a room at the Hotel Brittania. A once proud brick edifice, age had made it leprous with mold. Built in the late nineteenth century, it had originally housed sailors passing through the port of Vancouver. Despite its name, the hotel had been owned by a group of Chinese with deep ties to the old country, and it was rumored to have had its own brothel and opium den.

The years had not been kind to the building, and it had been slated for demolition. This being the case, the city council determined it would serve beautifully as an inexpensive place to temporarily store the city's undesirables. Some questioned whether placing the already mentally deranged in a vermin haunted ruin would be truly therapeutic. These concerns were ignored and about sixty down-and-outers now called the Brittania home.

I was assaulted by the sour odor of urine as I entered the Brittania's lobby. An indistinct figure sat behind a smeared and greasy window. I began to state my business in the building when a passkey was thrust through an opening at the bottom of this filthy glass barrier. The figure moved back silently without a word and was obscured in shadow.

The passkey allowed me to enter the elevator and rise to Percy's floor. The graffiti-covered plaster in the hallway had mildewed and crumbled, exposing the wooden slats beneath. I could hear the furtive scampering of rats in the dim hallway. They prowled among the used syringes and garbage that covered the floor, unconcerned by my presence.

I found Percy's room and raised my hand to knock. Before my hand could descend, a voice from within cried, "Come in, Johnny. I've left the door unlocked for you."

I had to push repeatedly on the door, as it was blocked by something on the other side. Eventually, I was able to wedge my way into the room, though it was impossible to completely open the door. It was blocked by a pile of notebooks. The room was filled with them.

It was an impossible scene given that he had supposedly only lived here a few days. I had seen cases of hypergraphia, the obsessive compulsion to write or draw before, but nothing of this scope. In parts of the room the heaps of notebooks touched the ceiling. Those nearer the floor were water damaged and had been trodden into a slimy pulp.

A man sprawled in a lawn chair which sat in a space that had been hollowed out of one of the heaps. He was smoking a cigarette, which seemed foolhardy considering the contents of the room. He inhaled greedily, exhaled a cloud of smoke, and regarded me through the haze.

Percy Oswald was a corpulent man with a ruddy unshaven face. His clothes—a sleeveless tee shirt, shorts, and sandals—needed a wash. A gallon of Old Grand-Dad bourbon was wedged between his legs. He offered me the bottle.

"Better have a bracer, Johnny. Get your day off on the right foot."

When I declined, he shrugged.

"Suit yourself," he said and took a long pull of bourbon.

"Well, Johnny," he said, "am I all that you expected? Mommy might have gotten your hopes up a wee bit too high when she gave you that Children's Book of Bible Stories."

"Mr. Oswald, I'm a social worker from the Eastside Clinic. I..."

He waved a dismissive hand to silence me.

"I know who you are, Johnny," he said. "In fact, I consider us old friends, though it's been a while since we last spoke. I appreciate your concern, but not to worry. I'm settling in nicely and, as you can see, busy at my work. Sorry about the mess, but it's the maid's day off. You understand."

There was a cardboard sign tacked to one wall. It was crudely painted with the words "CONFUSION NOW HATH MADE HIS MASTERPIECE." Percy noticed me reading it.

"It's from Shakespeare; *Macbeth* to be precise. Most of the Bard's stuff really bores me, but he was on to something with that little phrase. I've made it my own personal motto."

Percy exuded a false bonhomie, smooth insincerity, and barely suppressed mirth that made him somehow sinister. There was an artificiality about him containing something of both a department store Santa and a dealer of secondhand automobiles. He had the smug expression of a man who knows an inside joke, one that you are not privy to and quite possibly are the object of.

"I'll bet you're wondering just what an old loon like me is doing with all these," he said, gesturing at the heaps around him.

He thrust his hand into the pile and pulled out a tattered, filthy notebook. He held it up before me. On the upper right corner of the first page was a simple line drawing of a dog. He gave the notebook a flip that revealed similar drawings on each successive corner. By bending the corner of the notebook back with his thumb and then gradually releasing the pages he was able to create a crude animation. The image had the stuttering, jerky quality of an early silent film. The dog frolicked and leapt about as the pages fluttered beneath Percy's thumb.

"Just one of the amazing things you can do when you're God. Want to see another? Of course you do," he said.

He rustled around in the pile all the while looking me in the eye.

"Your special book is in here somewhere. Ah, here we are."

He pulled a particularly dingy notebook from the pile.

"Ready? You're gonna love this one."

Again, he caused the pages to rapidly flutter, and a new scene emerged. At first, it was vague and cloudy, but then a clear image of a woman in a hospital bed appeared. She writhed under the covers. The focus shifted to the woman's contorted face. With sudden nausea, I realized the woman was my recently deceased mother.

The scene changed and the bed was now empty. Sitting beside it, head bowed, was a man. I instantly recognized the figure of my grieving father.

Once more the scene shifted. My father stood on a chair, a noose around his neck. Stepping into space, he kicked the chair away. The entire tableau lasted only a matter of seconds. It was a feat of artistic legerdemain; not a line had been wasted.

Percy waggled his eyebrows at me in a Groucho Marx impression.

"Wadda ya think? Have I got a future in moving pictures?"

He settled back in his chair and lit a fresh cigarette.

"Why don't you ask me the BIG QUESTION? The question everyone wants God to answer," he asked.

"I'm not sure what you mean," I stammered.

"Oh, come now, Johnny, don't be coy. You know exactly what I'm talking about. But I'll play along. I know you're scared." He extended his hands and made a quivering motion of mock panic. "Happens to me all the time. You should have seen Moses' face when I spoke to him from the burning bush.

"The question is why is the world such a mess? If you have the power to make things better, why haven't you fixed things? Well, let me show you. A picture is worth a thousand words and all that."

He pulled another notebook from the pile. This time the images were of a cartoon pig. It was done in the style of an early Walt Disney cartoon. The pig strolled jauntily down a country lane, grinning happily. It walked into a fenced-in farmyard. There was a puddle of mud, buzzing with flies, into which the pig leapt joyfully. It began to cavort and roll in the mire, grinning all the while. The pig's face shifted out of focus and changed into Percy's face. He grinned manically and rolled in the muck until it was dripping off his face.

Percy slapped the notebook shut.

"Do you get it now, Johnny? The answer to The Big Question? You see the best possible world means different things, depending on one's point of view. You might even say it's a matter of one's particular tastes. Now...tell me the answer to The Big Question."

I stood silently before him.

"You have obviously become mute before my divine majesty, so I'll answer for you. The answer to The Big Question is I have fixed things. I'm God. I get to make the world as I see fit. The world is exactly how I want it." He grinned.

"Would you like a glimpse of my workshop? I'll let you look behind the Great Oz's curtain—-at the place where the magic is done—-the place where I create the world."

The walls of his apartment began to move rhythmically and go out of focus. We were standing in an open plain that stretched off into an infinite distance. The scene was like the vast, snowy expanse at one of the poles. As far as the eye could see there were heaps of notebooks. A white arctic wasteland, countless notebooks forming drifts of paper. Individual sheets flew about, twisting in the breeze. The silence was broken only by the rustle of pages.

There were hundreds of figures moving crazily among the drifts. They seemed to be frantically sorting, stacking, and reading the notebooks. A woman sat near us building up piles and then knocking them down. She shrieked with delight every time one toppled, like a child making sandcastles at the beach.

A man capered about, raising dust devils of paper in his wake. He paused at times to gather up armfuls of notebooks and hurl them into the air. Another flipped his thumb along a notebook's corner animating some scene repeatedly, his face frozen in horror.

"My helpers," Percy said. "Sort of like watching an anthill. Though ants generally conduct their business in a more orderly fashion. Still, they do their best and I like the company.

"I'm afraid the work has a high rate of burn out though. Many actually go mad. Of course, madness is not necessarily a disadvantage here. It helps one to deal with certain, uncomfortable realities about the world"

Percy paused to take a drag on his cigarette. He blew out a smoke ring and winked at me.

"You're a college boy, Johnny, you understand entropy. Everything in the universe is constantly falling apart. Complex things move toward chaos. I tried to keep up. My drawings of the world were all that kept it together. But there were so many problems, so many daily fires to put out. The fact is, I gave up trying to get it right."

He snapped his fingers theatrically, and we were back in his apartment.

"Johnny, my boy, I want you to be one of my helpers," he said. "You've got the right stuff, the proper attitude, for the job. I've been watching the carefree, slipshod way you deal with your patients. Never for a second believing there was the least chance to make things better."

I attempted to defend myself, but Percy only rolled his eyes. He smirked and shook his head.

"Dishonesty is so unbecoming of a gentleman. There's no need to make excuses for your actions. I see a kindred spirit in you. You understand the terrible secret: the world can't be fixed. It's too complex, even for me. It's a mess and we might as well accept it. Revel in it even. Have a bit of fun. There is a certain pleasure in kicking over the anthill and watching what happens next."

He reached out and slapped a stack of notebooks, scattering them across the floor. The unexpected violence of his action frightened me. I began to move towards the door.

"I need people like you to help me make my masterpiece," Percy said. He pointed to the quotation from Shakespeare hanging on the wall. "Oh, I could probably do it myself, being omnipotent and all, but there's nothing like a fresh set of eyes to solve creative problems."

"I want you to look for certain people, certain situations, where just the right touch will stir up all kinds of mischief. Then we can sit back and watch the results. The outcome is always unpredictable, and that's where the fun lies."

Percy leaned back in his chair and took another drink of bourbon. He swished the liquor around in his mouth, smacked his lips noisily, and then continued his sales pitch.

"Maybe we can throw your boss Norman a few curveballs. I bet you'd like that. You tell me what you'd like to happen, and I'll sketch it out in a notebook. We'll have a grand time. I tell you, you're going to love working for me."

"It's a job for life and with General Motors going to pieces, well, you know how hard those are to come by these days. No, no need to express gratitude, you'll be doing me a favor. Come back tomorrow, same time, and we'll get you started."

Percy dropped his cigarette butt on the floor. He put his foot on it, looked me in the eye, and ground the end of the cigarette into the carpet.

"And Johnny," he said, "don't make me come looking for you."

I headed east out of the city on the Trans-Canada Highway. There was no plan. I just drove. I had thrown a few clothes in a bag and left. I suppose it would have made more sense to get on a plane. But the thought of getting a ticket, going through the cattle pens at customs, and waiting for takeoff had been too much. I needed to get out of the city and the car seemed fastest.

I would drive for a few days. Stopping only for coffee and gas, sleeping in the car. Maybe get on a plane in Toronto. I could probably vanish in Paraguay or Argentina. Take in a few English students to make the rent.

Eight hours later I could see the shadow of the Rockies in the distance. Clouds boiled toward me in the overcast sky. It seemed late in the season for snow. But at this altitude, I supposed it was possible.

A piece of paper struck my windshield. A second and third page swirled past the car. The air was filled with clouds of notebook pages. Heaps of them began to build up, and soon the ground was covered as if by a fall of snow. I turned on the windshield wipers but only succeeded in making a pulpy mess.

I stuck my head out the window and drove on. The tires began to whine and spin as they lost traction. When I ground to a halt, he was there, standing in the middle of the road.

"Johnny, it's poor form to be late your first day on the job. You took a strange route, but I'm glad to see you all the same," Percy said.

He opened the door and dragged me from the car. Then with his arms outstretched, he let his head fall back and did a slow circle in the falling sheets of paper.

"We had better get busy, my boy," he laughed. "There's an awful lot of work to be done."

Disinfection

Matt Sadowski

Tell me you aren't afraid. The truth is your sense of scale has failed you. Monsters are real, measured in microns, mindlessly roving through microcosmic space as your cells are targeted for destruction by horrors unseen.

Germs.

They haunt me to this day. My father made sure of that. He tormented me with factoids about the microbial world at every opportunity. What was I then? Five? Six? He incited the worst aspects of my imagination with endless talk about microorganisms and their ubiquity.

"When you sit up in bed in the middle of the night, know that you're not alone. You're never alone, son. The microbes are always with you.

"There aren't any creatures in your closet. Not in the way that you imagine. But these creatures do exist. It's just that they're so tiny that you can't see them. Day or night—it doesn't matter. They're always there. They're always replicating themselves, making more and more and more."

I didn't believe him. Not at first.

Dad was a microbiologist at a nearby lab. It was his mission in life, he often told Mom and I around the dinner table, to do his damnedest to take out as many pathogens as he could before he died. Working at the intersection of biology and industrial engineering, he created environments free of bacteria and infectious microbes. He helped develop antimicrobial metals and graphene sheets. Nanopillars and cork. Any materials to stop the spread of germs.

And what he couldn't do at work, he did at home. Dad ruled our house with an antibacterial fist. He monitored our hygiene as closely as he could, made detailed notes of when we left and reentered the house. Notes above the bathroom sink reminded us to wash our hands while humming happy birthday twice from beginning to end. A note above the toilet reminded us to always close the lid before flushing and warned us of toilet plume.

We did our best not to sneeze around Dad. When we did sneeze, he'd holler about ejecting hundreds of thousands of bacteria and viruses into the air.

"It just takes one day for a single germ to multiply into more than eight million," he'd say. "And you just sneezed out 100,000. Do the math."

Our home often smelled like an indoor pool, rubbing alcohol and lemons. We never had visitors.

Dad instilled in me a deep fear of contamination. It was all he ever went on about. "You can't truly get rid of the bacteria," he'd say. "They're inside of you even now. Your eyes, nose, and throat. They're on your skin. There are mites living in your eyelashes. There's no escape. In your intestines, your gut. Respiratory tract. There are more bacterial cells in your body than human cells. You're more bacteria than human. In your anus, your genitals, your hair." My dad looked tired, beaten, a resigned look of acceptance in his face. He had declared war on germs and knew he couldn't win.

Before bedtime, instead of reading me stories, Dad used to show me large glossy photos of microorganisms blown up under the microscope. He had a way of describing their most monstrous features in vivid detail. There were bacteria stained with methylene blue, pictures of spheres, rods, spirals. Squiggly legs called flagella. Others were long chains or covered in something resembling hair. "It's good that you learn the true nature of your surroundings," he'd say. Blood would trickle out of the dried fault lines of his knuckles as he held the pages.

"The bacteriophage is my favorite virus. Doesn't it look like an alien spacecraft? Its head is an icosahedron—that means it has 20 sides. Its long fibers splay out like a spider's legs, lands on a bacterium, and pierces its surface with its sharp protein needle—like a hypodermic syringe," he said as he pinched my arm. I winced. "Its DNA slides down its tail tube and the injection is complete. It reproduces inside the bacteria until it explodes from the inside out."

Somewhere inside me, I imagined them whipping through the wet byways of my body.

"Other viruses wear a lipid coat—think of fat molecules. The coat is embedded with glycoprotein spikes that crack their victims open to infect them. Imagine roving spheres covered in spikes like a morning star. You know what a morning star is, son? It's a medieval club-like weapon with a spiky metal ball on the end used to SMASH" —and he slammed his fist on my nightstand— "the heads of enemies," and I began to cry.

"It's good to cry, son. Tears kill bacteria. Keep the tears flowing. They're cleansing."

And when I finally fell asleep, I'd dream of giant phages landing on my head and injecting their genetic material into my brain. Corkscrewed microorganisms and flagellates swam out from the hole in my head, and I'd wake up in a cold sweat. Dad would be standing there in the corner with spray bottle full of bleach and a rag, his twenty-faced head seeking germs in all directions at once with his forty eyes, and each of his twenty mouths would grin wide, and I'd wake up once more, for real this time, and go wash my hands until my nightmares had faded.

Dad got increasingly worse throughout the years, receding deeper into his mania. He got to wearing a surgical mask twenty-four seven. I'd forgotten what the lower half of his face looked like.

Dad started pasting photos of the microscopic bacteria he found on objects around the house. The pink rods of E. Coli would welcome us with every trip to the toilet. A photo of orange, rod-shaped Klebsiella was pasted to the backside of the TV remote. Blue chains of Enterococci on the charging cradle of our home phone. Purple grape-like clusters of staphylococci above every doorknob. He wanted to remind us of this unseen world, the risks inherent to uncleanliness. There would be no escape as long as Dad was around.

At the onset of one particular flu season, he stopped leaving the house altogether. Presumably, he had lost his job. I didn't ask, and he didn't tell. Mom worked from home writing emails, making phone calls. She began a Dad-approved side business making scented bar soap. Was she the one paying the bills now?

Not going out anymore meant Dad was always cleaning. Washing the clothes. Washing the dishes. Disinfecting. Decontaminating. It was a never-ending process. He forbade anyone else to help. It had to be done his way.

He'd put all the cutlery under UV lamps and when that wasn't enough, bleach baths. He bought boxes of toothbrushes for single use. Boxes of surgical masks that he forced us to wear. Gloves, too.

There was the time he found a water spot on one of the forks. He tore out the silverware drawer and tossed it across the kitchen.

Dad started wearing a full HAZMAT suit and carrying around a handheld fumigation machine at least once a week. He aimed the fogger's hose at the walls releasing a white mist. "Disinfectant ULV fogger machine with hypochlorous acid," he said. "Killer of bacterial, viral, and fungal pathogens. Why I waited so long to get this guy, I do not know."

He began dissolving germicidal tablets in his bottled water "just in case." He installed multiple UVC germicidal light fixtures throughout the house. There was always *more* to be done, more chemicals or light. More methods and more technology to kill more bacteria, more viruses. It would never end.

Dad called schools breeding grounds for microbes. Naturally, I was home-schooled. He certainly wouldn't have me becoming a vessel to transport germs back to his house. Even so, Mom made sure I joined some clubs at the park district to meet kids my age. *Small* clubs. Under ten kids preferably. This still presented a major problem for Dad, a breach in sterility. Lucky for me, he had a plan.

Whenever I came back home, "The Procedure" awaited. I'd go in the backyard, and Dad would make me strip off all my clothes. The fence and trees provided cover for my nakedness. My actions were all automatic at this point—they'd been long ingrained into me. Dad would be watching from the upstairs bedroom as usual. Deviating from the procedure meant I'd have to undergo it again. No exceptions. After tossing my clothes into a bin near the backdoor (to be washed ASAP), I'd then enter a contraption, a sort of human carwash. It was a tunnel with two rules labeled on the outside:

1. Close your eyes
2. Hold your breath

I'd first lie down on my back on a sled. The sled would automatically be pulled through the apparatus by a pulley system. Jets of antimicrobial fluid would shoot out onto my body followed by a cloud of antibacterial spray. A sign would flip out at the end reminding me to turn over and repeat the process. Once complete, I'd retrieve a fresh towel in a bin at the end to wipe away any extra fluid, especially around my eyes and mouth. A germicidal plastic liner would lead me into the house without my bare feet touching any grass or dirt.

Dad would be there to greet me for the final step. He'd wave his UV sanitizing wand all over my body and even under my feet. He had tried to install the UV wand in the human carwash but after several failures, he decided to do it manually.

He never put Mom through the same process although he ensured she showered and cleaned her clothes as soon as she got home. No exceptions. They slept in separate beds too, of course. The only dead skin cells and bacteria my dad slept in were his own.

"Your father is a sick man," my mother once told me. "I wish there were sanitizer to clean out his sick thoughts. Your father didn't always used to be like this, you know. I remember when he slipped a ring on my finger and didn't concern himself with washing his hands right after. There were times when we shared an ice cream cone. When he trusted the air he breathed. When he walked barefoot on the grass."

I saw them interact less and less. Sometimes, Mom would disappear for days at a time. To where, I did not know. But she always left a number so I could call her in case of emergencies. I imagined her going out and lying on the grass, getting dirt under her fingernails, taking in the filth of the world, and loving every second. And Dad would await her return, a UV wand in hand.

Dad regularly took samples from around the house to look at under his microscope in his mini lab in the basement. I remember the first time one autumn night that I was allowed to look through the scope.

We were both sitting on the front porch, a rarity for dad. A few feet in front of the house was the farthest Dad would venture. He had just vigorously cleaned off the bench before sitting down. The chemical smell lingered in the air.

We were both looking up at the night sky, watching the clouds go by. It had just rained. Dad was inhaling deeply through his nose from behind the mask.

"Smell that?" he asked, and I knew he was referring to that musky after-the-rain smell. The acidic tang of the cleaning chemicals had since dissipated. "It's the smell of dying bacteria. Streptomyces, to be precise. They release a chemical called geosmin." He seemed to enjoy it.

We sat there under the awning. Raindrops dripped off the trees above, their fall muffled by the shingles.

"Even the clouds," he said, pointing at a roaming mass of nimbus, "have bacteria. That's how they form. Bioprecipitation. Humans don't rule this planet, son. It's the bacteria."

He pointed to the mason jar I had left under the gutter to collect rainwater per Dad's instructions. "Get that and come with me." I followed him back into the house and down the steps to the basement. There was more equipment down here than I remembered. A few microscopes were set up on a desk beside vertical computer monitors. A mini fridge containing what could only be various microscopic samples hummed beside the desk.

Dad gestured toward the desk, and I placed the mason jar down. He used an eyedropper to suck up a drop of water and released it onto a transparent slide. After covering it with a thin square of plastic, he slid it under the scope. "Look."

Once my eye peered through eyepiece, a new world emerged. Semi-transparent lifeforms swam around an alien ocean. Long stalks undulated from ovular bodies. Squiggly lines of cilia whipped flamelike at one end. Wriggling appendages squirmed from snakelike bodies. My mouth tasted of acid as my stomach roiled, but I couldn't look away. Gastrotrichs, rotifers, amoebas, stentors, and other denizens of the microcosmos—their names I'd learn later.

"We're waging an invisible war," he'd say. Their invisibility to the naked eye made them all the more frightening.

Dad then took an adhesive strip and placed it on my forehead. He yanked it off, taking a thin layer of skin with it. He placed it under the microscope and turned the dials. "Come look," he said, and I did.

Through the eyepiece, a monstrous little creature wriggled its eight arms and fat tail.

"That's a face mite. It's an arachnid that lives in your skin down in the follicle where your hair grows."

I always thought you could run away or hide from monsters. Never before was I faced with incontrovertible proof that they had already made their home *in* me.

Why hadn't I been aware of this world before now? Sure, Dad had showed me photos, but they always felt like they were somewhere *else*, never here and now. This changed everything. My dad had revealed a new layer of reality, never to be seen the same way again.

"Do you see, son?" The desperation in his eyes scared me more than what I had just seen. "Do you see what I'm up against?" I began to understand my father's plight. "But this is just scraping the surface. The bacteria—the pathogens—they're even *smaller*."

Most of the next day I spent in the shower scrubbing my skin raw.

With Dad around, it was inevitable that his behaviors would become my own, his phobias my phobias.

Between increasing trips to the bathroom sink, visions of writhing cilia bloomed in my mind, moving their infectious load through my bodily fluids, spreading, proliferating. Scrubbing couldn't stop them. My knuckles began to look like tools to sand down wood. Dad took notice.

"Good, son. Kill as many of them as you can. But just know that washing your hands doesn't do a lick of good in the grand scheme of things. Not even death will destroy them all. In fact, that's what they're waiting for. They lie in your body for your whole life just waiting for your heart to stop. That's when they begin the work of consuming you." It was never good enough. It would never be good enough.

Some nights, I'd wake up from bacterial nightmares and hear him across the hall humming the birthday song in the nightlight-lit bathroom with the water running so hot it steamed up the mirrors. Joining him in the adjacent sink, we'd hum and wash together.

Everything changed when Dad got sick. He'd never had a cold before, which helped convince me that his obsession with cleaning held some merit. It started with a few too many sneezes and some light coughing.

"Which one of you brought disease into this household?"

He quarantined himself in his room and was very clear that we should "stay the hell away" from him. He'd not allow the contagion to spread.

I decided to try and help my father, as any good son would. I gathered isopropyl alcohol, hand sanitizer, and bleach. With a "galaxy of bacteria" inside of him—he had told me that there were more bacteria in my belly than there were stars in the Milky Way—I knew what I had to do.

The first step? Mix sanitizer into his water. It wasn't easy. Despite Dad's hypervigilance, I managed to sneak it into his drinks at strategic periods. His congested nose must have prevented him from tasting it. He started getting sicker, so I gave him more. Next? Slip traces of bleach in his food. Mom would deliver meals to his door, so I was careful not to overdo it. Dad only seemed to be getting worse. He complained of stomach pain. The bacteria must have been spreading.

And what about Dad's fogger? Confined to his room, Dad hadn't used it in days. I imagined its disinfecting mist swirling around him in a curative cloud. He'd wake up in the morning feeling better and thank me for healing him.

Once he was sleeping, I used a step stool to reach the fogger from a high shelf in the garage. The tank was already full of solution and the hose attached. I strapped the machine over my shoulder and made my way to my father's bedroom, slipping on the respirator along the way. All I had to do was toggle the switch and the solution misted out. It was a little noisier than I had remembered, but Dad didn't stir. I sprayed for a couple of minutes around the room trying to avoid direct contact with Dad. The mist settled into the carpet as minute particles illuminated in the moonlight through the blinds.

I woke up to Mom screaming, and I knew the bacteria had gotten him. My efforts had failed. I ran across the hall, and she was shaking my father. His head lolled as his surgical mask slipped down to his chin. I started crying and remembered how Dad told me it was good to cry. Mom called 911, and the paramedics took Dad out on a stretcher shortly after.

Dad went blind first and then fell into a coma before his death. This truth was concealed from me for many years. He had always insisted that he be cremated when he died. "Don't let the bacteria win. Incinerate them all," he'd say. And so he was. Where Mom keeps the ashes or whether or not she kept them at all is anyone's guess.

Sometime afterward, the police questioned me. What was I then? Eight? Nine? I told them I just wanted to kill the bacteria, that they were everywhere, don't you know? My father was sick. My dad needed disinfection, defense against foreign invaders. I told them not to touch me. I asked them when the last time was they had washed their hands. Did they have any hand sanitizer?

It was just Mom and I after that. The house quickly lost its antiseptic smell. The floors took on a layer of grime. Dust clung to shelves. Crumbs littered the kitchen. How quickly the house devolved from its pristine state of cleanliness.

Mom became silent. Contrary to Dad, her every movement around the house seemed to make it dirtier, not cleaner. I understood. This was no time to clean.

But I now had the freedom to go outside at will. In the months to come, I played in the yard with the neighbors, went to the playground and swung from the monkey bars. Dad's human carwash apparatus sat in the yard, a relic from another time, now coated with mildew and insect colonies. The world embraced me in its dirty arms, not nearly as threatening as I was led to believe.

Over the years, I faced uncomfortable truths during countless sessions with various therapists. Did you know what you were truly doing to your dad that night? they'd ask. Any idea at all? I'd think back to that night and the valence of my thoughts. I honestly couldn't say, couldn't truly remember. Maybe time had served to scrub this memory clean, washing it beyond recognition. It's true that I never really mourned my father. His death only served to free me from his obsessive repression.

I grew up, married, and got a job as a psychologist, perhaps in an attempt to understand the disease that dominated my father's mind. It took years to undo the damage done during those years of my youth. But my perception of the pathogenic universe surrounding me never quite left my mind. My wife would notice the antibacterial handwipes filling up the waste basket, the inordinate amount of time spent in the bathroom as the faucet ran, the lingering smell of rubbing alcohol and lemons that followed me like a shadow.

In time, her belly began to swell with new life. I began to see her body—all bodies—as mere vessels for the proliferation of microbes—in line with the primordial objective of all bacteria. In the early days of her pregnancy, during her bouts of morning sickness, I couldn't help but feel that I had infected her. For what is conception but sperm infecting an egg? Her body grew ill, as if her immune system rejected what I had placed inside her.

So now here I am in the maternity ward as my son enters the world, sliding through his mother's bacteria-laden birth canal and in this ellipse of flesh I see the gaping maw of my dead father, his slumped head, and it's through this slit that my son's head crowns, enveloped in what will become his first microbiome, and it strikes me how odd it is that all human life begins coated in bacteria, how they greet the newborn in a bacterial hug before any human embrace. It's there for us at the beginning and at the end.

My son slides out, lubricated with amniotic fluid and a waxy glaze of vernix, and a sudden wave of repulsion hits me. Barely make it to the bathroom sink before the bile spurts from my mouth, and I know that forevermore, the first memories of my son will be of absolute disgust—a vile, fetid creature—and I wonder if my birth was the moment that changed my father. It's then I begin to think of him for the first time in a long time. Thoughts of germs, about how we're never truly alone.

When will my son be cleaned, I ask the doctors, and all I can think is how vulnerable this newborn is, how dirty the world is, how I will be the one to teach him. There will need to be changes at our house. It's not clean enough. No, not clean enough at all.

Laugh Track

Shaoni C. White

I used to worship Our Lady of the Truth Geometric,
learned topology, norm, infima. Every Sunday
Pythagoras smiled down at me, trapped in stained glass.
Then one day I heard it: the laugh track.
The rest of this proof is left as an exercise for the student
the choir sang, and the light all bright and broken
chanted *ha! ha! ha!*

Now I find Midas Margarita, clown and saint,
at the altar on the catwalk in the abandoned theater.
He wants to rent out my intestines, just a part-time thing,
basically a timeshare. I say no thanks.
But they're so neon, he says, *so slippery.*
Answer's still no. He scowls and switches topics
like a train headed face-first into a river.
He wants to know where his money is. I owe him
just a little bit—he kept my liver for safe-keeping
while I was busy courting death dressed in whiskey.
I hand it over and he says *that check better not bounce*
or you're a dead motherfucker. He's a swell guy, that Midas,
the last bodhisattva of self-destruction. *God*

he says, *you're such a sad sack*
the only guy here who can hear the laugh track
and the light all bright and broken
chants *ha! ha! ha!*

Days later Midas Margarita finds out
the check is rotten as a carcass on a roadside.
I'm gonna peel you, you son of a bitch, he howls
I'll be the beginning and the end of you
just you watch. I will hunt you like a goddamn addiction.
He's a swell guy, that Midas.
I stumble back toward somewhere
that in the half-light might wear the word *home.*

My skins won't shut up. In storefront windows
Pythagoras winks.
I pass kids on the street skipping rope, singing
sad sack, sad sack, the only one
who can hear the laugh track
and the light all bright and broken
chants *ha! ha! ha!*

Bird's Eye Rhyolite

Sara Wilson

Under every bird's nest the tossed
mulch is pocked with egg teeth,
fragments of the brittle
husks, the ashy sighs
of mushroom caps.
Spent chicks.

Pine needles, like fingertips
or stripped feathers, gilded
and tinder, bed them
pink eyes rolled deep
into the tiny skulls,
like eggs themselves
folded into this new
deeper nest, like the dirt knows
a better way to incubate.

No Visitors

Charles Wilkinson

ALTHOUGH THE LACE curtains filter the glare, Lenthall knows the worst of the winter's light is out there, whitening the morning from the top of the tall sky right down to the grey gravel path, which will now appear frosted. It has been like this for a week: cold Arctic air keening in the grass, every blade burnished to a sparkle; the wind that freezes on the face like a visor. The wrong month to bury the old man. He imagines a Rector, purple-fingered at the graveside, tossing a prayer into the gale; Lenthall the only mourner.

The house is quieter now it no longer has his uncle's breathing in it. Neither of them pretended to a taste for music, so there were few sounds to disturb the silence: the water hammer when the hot tap in the kitchen was turned on; the kettle, its boiling abusive with bubble and steam before scathing a sigh. And the old man, Uncle Samuel, dying on the sofa; every day the rattle of respiration, the phlegm-thickened cough.

Lenthall has breakfast in the kitchen. There's a radio in the left-hand corner beyond the sink, but he can't recall that it has ever been turned on; at least, not during his time in the house, a good ten years and as many months. It had seemed generous of Uncle Samuel to take him in after the job in the garden centre had come to an end. At forty, Lenthall had exhausted his options, his curriculum vitae curdled with early failed careers, these disasters followed by the ignominy of temporary appointments and odd jobs, many of them terminated in humiliating circumstances. "Why not move in and give me hand?" Uncle Samuel had said. "I'm too old to keep the garden under control and I could do with some help with the security."

He hears the clink of his teaspoon on the saucer. The room is a repository of ancient hostilities. Hacking at a boiled egg, he only half decapitates it before becoming aware of footsteps on the garden path. A moment later the sound of the bell, the hand held down on the buzzer for too long, the tone imperative, less than polite. With a sigh, Lenthall gets up and makes his way to the front door.

It's his next-door neighbour, a short man wearing a flat tweed cap, a bureaucrat's moustache stuck to his upper lip as a badge of authority, a gleam of a long-held grievance in his watery eyes. Lenthall tries to remember the man's name. Pursglove or Purslow? Or perhaps Purslove. Something like that.

"Yes?"

"Where's the old man. I want a word with him?"

"He's unavailable?"

"What you mean by that? He never goes out."

"He's at home, but he won't to speak to you."

"Why ever not?"

"He's dead."

"When did this happen?"

"About a fortnight ago."

"There wasn't much about it was there?"

"It was sudden though not unexpected. He died peacefully at home. On his sofa."

"No, I meant there was nothing about it in the papers. No notice of a funeral."

"The ceremony was a private occasion."

Lenthall wonders why he's allowing himself to be held at bay on the doorstep, answering impertinent questions. His uncle had hated the Purslows: never socialised with them, mentioning them only as a possible security risk. On Saturday nights there were too many cars outside their house.

"And so you'll be in charge here, I expect."

"I'm sorry but I'd like to finish my breakfast."

"Breakfast? It's a quarter to twelve in the morning."

"If you must know, I'm a little behind schedule. And now ..."

"It's about the hedge."

"Another time, Mr Pursglove."

"Purslove. The name's Purslove,"

His neighbour nods, proud to have put him straight. Lenthall watches the man walk back down the path. Just as he's about to open the gate, he swings rounds, wipes his moustache with the back of his hand and then hollers: "The hedge. At least three feet shorter. Understand?" Then he nods again, as if it to underline that the matter was to be dealt with – and soon.

An old antagonism that Lenthall's unhappy to have inherited. A legacy of Uncle Samuel's aversion to his property being overlooked. The thought that so much as a sliver of the garden might be visible from the Purslove's attic window was abhorrent to him. Hence the hedge, fast growing and evergreen, a way to protect the west-facing border. Although Purslove had responded with talk of easements of light, the dispute never came to court.

As he went inside, Lenthall picked up two brown envelopes from the mat and took them to the breakfast table. Brochures from travel agents. He flicks through the images: white hotels, dazzling in reflected Mediterranean light; superlative blue of repeated skies; swimming-pool shapes: the containment of water as gemstone sheen; white parasols and the perfectibility of early morning sand, a suggestion of softness; the arc of beaches unblemished by footprints; the small waves waiting to come in. A holiday. What he hadn't been able to take since childhood. Then he recalls Uncle Samuel, sitting up on the sofa, some years before his final illness but still in his pyjamas at mid-afternoon, his paunch the shade of cheddar, protruding from a partially unbuttoned top. His round face was paler than the rest of him, the sagging skin a perpetual stranger to the outdoors.

"What do you mean, you need a break?"

"A short holiday. A week by the sea."

"You need a break from me. Is that what you're trying to say?"

"No, not at all. Why don't you come too?"

"Huh ... you know you're on safe ground saying that, don't you. I'm not going abroad."

"We don't have to go abroad. Why not a trip to Cornwall – or somewhere on the east coast, if you'd prefer it?"

"What! And leave this house wide open for any old riffraff to come in and strip the place bare or burn it down."

"We'd lock up. Take extra precautions"

"I daresay we would. But you listen to me – as soon as a house is left empty it's open season. Nosy neighbours, kids, cat burglars, squatters. You might as well put up a great big sign: 'Help yourself. We don't care. We're on bloody holiday.' And anyway, who's going to subsidise this jolly of yours? Me, I suppose."

"I've some savings."

"Then hang on to them. We're staying here. There's a property to protect."

Since his uncle's death, Lenthall has turned the central heating down. He didn't want large bills ruining his chance of a break. He went over to the window. The air was nicked with silver, rain on the verge of snow. Apart from the kitchen, a chill had established itself through the house. He'd have to do some research: find out what were the nearest destinations with some warmth in winter. He repeated the phrase: warmth in winter. That was what he wanted, and for the first time it was in reach.

As he bends double to draw back the bottom bolt on the front door, Lenthall asks himself why he has yet to simplify his late uncle's security arrangements, its systems of paranoia and impeccable intricacy, a tribute to an adamantine aversion to the world and all its occupants. A bulwark against the phantoms of rampaging criminality. Only during his last months had Uncle Samuel relinquished all oversight of the nightly ritual of locking up. When Lenthall had first moved in, his uncle explained that although they might live in a respectable neighbourhood it was far from free of felonies. Many burglaries. Property stolen, sometimes with the assistance of brute force. Nowhere was immune. But at least one could have the satisfaction of ensuring that entry would not prove easy. The main points of ingress, the front and back doors, sites of maximum vulnerability, were both secured with multiple locks: the minimal protection offered by the Yale augmented by bolts at the top and bottom, in addition to no fewer than three mortise locks. All the windows had been fitted with special fastenings. At night, wooden shutters, not original features of the house, were closed.

There's also a complex system of alarms and CCTV cameras. In the early years, Lenthall accompanied his uncle on his nightly rounds, the first of which took place at 7.00 in the evening, the aim being to secure the property before tiredness, with the accompanying possibility of mistakes, crept in. Despite this precaution, a final inspection would be made before bedtime at ten o'clock. During the day the house was kept as tightly closed as practicable. As his uncle ailed, so Lenthall's tasks became more burdensome. First, he took on the responsibility of the initial locking up, which was then checked by his uncle later in the evening. In the final year of his uncle's life all duties devolved to him, although never without a comprehensive debriefing before he was free to retire to bed.

It has taken him so long to unlock that he is not in time to wave at the driver of the delivery van, who would sometimes wave back: an interaction, a source of solace. He picks up the groceries left on the doorstep and takes them into the kitchen. Now that his uncle is dead wouldn't it be better if he went to the shops, as he'd done years before? If he was to muster the self-confidence to take a holiday abroad, which would involve taxis and trains, not to mention airports and the elaborate rituals of arrival and departure from his hotel, he should re-engage with the world. How many years was it since he'd been inside a shop or a bank? Eight, perhaps even nine. True, he'd mastered the art of ordering over the phone, but that was unlikely to prove an adequate preparation for what lay ahead.

Once he's deposited the vegetables in the fridge and put the fruit in a bowl, he returns to the sitting room. The sofa, without the encumbrance of his uncle's corpse, appears larger, although the declivities of long use, even the shape of the old man's body indented on the cushions and headrest, remain indelible. Yellow-brown and stained with mould, it reminds Lenthall of a rind of cheese. On one of the armrests, just to the right of where his uncle's head rested, is the one surviving patch of the pattern, a yellow flower. To sit on the sofa, even to touch it, would be to risk uncontrollable nausea. He must find a way to be rid of it. If he left it on the forecourt, by arrangement with the Council, perhaps the refuse collectors would remove it. But this seems unsatisfactory: too like leaving an open coffin at the front of the house. With the springs long gone, selling it for restoration would prove impossible. There'd be no profit in it. The likeliest solution would be to pay someone, the owner of a junk shop or second-hand furniture store, to take it away. He flicks through the parish magazine and finds a number. He explains and gives his address.

"That's Sam Lenthall's place, isn't it?"

"Yes. I'm his nephew."

"I haven't seen him in thirty years. Used to do business with him back in the day. How is he?"

"He's in hospital at the moment."

"Nothing serious, I hope."

The voice is flat, unconcerned. There's no need to enlarge on his lie. "When do you think you'd be free to come round?"

"It's just the sofa, you say. Nothing else."

"Well ... we have plans to downsize. There are other items that you'd be welcome to take a look at."

How much furniture does one man need? Lenthall glances round the room. There's a sideboard of some antiquity and a Windsor chair. Why not sell those and throw in the sofa for free?

"All right then. We're busy tomorrow. How about Thursday?"

Once a time has been fixed, Lenthall goes over to the window. He takes pride in the arrangements he's made. Manoeuvring the sofa out of the house and onto the asphalt forecourt would have been an impossible task for one man. It's prudent to have the men come to the house, even though it involves breaking the 'no visitors' rule. He must keep his presence outside to the minimum. Leaving the sofa in public view would only provide a talking point for the curious. Lenthall pictures Uncle Samuel, at rest in the garden shed, his upper body supported by a wheelbarrow, his legs straddled over two bags of ancient compost. The spades, rakes and shears leaning against the wall had acted as witnesses of the interim funeral service. The truth of the matter was that Lenthall couldn't tolerate doctors, funeral directors, all the manifestations of officialdom, until he'd had a holiday.

He unlocks the back door and goes out into the garden. It is cold, below freezing. The sheen on the white-grey clouds and the pale blue sky are suggestive of icebergs drifting on Arctic waters. His uncle's corpse shouldn't decompose too quickly in such weather. He stares around him. How long is it since he's tidied up let alone performed any task that could be categorised as gardening? Tangled alder; plants that outstripped their names, jumbles of leafage; the lawn's verges long since overwhelmed by the anarchy of grass: a ruination so complete it is impossible to imagine what it looked like before his uncle's arrival. Today any residual verdancy is subdued by coatings of frost: a bush like a half-formed ghost struggling back into the afterlife; the hedge a wall of a chainmail; the rigid evergreens, their armorial glimmer. The only sign of recent activity is the path he hacked through to the shed. A brutal exposure, leading the eye to a flimsy door.

The next morning, after considering the matter for no more than a moment, Lenthall resolves to put the house on the market once he returns from his holiday. Of course, Uncle Samuel's remains must be dealt with, along with the legal formalities. But as soon as these obstacles have been overcome, he will have enough money to start a new life.

His hand hovers over the telephone. Admittedly, he is not yet able to instruct an estate agent, but no harm can result from finding out what the property is likely to fetch. As he's about to dial, he's startled by an unexpected thought: he's no idea what the house looks like from the front. There was a time, of course, during the days he went shopping, when he would have known this. He can picture the view from the front doorstep: the asphalt forecourt, the gravel path, the iron gate, and the fence. He can even visualize, with absolute clarity, the details beyond. A red-brick house with bay windows and a pitched roof, the television aerial at an odd angle. The house next to it smaller, with a flat roof and a tree shaped like a green spear in the front garden. The blue van that is sometimes parked outside, especially at the weekends. He tries to imagine himself walking along the road, with a shopping basket full to the brim, and then reaching the iron gate. He opens it, steps onto the path. What does he see? The front door, he's certain, is dark green. But apart from that he recollects nothing. He's about to return the receiver to the cradle when he asks himself why an estate agent would demand a description of the exterior of the house. Surely information about the number of rooms would be sufficient. He dials. A crisply resonant voice that reminds Lenthall of a radio announcer. The details are taken.

"Of course, if you want us to give you a valuation, we will have to fix a time when we can visit you."

No visitors! How many times had he heard Uncle Samuel insist on this? Delivery men allowed as far as the front step, but no one to venture beyond the dark green door: no gasmen, no one from the electric (we read the meters ourselves), no one from the council, no doctors, not even a plumber. Uncle Samuel knows how to fix the dripping tap, the cistern, the overflow, the problem with the kitchen sink.

"Is that necessary?"

"Detached properties with five bedrooms in your area are going for around £750,000 pounds, but you say yours is in need of restoration. I am afraid that without making an inspection any estimate is going to be little more than guesswork."

Uncle Samuel is dead. There is no longer any necessity to think like him.

"When can you come round?"

"Thursday between ..."

"Thursday's difficult. How about Friday?"

He writes down the time. For an instant, it is as if he's aware of Uncle Samuel's envious spirit, watching him, listening to him, seeing how well he is coping: making arrangements, agreeing to times of appointments, and above all planning. The sofa gone, the house to be sold. Their lives together dismantled, taken to the tip. Every room in the place, even the air they owned, purchased by a stranger. He doesn't normally drink, but some sort of celebration is justified. In the kitchen cupboard there's a bottle of sherry, matured for more than a decade. He unscrews the top; the smell alone is sufficient to make him heady. The first sip conjures thoughts of Spain: brown shadows in a courtyard, scents of an orange grove; depth of afternoon sunlight. The level goes down. Warmth wraps itself within him, glows in his veins. There's still some left. One more measure and then a siesta. He is half collapsing, sinking down to a place of safety. He drains the glass, shuts his eyes, and stretches himself out. Welcome to the retreat of the room.

Even before he opens his eyes to the blade of light severing the air beyond the crack in the curtains, Lenthall's aware of the swirl of nausea in his stomach, the iron helmet screwed to his head, the flow of heavy poison in his veins. There's a taste of vomit thickening on his tongue; acid-stab in the oesophagus: if moves now, he will be sick. After a minute, he forces himself to breathe deeply. The truth of his vague recollection of having woken at one in the morning to banish his hangover with the aid of brandy, which his uncle kept in the bathroom cupboard for medicinal use, is confirmed. The half-bottle is next to the sherry on the side table: both are empty. A glass has rolled onto the carpet. What day is it? Thursday. He groans and glances at his watch. The men from the second-hand furniture store are due to collect the sofa in half an hour. The sofa on which to his disgust he now rests. He shifts his position, so that he's lying on his side, and angles a leg down towards the floor. The smell of a dying man, ripened by a long sojourn on the sofa, rises into his nostrils, where it almost displaces the sour scent of vomit. The cushions are soft and greasy with mortality's sweat; every centimetre of the fabric is imbued with the juice of suffering. The telephone rings. Lenthall holds his breath and levers himself upright.

"Yes."

It's Toby Sopwith, from Sopwith and Melrose. I'm sorry we won't be able to come round tomorrow for the valuation. And we're rather busy next week. How about if..."

"Later this afternoon. Around teatime?"

"I thought you said Thursday wouldn't suit you."

"I do have another appointment, but I should be free by four o'clock."

"That's fine. I'll see you then."

He puts the receiver down. Lenthall tells himself he mustn't allow himself to subside onto the sofa. To do so would be worse than flinging himself into a newly dug grave, where at least the fresh earth, just turned, would not yet be tainted with corruption. The smell in the room has worsened. Is the stench issuing from inside him – or is it rising in necrotic clouds from the sofa? He must go into the garden; let the harsh winter air scour his lungs. He's surprised to find the back door ajar. At some stage during the previous night's debauch, he must have gone out to be sick or take the air. The cold freezes the night sweat to his face; it's as if he's wearing a death mask. Every leaf and blade of grass is frost-sharpened, stolen from an armoury – and, despite the grey sky, glinting with the intent to wound. Something has been disturbed in the garden: an unwarranted change. It's a moment before he's aware of the cause; the door of the garden shed is open, a mouth laughing. He half runs and staggers up the path, then peers in. Uncle Samuel's corpse has disappeared. The wheelbarrow that supported it has been moved and propped against the wall. One of the bags of compost is stretched on its side: a flabby boxer out for the count; the other is still upright but sagging, as if winded. He steps into the shed, searches under a tarpaulin, a bench, and a pile of sacking, even though he knows that the body is far too bulky to be concealed in such a small space. Of course, he'd checked his uncle's pulse and breathing: a definite, irrevocable death. How could the old man have absented himself in this manner – and where was he now? In his bedroom perhaps. No, it was absurd to imagine that he'd somehow dematerialised and then reassembled himself in a place he'd been too ill to enter for over a year. But if all plausible explanations had failed the impossible had to be considered.

The instant he's back in the kitchen, Lenthall hears the bell ringing, followed by a peremptory pounding on the front door. The men must have arrived to collect the sofa.

He thrusts his hands into his jacket, his trouser pockets. No keys. There's a hook in the hall where he sometimes leaves them. Nothing. The ringing resumes. A voice calling out. Further knocking, then frantic beating with the flat of the hand.

"I'm coming." Lenthall's pitiful croak, the phlegm crackling in his throat.

The keys must have slipped out when he was asleep on the sofa. He hurls the cushions across the room and works a hand round the cracks in the side until he finds a hole. He pushes deeper into the sofa's soft belly. There's something cold and hard. He pulls at it, then rips the fabric with his free hand, widening the cavity. He drags the trophy upwards:

Uncle Samuel's false teeth, the lower set, lost six months ago. He dives his hand down again and touches metal, but it won't give. It's long and slender. A spring? Footsteps crunching down the gravel drive, away from the door. He runs to a window and hammers on it and waves, but the man does not look back as he steps up into the driver's seat. Within a minute, the van, indifferent to Lenthall's cries, starts up and moves off serenely down the street.

He must find the keys before the estate agent arrives; but first, despite the evident absurdity of such an undertaking, he must search the house. The downstairs has already been checked. Is it possible that the cold weather has somehow revitalised Uncle Samuel, plucking him from apparent death and providing him with sufficient vigour to crawl into the house and up to his bedroom? No, but at least there's some advantage in knowing where the corpse is not, especially as he will have to show the estate agent around in a matter of hours. Ludicrously, he finds himself opening the largest of the wardrobes – and even the airing cupboard, in which his uncle's body could only have been stored if it had been dismembered. It takes him ten minutes to establish that there is no trace of the old man and nothing to indicate what might have happened to him.

As soon as he's back in the sitting-room, he spots that the sofa has been moved. It's now at an odd angle to the wall, as if on the offensive, ready to exact revenge for its recent violation. Yet the explanation is simple: it shifted when he was searching for the keys. He tries hard to remember if it was in that position before he went upstairs. Then the memories blaze back, awful in their immediacy.

Uncle Samuel's last night: his ragged breathing punctuated by the way his mouth widened, gulping and avid for air; his yellow face-flesh beginning to whiten; every cough adding a tremor of blue; the chest thick with liquid, crackling with his gasps.

"Phone a doctor."

That was what the old man had said.

"No visitors, Uncle. You've always been very clear about that."

"A doctor!"

"Surely not. You'd be breaking the principle of a lifetime."

Lenthall went into the kitchen and shut the door. He was never one to gloat for long. And the spectacle was displeasing, a slow death of little medical interest. He went back after he'd eaten a light supper. His uncle lay beached and unbreathing on the sofa.

He forces himself to concentrate. It's imperative that he pulls himself together.

The keys, they must be somewhere. They could have fallen on the carpet or be underneath the sofa. It's little over eleven minutes before he understands that the simplest remedy is to phone a locksmith. But the ringing starts before he puts his hand on the receiver.

A second of silence and then heavy respiration, the fight for thin air underscored with water rasping on shingle.

"No need to unlock the door, lad. Always a way in for those who know how."

His uncle's voice, but as if hauled up from fathoms down, the vocal cords barnacled, the salt still thick on the tongue.

"What... who is this ... speaking?"

A sigh like spray on a rocky shore. "Should be with you soon. Just a short journey."

He bangs the receiver down. When he turns round, his uncle is re-establishing himself in the room, although now it as if he is part of the sofa: his features emerging from an armrest: his left check imprinted with the faded pattern of a yellow flower; his stomach enormous, augmented with stuffing and re-sprung; his feet, half flesh and half fabric. One of his eyes is rheumy; the other well buttoned. His chest has dried out now. Uncle Samuel unstitches a smile; triumphant in textile, he is at one with the supremacy of furniture: the sofa's suzerain, an emblem of eternity within the sitting-room. And then the vision fades: the face dissolves – the lineaments lose their outlines; the stomach subsides; the feet dwindle as skin, veins and bones are unspun. Instead, the stink rises, physical in its re-creation of all the odours of illness, the year-long detritus of decay, the spilt medicines, the offerings of sweat, piss, and vomit.

Lenthall craves air, clean and cool as water. He rushes to the window, but it is stuck fast. No one has opened it living memory. The same unaltered view: the iron fence, the houses beyond, the blue car parked in the road. Then Purslove comes out onto the pavement, turning from left to right, scanning the street. He must be expecting somebody. His moustache twitches on his upper lip. Then a man who is unmistakably Uncle Samuel crosses the street and walks towards the iron gate. He has awoken refreshed from his temporary extinction; yet he ignores Purslove, who must wish to speak to him about the hedge. The day is bright with the cold normality of winter. The sky is an irreproachable blue, fit for daily use. And now Uncle Samuel is walking down the path, dangling the keys to the house insouciantly in his dead hand. He is an old man, but from now on he will be everywhere.

The Merchant of Places and Precious Things

Sofia Ezdina

SACKS APPEARS the Station, knowing nothing but her own name.

She had a nightmare before, where she was lost. This time, in a large hotel with many rooms and no light in the corridors. Gasping, she ran around in the dark, her hands extended. I'm hungry, a whisper. I think I will always be hungry.

Sacks has long tangled hair and a white nightgown. It is vulgarity and bad taste, but this is not her fault. Sacks is not involved in the fact that many are afraid of girls with long tangled hair and white nightgowns.

In the Station's restroom, Sacks cuts her hair with manicure scissors and airs what's left under the hand dryer. She flushes a wet clump into the toilet, then changes the nightgown to the pair of jeans and sweater, carefully folded for her next to the washstand. "We provide a safe place for humans." the hostess of the Station has said. "Hopefully, we can offer you a shelter too." The hostess considers this trade profitable. Same does Sacks.

It is always a transaction, Sacks learns, is a metathesis, even beyond the establishments of professionals. The transaction is when you give something in exchange for something else. Each party involved wishes somewhat of value from another. In that respect, it is not very unlike friendship, or love.

Sacks does not know that at the Stations one cannot eat what comes of itself, so she doesn't linger for long: after the first misunderstanding, the hostess asks her to leave. Sacks regards this as an overreaction and wonders what hostess could have taken from her in return instead, as her price or by her nature, and whether it would be worth it. She wonders if she would miss it when it's gone.

"What are you?" the hostess asks before they part ways. Sacks do not know. Identity is what she is uncomfortably lacking. An empty vessel is not worth much, is not legal tender, but it can be filled with other memories and aches. Self is a currency you can pay for goods and services with.

Nothing is void of a price. Including theft.

She does not wander for long: almost immediately she descends to the subway and realizes that she likes this place.

There is impenetrable darkness on one side and the impenetrable bright gleam of the headlights on the other. The train is coming to the platform. Monumental and tall, copper, gloomy, mournfully brilliant, like a huge iron.

Sacks stares at the reflection in the train's glass, murky and quivering, and tries to smooth her hair and do something with her face. The first is managed, the second is not: her face is still frozen with frightening anguish. Her eyes are vacated, guarded with something she has no name to. Sacks leads her palm from forehead to chin and sees an empty white spot in the glass. She leads again, now from the bottom up — and her face becomes the face of a thirteen-year-old. Once again, down and up — and now Sacks is sixty years old, then thirty, wreathed in cuprum and kelp.

A few types of hunter prey here. Sacks, locals, and trains. The last two hardly appreciate the cooperation. Perhaps, they sensed how untenanted she was, and thus prefer to keep their distance.

She does not stay for long in the subway either: there are few guests here — lesser than it might seem. Trains are greedy, loud loners, apex predators of the underground. Locals, those who live in tunnels, do not have any business for Sacks and she, too, has no enmity to offer; they exist by themselves, silent and hungry, and rarely even spare a word for a newcomer. Sometimes their feasts splatter on the railways; Sacks hears them, although they have said nothing, and she returns their talk. But every drip, drip, drip beckons her forward, forward, down the tunnels that twist like a snake swallowing its own tail.

Sacks leaves the train and, without disturbing the tranquility of thick gray dust, rises on the dozing escalator upward, into the stuffy somnolent summer of the abandoned town. She whispers a word of farewell back to the darkness, to the hungry places, forsaken along with everything that isn't hers any longer. When spoken, it withdraws from her and leaves her hollower than she was before.

The town seemed to wither, covered with cobwebs and yellow mold. Dry cellars, strangled with thistles; rusty iron rods bursting through cracked concrete; broken bottles in the sun. Fishy smells and dead eyes in doorways; neglected quarters, streets half full of sand; the deep calm of a place where no human longs to be.

Yet not everyone had fled. A few types of strangers still haunt the city. Sacks, whispers, and city frogs. Grey-green; bony and slimy. Merging with roadside grass. Dwelling in sewer wells. Scavengers. It is unpleasant to observe how the congregation of these amphibians clung to a dead pigeon, devouring it with a peculiar croaking at the sundial shadow. Sacks hunts them down. Teeth fouled with gore. Red. Dripping. More.

She does not know how to look for habitable places, so she roams around empty houses, changing dresses she finds in the cupboards. She gets out on the roofs through attics and looks over the dead city.

All furniture is covered with a thick crust of soot, under which is nothing but ashes and coal. Sacks quickly grows bored and wishes to go somewhere else. She is lucky: in one of the six-story houses in the city center, she finds an elevator.

Sacks and the elevator fancy each other: like her, it possesses no immanent face; like it, she is an unhaunted object; but rough approximations of what both understand to be friendship will not last long: the elevator cannot stand still, and Sacks cannot always live on the road. Sometimes the elevator will find good friends for her, and Sacks, in return, altering several faces, will serve as a bait for travelers looking for transport, so both she and elevator can prey. But in the end, for the last time, she will reach to the button panel, which she will remember both brand new, sparkling chrome, and dull, lit by matches, and splodgy with gums and inexplicably sticky; for the last time, the elevator will shut the doors and go sideways, away from the mine, ready for anything to find a better place for

Sacks. It will stop almost immediately, the doors will divide with a wheezing sigh, and a crimson carpet with a worn gold edging will unfold in front of Sacks.

The concept of a transaction is this: there are participants, each of them possesses something of value. They each price the other's possession more highly than their own, thereby they agree to barter. But if the object is not something possessed, but, instead, something inhered. In such an exchange — what, then, would be the terms.

So, Sacks gets to the hotel.

Here she will stay for a while: the hotel is full of guests, and the place fits her well. Guests will be nice to her, and she will be kind enough to them in return. They will scud up to her, they will whirl around her, asking of her, summoning her; soon Sacks will be renown in the hotel, and many will come back to her. 'We provide valuable services", the hotelier will say, 'Hope you can become an inestimable asset to our endeavors'. In the hotel bar, residents who pass the time in the absence of guests will tell her, at last, what she is, and Sacks will believe them. In the bath's sink, she will find her hair and decorate the room with it; deep down she will consider it vulgarity and bad taste, but first of all, she cares about the guests and their comfort. In the black wormy waters, which the hotelier will begin to flood the sacrificial pool with, she will float: soft long hair, carefully groomed, will look delightful, but her eyes would already fade and darken: she will replace them with stained glass and try to stay away from the mirrors.

Long time Sacks will spend at the hotel, spinning a web of her own hair, entertaining guests, and shifting faces, and everything will be all right. But one day, a certain visitor will realize that in fact, Sacks does not have any face; he will shuffle, retreating, trying to get out, leave the hotel earlier than his time will come, and Sacks will flow after him, slip on the walls, on the ceiling, turn herself into a room, into a mirror, into a crimson carpet in the corridor, into the hotel itself and into everything that is around. She will twist into a helix, close, open, like giant jaws; she will change and shift — until it will become clear that it is not just one more nightmare has settled in the hotel, that nobody can enter and nobody can leave; until the guest will stumble into the merciful darkness, beset by the sensation that in these corridors, he will lose something more precious than the thing he used to call himself.

UNRAVELING

Barbara A. Barnett

I.

"Though unwittingly I have stumbled upon these ghastly truths, more mouthpiece now than woman, in another life I will seek such things with purpose, like the ghoul who borrows damp fire from the dead. On that day, I will but scratch the surface. And when I do, muddied scarlet will pour forth from the unfathomed depths. Existence will cease to exist."

— An excerpt from *Meaning Veiled in Madness: The 16th-Century Writings of the Mad Prophet of Carrowmore,* as translated by Esther Elizabeth Conroy, March 1887

Locked away in her study, Esther tried to push thoughts of Petya Aleksandrov from her mind. Succumbing to his charms was a momentary madness she refused to repeat. Passion like that could undo a person, and so Esther would have none of it. Instead, she focused on her latest translation project—the journal of a self-proclaimed prophet written in a bastardized hodgepodge of Scots Gaelic and Latin. She was puzzling over a mishmash of a word she could translate as either *ploughman* or *ghoul* when she heard the swish of parchment sliding across hardwood. A familiar sound, but one that should *not* have come from the closet.

Esther cocked her head in surprise. A note slipped under her *study* door would not have been unusual. The servants knew better than to interrupt her while she was working, especially so near the end of a project as all-consuming as the Mad Prophet of Carrowmore. And so rather than knock, they pushed their little missives through that sliver of space between hallway and study. Dinner or lunch or tea was ready. So-and-so had stopped by to deliver such-and-such. Petya Aleksandrov had called on her again and said he is only in London for another week, would she not deign to see him?

A note slid beneath the *closet* door, however—well, that was most strange. Esther pursed her lips and stared hard at the folded square of paper, then at the closet, shut as always. A jest, she concluded. An obvious jest. But whom was her trickster? The gardener? The cook's little imp of a son, perhaps?

"Sneaked in there during my morning constitution, did we?" Esther set aside her dip pen and replaced the cap on her inkwell; no sense risking it drying up or accidentally spilling on her papers while she dealt with this distraction. "Come on out now and show yourself."

Silence.

Esther took out her pocket watch and let a full three minutes tick by, during which time neither reply nor rustle was forthcoming. A trickster as patient as she, it would seem, not undone by the drawn-out silence of unresponsive prey. Begrudgingly, Esther allowed herself to be impressed. It had to be most cramped inside that tiny space.

After another two minutes passed without incident, Esther stood, smoothed out her trousers, and straightened her frock coat with a tug. She took slow steps toward the closet, exaggerating the heel-to-toe roll of each foot so as to prolong the creak of the floorboards. But she would not let her trickster believe her patient to a fault. As soon as she reached the closet, she opened the door with a swift, clean yank.

Empty.

Esther's eyebrows raised in astonishment. There were *things* inside, of course. A box full of books and parchment. Folded blankets for when she slept in her chair. The scent of mothballs. A down-like coating of dust; she would have to chide the servants for that. But no trickster.

Had she been mistaken? Could the note have come from the other door, shoved so hard by an over-eager servant that it sailed clean across the floor? No, impossible. She had heard the swish quite clearly from this direction. Besides, the sound had been too brief to cover such a distance, and the path between the study door and the closet was littered with too many obstacles: a thick-piled rug; the wide copper base of a floor candelabra; precarious piles of books.

Could there be a secret compartment of some sort? Unlikely, yet Esther pushed at the closet walls and poked at the ceiling. Nothing. She dropped to her knees and pried at the floorboards to see if any came loose. That was when she noticed a trail in the dust, the exact width of the mysterious missive, beginning in the middle of the closet floor. The dust around the trail's point of origin lay undisturbed, void of any footprint or impression other than the few Esther had just made.

Most peculiar. Her trickster was clearly clever, but then, so was she. And in her favor, the next obvious step was the very thing she excelled at: looking for clues in words.

Esther reached for the note. As soon as her fingers touched the paper, her skin prickled with a sudden chill—the feel of a spectral hand brushing along her cheek, down toward her neck, ready to squeeze, ready to sink into her flesh and tear.

Esther shook the preposterous image from her mind. It was nothing more than a draft, she told herself, unfolding the rough, filmy parchment. A rational explanation for the chill, and a possible answer to this mystery. The note could have been sitting there on the floor when a good strong draft blew it out of the closet.

You would presume to unravel me, the note read in jagged, undisciplined letters, *to mock my prophecies yet know their meaning. But I, your mad prophet, shall be both your doom and your legacy. For in another time when you have turned to dust as I have, Miss Conroy, someone else will presume to unravel you. They and not you will decide for posterity why you adopt the trappings of a gentleman in dress yet wear your hair long and loose in defiance of all current fashion. Why you have taken no lovers since that ballet dancer from Saint Petersburg. Why your obsession with language has left you with so little to say. They will take a scalpel to your life and dissect it and display it as mangled strips of flesh.*

Esther started to crumple the letter, her hands on the verge of trembling, but she stilled herself. *Come forward and I will show you how much I have to say, coward.* The thought quivered in time with her simmering anger. To adopt the guise of her long-dead translation subject, to know of her one-time tryst with Petya, to mock her work—her would-be tormentor most certainly had to be watching or listening, waiting to gloat over her reaction. But Esther would not let her trickster have the satisfaction of seeing her so unnerved.

There were explanations to be had for this letter, for its presumption to know what was in her mind and heart, and she would find them. She would *unravel* them.

2.

> *"Sometimes, the war dreams and existence prays. Sometimes, the servant inside a lover awakens. Sometimes, an ocean trembles and the unearthly coin is false. But much more dangerous is the green exploration."*
>
> — An excerpt from *Meaning Veiled in Madness: The 16th-Century Writings of the Mad Prophet of Carrowmore*, as translated by Esther Elizabeth Conroy, March 1887

After the letter's appearance, no one was permitted to enter the study without Esther. While she worked, she had a servant watch the closet. One nodded off after an hour; Esther threw a shoe at him to wake him. Another questioned the purpose of her task; Esther threw a shoe at her as well.

For the first two days of their vigil, Esther left the closet door closed. For the next two, open. Not a single note appeared.

Other servants brought Esther the usual messages: Dinner or lunch or tea was ready, she really should eat. It had been four days since her last bath, should another be drawn? Petya Aleksandrov no longer believes that she is out or indisposed, what other excuse should they give?

Tell him I cannot lose myself like that again. Tell him I have built these walls around myself for a reason.

"Tell him I am stalking shadows," she said.

After five days without another note from her trickster, Esther barred her servants from the room. She gathered her books, her ink, her paper, even the chamber pot, and sat beside the closet door, this time left ajar. The slightest stir within, and she was determined to hear it.

Though her back protested the awkward angle that working on the floor required, Esther continued her efforts to unravel the Mad Prophet of Carrowmore. She found it intriguing that her trickster had put question to her own choice of garments, for Esther's translations supported the legends that the Mad Prophet had worn no clothes at all. And yet, Esther found the prophet's dense, rambling words, unlike their author, to be far from naked. Their frequent incoherence was a mere gown, with glimpses of meaning displayed like the teasing baring of an ankle. As she worked, Esther imagined herself rending the fabric of that gown to reveal the bare flesh beneath.

They will take a scalpel to your life and dissect it and display it as mangled strips of flesh.

The parallel between the trickster's words and her own thoughts gave Esther pause. Where her pen had come to a stop on the parchment, the ink pooled, obliterating an unfinished word. Was she cutting skin as well as satin with her translations, revealing not just flesh, but blood and bone and sinew?

And so what if I am? Is that not my vocation?

If the cut was skilled enough, flesh could be stitched as well as cloth and leave but a scar. Meaning could be enhanced by that studious peek beneath the surface. Why should she fear unraveling the Mad Prophet's threads?

Esther returned her attention to the manuscript in front of her. "But much more dangerous is the green exploration." There was another thread to pull. "Green" meaning inexperienced? A naive soul unknowingly venturing into a dangerous place? Or did the text speak of an expedition into a verdant yet dangerous land, "exploring green" rather than a "green exploration"? But in the prophet's bastardized tongue, there was a hint of the Scots Gaelic that could more specifically mean "research." So not a physical exploration of place, perhaps, but the work of a scholar. Her own work, she thought with a shiver.

Esther shook her head. There lurked another parallel, but a poor one. She was a scholar, yes, but not by any stretch a green one. And yet, as she sat there in silent expectation of another mysterious missive, her mind threatened to run free with gullible imaginings. How easy for the room's creaks and drafts to transcend their mundane place as structural imperfections and become the sounds and motions of a ghostly trickster. How easy to imagine the Mad Prophet no longer dancing naked around the stone tombs of Carrowmore, her wrinkled breasts swinging wildly, but instead standing here in Esther's study, waiting. The Prophet and her trickster, one and the same.

Waiting for what? Esther wanted to demand, yet dared not. She would entertain the thought of shadows, but she would not abandon reason enough to question them aloud.

Across the room, papers rustled on Esther's desk. Then came the groan of her chair, the exact sound it made whenever she sat, ever so slightly different in timbre and duration from the sound it made whenever she stood.

That was no gullible imagining, Esther realized, pulse quickening. That was the sound of someone sitting in her chair. And yet, as with the closet, the chair was empty.

Esther pictured the Mad Prophet seated there, scrutinizing her with eyes like green ice, hair spilling over her shoulders, as long and red as Esther's, yet dirty and matted. Scarlet, pus-filled slashes lined her skin, wounds where history had sliced her. And in her madness, the Mad Prophet smiled.

Esther stared into those imaginary eyes, meeting intensity with intensity, putting challenge to feral mischief. *Tell me what you are waiting for, my trickster friend. Tell me what you want.*

And while Esther focused on shadows, the closet door slammed shut. A note slid through the crack with a dusty swish.

Damn you! Esther leapt to her feet, scattering paper and spilling ink in her rush to open the door. As before, she found no one inside the closet, nor any secret panel sliding into place.

Esther grabbed the new note. As she unfolded it, a frayed edge sliced into the pad of her finger, drawing blood.

Do not address me as friend, the note read, *for I am anything but. I am your shadow and your doom, Miss Conroy. I am that which you would presume to control. I am that which you both seek and hide.*

"You . . ."

No. She would not rant aloud at invisible people as the Mad Prophet of Carrowmore was said to have done. The servants thought her eccentric enough already. But eccentric was acceptable. It made one memorable, yet off-putting enough to keep people at a desirable distance. Madness, though, lacked cultivation. Restraint.

Esther gathered her ink and her paper, stood, and returned to her desk with a determined yet unhurried stride, leaving the spilled ink for the servants to clean up. *You best be out of my chair*, she thought as she sat. Doing so elicited no ghostly cries or spectral chills, only that familiar groan of weight settling on wood.

Esther set out a blank sheet of parchment, dipped her pen into ink, and began to write:

My dear trickster,

You would presume as much of me as you claim I do of you. You contend that my obsession with language has left me with little to say—a statement that wears but a varnish of truth. Days spent twisting words from one tongue to another leave me with little tolerance for the idle chatter that others insist upon. It is therefore not that I am left with too little to say, but rather that others are left with too much.

And so, because my words are limited only to those that need be spoken, let us be blunt with each other. Tell me plainly what it is you want of me. If you seek to rectify some error in my translations, to see that I do justice to your words in my tongue, then I welcome your corrections. But if you wish for me to cease my work entirely, to stop 'unraveling' you through translation as you would put it, then I am afraid I cannot, and will not, comply.

I eagerly await your response.

Ever your friend, though you would have me not,

Esther Elizabeth Conroy

With a smug sense of satisfaction, Esther slid her letter under the door and into the closet. That seemed the obvious way to deliver it. She had no doubt her trickster friend would respond in infuriating fashion, but that was the game now, wasn't it? To unnerve each other, to poke and prod until one of them finally gave the other what they wanted.

Esther sat at her desk and resumed her translations. Daylight had faded, and so she worked by candlelight. Every so often, the wicks would crackle and flickering shadows would dance across her desk. The motion drew her attention toward the letters from her trickster, the ends of each held down with thick tomes so as to keep them neatly unfolded.

I am your shadow and your doom.

Esther scoffed at the threat. Shadow, yes, but far more distraction than doom.

Why you have taken no lovers since that ballet dancer from Saint Petersburg . . .

Esther tried to focus on a string of words that eluded adequate translation, but her gaze strayed again and again to the candles. The rhythm of the flames' undulation unearthed a melody from her memory, the swell of an orchestra to accompany a dance.

No, Esther silently pleaded, but her thoughts refused to obey. They turned to Petya, to the devastation of a lover who knew the choreography of pleasure as well as the dance, who could reduce her to a wordless state of instinct. Esther had both loved and despised that feeling, and so fled from it.

That was what could unravel a person. Not ghostly letters, but passion, losing all sense of self in another.

And therefore, I won't have it. One after the other, she took the trickster's letters, turned them over to the blank side, and replaced the tomes that held down their edges. Remove the reminder of Petya, remove the desire. And by removing it, control it.

"Now back to you, my friend," she said, puzzling over the Mad Prophet's patchwork of words before her.

The closet door opened, the groan of its hinges pained and prolonged, as if the dead had been given voice. What the dead spoke, Esther could not translate, but in their voice she sensed an invitation.

As with the arrival of that first damned note, Esther stood, smoothed out her trousers, straightened her frock coat, and made her way toward the closet with slow, deliberate steps. Her breathing threatened to quicken, but she wrestled control away from instinct. Inhale, exhale. Slow and deep until her chest ached.

This time, the note remained far inside the closet, unfolded, the paper crinkled and torn. Esther imagined herself a fish staring at the lure on a hook.

Outside, an owl hooted. *Woo-hoo-hoo-hoo. Woo-hoo-hoo-hoo.* Her heart beat in time with the quick, percussive sound. A warning? The owl, a symbol of wisdom—the very thing she was about to disregard. The feeling that something dangerous lurked inside the closet was like a swarm of spiders crawling over her, their needle-thin legs raising the gooseflesh on her skin.

A wise person would heed such warnings. A wise person would close the door and flee. But Esther had never been one to be dissuaded by dark feelings and the instincts of animals. The words of her trickster were scrawled on that note, and she needed to read them. She needed to *know*.

Esther stepped into the closet.

Run. Grab the note and run.

No, she told herself. She would not be commanded by fear. She would not surrender control. And so instead of heeding that small, scared voice within her, Esther plucked the note from the floor with the slow care of one uncovering an ancient, fragile artifact.

The door slammed shut behind her. The darkness, so instant and deep, swallowed the note's black words before Esther could read them.

No! She tried the door handle, but it would not give. She rattled it hard and turned it until her hands ached and still it would not yield.

"Let me out," she said, her chest so tight that the words came out as a choked whisper. Who was she even crying out to? The servants? Her mad prophet?

Esther grasped the handle and shoved against the door with all her strength, again and again until her shoulder struck so hard that she cried out in pain. Nothing. Beyond the door, as if in mockery, came the *woo-hoo-hoo-hoo* of the owl in the night.

"Please!" Oh god, she could feel it now: control tumbling away with each quavering breath. No passion infecting her this time, but darkness. Ice instead of fire. A tremble of pleasure, a tremble of fear; why could she only now tell them apart? Petya the former, this darkness the latter. Sharp like a quill, black like ink. Like letters. Words on paper.

The note. In her struggle with the door, Esther had dropped it. It sat now by her feet on the floor, next to the crack beneath the door. There, dim light from the candles in her study crept into the closet, like searching, uncertain fingers.

Esther dropped to her knees. She clutched the note and held it near the crack. The shadowy words came into focus.

In unraveling me, you unravel yourself.

Arms wrapped around her from behind, unyielding in their grip. As much as Esther willed it, as much she tried to claw and thrash at her captor, she could not move. Fingers pinched and pulled at her skin. Flesh uncoiled like thread. A scream poured out of her, and then blood, thick and dark like mud. It blackened the floor just as the Mad Prophet's words blackened her mind.

3.

"Popular theory is that Conroy's death was one of self-mutilation, and that she authored the mysterious missives, carrying on a kind of mad correspondence with herself. These scholars argue that Conroy, always the eccentric in the public eye, had maintained enough outward appearance of self-control that her mind had unraveled before anyone could notice.

"The evidence, however, suggests otherwise. Close analysis shows little similarity between Conroy's handwriting and that of the notes she received. And given the extensive and gruesome nature of the mutilations to her person, it is unlikely she could have remained conscious long enough to inflict them all. And so, in these pages I shall posit a different theory: that Conroy was not mad, but murdered.

"Still, as I continue where Conroy left off in analyzing the Mad Prophet of Carrowmore's writings, it is easy to imagine a person of delicate constitution succumbing to the pull of madness. It would be disingenuous of this scholar not to admit to feeling a chill while pouring over the manuscript, like a spectral hand closing around one's neck . . ."

— An excerpt from *Unconventional Translations: The Life and Death of Esther Elizabeth Conroy*, an unfinished work by Victoria Todd Williams (Miller Creek Press, 1952)

Word of Mouth

Stephen Hargadon

WALKING HOME FROM the Gull late one afternoon, as the sun faded over the city, Cottle heard his name being called. A soft voice. Gentle. Not like the others. Perhaps it was an old pal, someone he hadn't seen in years; or the barman from the Gull bringing him something he'd left behind – an umbrella, a bag of groceries. No. He'd gone out with only the clothes on his back and the thoughts in his head, plus money for no more than five pints. He still had his clothes and thoughts (he liked neither) and the money was almost gone. The voice came again, soft but insistent – clear – and he looked for the caller, a friendly face, but the street and its occupants held no welcome. Everyone was a stranger. People rushed by as if he didn't exist. The young, the busy: he was invisible to them. He looked closely at the mouths and eyes of passers-by, searching for a trace of recognition. Nothing. It was just like any other day. He looked at the sky, seeking release from the human world and its erratic potencies, but the vast prairie of cloud filled him with sadness.

He was reminded of all the things he would never do, the bodies he'd never touch or kiss or wake up next to. He thought of all the places he'd never seen: the mountains, the cities, the golden beaches. He thought about money and how it had never stuck to him. He thought about his son.

He didn't want to think any more. The sky was just too big – it held too much information. It was best to keep your eyes down.

And this is how madness starts. Or how it ends. Or turns into something else, something criminal, something to be measured by judge and jury. Hearing voices in the middle of the city, in open daylight: that's worse than hearing voices when you're alone. We're all mad when no one's looking. But this madness, Cottle knew, started long ago.

His son had heard voices. From an early age, from the start. Perhaps he'd heard them in the womb: *Stay where you are, little one, stay there ...* Poor Martin. Martin and his imaginary friends. Friends that turned against him – killed him. Martin is dead. But his friends are out there still, not living, not dead, in the streets and precincts, and if you listen carefully, you will hear them. They never die. They cajole, they whisper, they tell you a truth others cannot bear.

How long ago was it now? Seventeen, eighteen years, something like that. Hanged himself. The authorities didn't help. They hounded Martin for being different, for thinking strange things, for hearing what he was not supposed to hear. They said he was unwell. He was not. He did bad things because bad things kept happening to him. He should not have been in that place, that pit.

Cottle was almost at his bus stop. He couldn't hear the voice anymore: its words had been blown away, scattered into the city. The thinnest of grey rain filled the spaces between people and buildings. His bus pulled away. He'd catch the next one. He never had to wait long.

There was a pork chop in his fridge at home. Soon he would be sat on the sofa watching the news with his dinner on a tray. A dollop of brown sauce. A glass of milk. The voice had not revealed its purpose. It didn't matter. Soon there would be new annoyances to think about: the news would be full of them. Death and corruption. He'd forget about the voice in the street. Or it would come back to him in a dream, turned inside out like a jacket, full of malice and threat because he had not answered its call.

But it wasn't his fault. He had tried to listen, to tune in. It was the voice that gave up, not him.

Cottle turned away from the stop. He knew the timetable by heart. Everyone around him was in a rush – chasing or fleeing but always moving closer to death – every tense face held together by unknowable thoughts. Cottle did not want to know what went on inside those heads. Their faces were bad enough. But once you studied the swarm for a few moments you saw people who were in no hurry at all. Dawdlers, strollers, smiling idlers. Some of them were looking and listening, just like Cottle, alert to the neglected frequencies. A man in fluorescent running garb knocked Cottle as he bounded by. *Sorry pops.*

Cottle looked in the window of a jewelry shop. He saw a watch the price of a house he had nearly bought many years ago. The Gull had not been a good idea. He had imagined a jaunty afternoon bumping into old faces who would buy him a pint. But that didn't happen. Sat alone in the corner with his pint of the usual, he felt the old sadness return and wanted to go home almost immediately. The only remedy was to wait. Or to drink. Or to keep moving, to move to the next moment, the next pub. Only in these ways could the pain of the present be overcome. Everything passes. Everything returns. And what other folks want and get is none of anyone's business but their own. The barman in the Gull was a miserable bastard.

"This way, Mr. Cottle. Yes. It's time for your trim ..."

Cottle looked up. The voice. He had been warned about this. He had been told stories of catastrophe and madness, of unconstrained drinking, of what happens when a man lives on his own and fumbles into old age.

Think yourself lucky. There's always someone worse off. That was another thing Cottle was always hearing, usually in the pub. And it was true. You saw it on the news. And he'd see it tonight, while eating his chop. Wars, famine, rape. Bombs and blood. Houses flattened like cardboard boxes. Fire and dust. Children screaming, pleading for mercy. But it wasn't real, not for the viewer.

Step this way, Mr. Cottle, step this way ...

Cottle has friends. Cottle has enemies. The whisperers in the kitchen, the insinuators and persuaders who follow him from bathroom to bedroom, who mock him as he spoons baked beans onto a slice of toast. But there's only one voice that counts and he knows it. All the others—they're not even voices, they're just idle thoughts. He's frail. He's too old for this lark. He scarcely knows if the voices come from inside his skull or from the cracks in the wall. The world is rich with suffering. Cottle has it easy compared to most of the world. But that's no good to him. He doesn't feel lucky.

A woman barged by, talking loudly into her phone which she held in front of her mouth like a slice of toast. *I told him hundred per cent no way, but he was like not having it and that's when it all kicked off you know, and I was like I don't think so yeah ...* Cottle leaned against the window of the pawn shop. He wanted to get away from these frantic weirdlings. Why couldn't they go about their business without bumping into him or contaminating him with their noise? Cottle himself had no business other than to stay alive, to follow each day from beginning to end, from first yawn to last; to breathe, eat and drink; to look and listen. Every waking day seemed as long and involved as a century, with its own traditions and fads, its peculiar politics. But put all those days together, accumulate the moments, and what did they amount to? A life. Which was something quite different. Something elusive, unquantifiable. A life, when lived, is nothing. Or nothing much. Those voices in the afternoon. Telling him this. Telling him that. The pub philosophers. Garrulous strangers. And the surly barman with his tabloid, leering over the smudged pages, turning from one perversion to the next.

Time to go back to the bus stop. Cottle passed an open doorway, wedged between the pawn shop and a chic bar done up in the style of an old-fashioned classroom, with wooden desks, faded wallcharts and a blackboard.

"This way, Mr. Cottle ... I'm here to help ..."

A red and white striped tube, scabbed with rust, dangled over the doorway. Cottle looked inside: he saw long, shadowy hallway with a staircase at the end. Was this someone's home or a business? Hard to tell.

"Come, Mr. Cottle," said a voice in the gloom. "Take the weight off your feet. It's time for your appointment. We'll have you looking as good as new in no time."

He was about to move on, into the pulse and curse of the crowd, when the hallway filled with yellowish light, and Cottle saw a man, a short man, standing at the foot of the stairs.

"Come in, Mr. Cottle, come in. This is such a pleasure." The man shook Cottle's hand. "You look tired, if you don't mind me saying – this city air is bad for the complexion, it's bad for everything – but we'll soon have you right as rain ..."

Cottle didn't know what to say. The man was so friendly. He steered Cottle into the hallway. He had strong arms.

"Put yourself in the safest of hands, Mr. Cottle, the nimblest of hands ... Relax and luxuriate – let your worries fade away. You'll come out feeling like a new man, believe me. I'm not just a barber, you know."

"Barber."

"Yes. It's in the blood. But I'm expanding. This way, this way. Do you like tea?"

They were on the stairs now.

"Tea?"

"Tea. Yes. The finest Assam. A proper brew for a proper gentleman."

"I missed my bus."

"They're no good. The council do nothing."

"I got there a bit late, that's all. They're pretty regular. I've got a pass."

"This way. It's not far." The man was pushing Cottle up the stairs. "I'm Sneck, by the way, Nelson Sneck. I've taken over from Winston – my cousin. You probably know him. Course you do. Everyone knows Winston round here." The man fingered Cottle's thick white hair. "I'd recognize Winston's artistry anywhere."

Cottle didn't know what he was talking about. The stairs were taking it out of him.

"Winston's retired, of course," the man continued, "no doubt he told you his plans. He told everyone. You couldn't shut him up, could you? The way he carried on, you'd have thought he was going to Florida not bloody Morecombe. But that's Winston. Full of joy, always the life and soul. He's got bungalow up there now. A little garden, front and back. Civilized. A different kind of snipping."

Sneck pounded up the stairs. Cottle struggled to keep up.

"This way, this way," said Sneck, but from what Cottle could see, which wasn't much, there was no other way to go except down. The air was damp. There were blooms of black mold on the walls. They climbed higher and higher – surely the building wasn't tall enough for all these stairs and floors. On one landing Cottle saw a portrait of a chubby man with grim little eyes and a lush moustache waxed into glistening points. Cottle stopped to catch his breath. The waxed ends of the moustache made him think of a snail's antennae. Cottle had been fascinated with snails as a child. He had taken them apart. He had performed meticulous experiments using razor blades and bleach. He remembered trying to burn the eyestalk of one. Another he had dropped into an ants' nest. But childhood was so far away. He found it hard to believe that such an innocent or enquiring Cottle could ever have existed. He distrusted half the things his memory presented to him as biographical fact. Only in the moment could he be sure that he was Cottle, for the world was full of Cottles he had left behind. The Cottle who had sat in the Gull drinking Bass. The Cottle who had made a baby and given it his name. The Cottle who had told a woman he could change, would change. The Cottle who had muddled through. And continued to muddle through. Did all those Cottles add up to this Cottle, the Cottle short of breath on a strange stairwell? It seemed a poor result for so much time and effort.

"Handsome, isn't he? My uncle Harris. Harris Sneck. Come on. Not far now."

Sneck helped Cottle up the stairs. The light here was almost non-existent: Cottle found it hard to see the steps. His eyes tried to decipher the murk. The windows were covered in newspaper: through holes and rips came knives of light. Not that there were many windows.

"Don't you have a lift?' asked Cottle.

"This ain't the Savoy," said Sneck.

"You can't get many customers up here."

"I get plenty. Word of mouth. They are loyal."

They came to a landing. Four doors, a flickering lightbulb. There was a strong smell of boiled pork and mold. Cottle noticed a sign on one of the doors: Sneck & Son.

In they went.

"My salon," said Sneck.

Cottle nodded without enthusiasm.

"Take a seat, Mr. Cottle. In the big chair. Yes, yes. Over here, in front of the mirror. You are handsome, Mr. Cottle. Still handsome. I bet you have your share of the ladies, hm? But I will make you more handsome. Of that you can be sure. Oh yes. Shall I take your coat. No? OK. Make yourself comfy."

Sneck settled Cottle into the big leather chair. It had chrome appendages and various straps and buckles.

"Don't be nervous. I'll see about that tea. Please, relax."

Sneck buckled one of the straps around Cottle.

"The traditional way," said Sneck. Then he looked at his phone. He seemed to be sending a message.

"My niece's birthday," he said. "Serendipity Sneck."

The salon was small, with mirrors and sinks, aeronautical magazines scattered on a low table, a glass cabinet filled with pots of ointment and complicated tools, and a single window covered with a square of frayed, greying lace through which Cottle could just about see aerials and satellite dishes and sagging wires – a world of rooftops and fire escapes. Possibly there were clouds out there, too, and fat pigeons, but it was hard to tell.

Cottle looked at himself in the mirror and saw an old man, a pinched grumbler. This was the disgusting old man who squatted in his youthful soul, the imposter who haunted every moment of his day, trailing him through the city, who slept in his bed and filled his flat with empty beer cans, who wrote indecipherable notes on scraps of paper and taped them to the fridge door, who left soiled underwear in the kitchen sink; the shriveled creature who farted on the bus.

Is this why he had come into town today? To get his hair cut? Is this what the voice was all about? He felt cheated. He seemed to have been sat in front of the mirror for a long time, a pint's worth of time. The street, with its noisy strangers, was part of another lifetime. Sneck, he told himself, was no more than a voice, a voice inside his own head. A stupid, prattling voice. Cottle strained to hear the noise of city. But he heard nothing, not even the rumble of distant traffic, just the ticking of a large antique clock above the mirror.

A door opened and out came a fat man. A jabbering noise followed the man into the room – the sound of many humans, most of them querulous or scared. He closed the door and the jabbering stopped. The fat man was wearing a greasy white jacket. Without saying anything he placed a cup of tea on the small table beside Cottle's chair.

"Thank you, Anderson," said Sneck. "There's your tea, Mr. Cottle. The finest Assam. Enjoy, savor, luxuriate. Anderson's a great chap by the way. Regularly visits Winston up in the bungalow. Loves his Schopenhauer, does Anderson. Always ready with a quote or anecdote."

Anderson disappeared into his room.

"Thank you for the tea," said Cottle, sipping cautiously, "but I think there's been a mistake." The tea tasted terrible, but he continued to drink out of politeness.

"Life is full of mistakes," said Sneck. "Indeed, it's mostly mistakes, as you well know. The trick is to make the most of them. Planning will get you only so far. The rest is ... well, the rest is ... luck, that's all, and luck is all about character."

"I think I should be going. You've got the wrong man. I mean I've come to the wrong place. I was on my way home, you see. I missed my bus." Cottle looked at his watch. "I'll get the quarter past. I don't need a haircut. Not for another few weeks. I don't know how I've ended up here. I'm sorry for wasting your time. I see a man in Northenden. And I don't have enough money on me anyway."

Sneck flicked through an appointments book, the pages thick and warped, almost corrugated.

"No, no, Mr. Cottle, you're in the right place, that's for sure. Our rates are not exorbitant. Your credit is good."

"I always pay my way."

"I know you do."

Sneck settled himself into a low leather armchair, setting off a series of crackles and squeaks as he adjusted his weight. He lit a cigarillo.

"You don't mind, do you? Good. Calms the nerves. My father started this business. Wellington Sneck. Have I told you that already? It's a foible of mine. I'm a Sneck through and through, as you can see from my nose. That portrait you were admiring downstairs - you can see the resemblance, can't you? The Snecks of Collyhurst, the famous Snecks – with a few infamous ones chucked in for good measure – that's us, not to be confused with the Snecks of Winsford, who are just a bunch of chinless loafers."

Cottle fumbled with the buckle on his seat strap. He felt woozy. He could not coordinate his fingers. Perhaps it was that rotten foreign tea. He had the curious sensation of being outside the room, of being spread across the ceiling, like paint.

"I'm sorry," he said. "I don't feel too good. I must have had a funny pint."

"It can happen."

Sneck looked at the glowing tip of his cigarillo, puffed and coughed, disappeared behind quivering whorls of blue smoke, then reappeared, red-faced and sweaty, as he waved away the fumes.

Cottle had given up on the buckle. He had no feeling in his fingers. He tried to concentrate on his surroundings. The walls now looked as insubstantial as clouds or steam, slowly shifting, their surfaces prone to subtle tremors and sudden bucklings. He thought of tectonic plates, of how they moved on currents of molten rock: he had been told that in school. He took it for granted that it was true.

Sneck continued to rhapsodize about Sneck heritage. Herbert Sneck, Hermione Sneck, Hector Sneck. Ridiculous names. The world is full of people who can't shut up, who fear silence. Babblers and prattlers.

"There's no problem that a decent haircut can't solve. The simple things are the best things. Sex, food, a decent haircut. My nephew Enzo isn't here today but he knows all the contemporary styles. He does the youth. Not that I'm suggesting anything *avant garde* for a gentleman such as yourself."

Cottle closed his eyes. Maroon clouds, a black sun.

"Enzo's the sociable type. A people person. I'm the same. Now Gordon, my eldest, he's a different character entirely. Reserved. A thinker. A bit like old Anderson, I suppose, in temperament, but he's definitely got Sneck DNA in him, no doubt about it, he's got the Sneck nose. For sure. He's Sneck all over, I guarantee it, from head to toe and back again.' Sneck turned to the left and then to the right, his index finger on the end of his nose. 'Unmistakably Sneck that is. But personality ... ah, that's something else. The mysteries of human character. Gordon, the thinker, he's always been quiet. But that's not necessarily a bad thing. He designs our promotional material. I've got big plans for this place. I've got a vision. Winston was a plodder – he did his work, made some money – but he didn't see the bigger picture. The potential. I'm different. I make things happen. And Enzo, dear Enzo. What a lad. You should see him with the girls, you know, in the supermarket, down the pub, on the bus, in the post office, always on the pull. He's gifted, knows what to say and when to say it, with a little joke here and a quip there, puts 'em right at their ease. It's a natural talent. The sort of talent that goes well with a pair of scissors. But I'm not sure I'll be able to keep him here. He'll be off. And quite right too. He'll make good with an actress, I expect, a proper one off the telly."

Cottle, nauseous, had no idea what Sneck was on about. Gordon, Enzo, Winston. They were just names. More names. Every day was full of names and talk and numbers and names. Somehow Cottle must block or deflect the words coming out of Sneck, for if he let these words take root in his own skull there would be no room for anything else. He did not want to become a mere name in a stranger's gob: a joke, a dirty story, a pub tale. "Remember Cottle? Skinny bloke with white hair? Used to drink on his own in the corner. The one with the loopy son ... Yeah, well guess what happened to him ..."

Sneck was a man whose words did not fit together.

Cottle's son had something wrong with him. An illness of the mind. That's what the professionals said. Cottle did not believe them. There was nothing wrong with his son. There were questionnaires and tests and interviews. It made no sense. Martin was fine. Anyone with half a brain could see that. But once the professionals got involved there was no escape. It was pills for this, pills for that. Endless conversations. Interviews. Interrogations. They called it therapy. They were determined to make Martin live a different life from everyone else. They put new forms of unhappiness and confusion into his skull and tried to cure them. It was an elaborate game for the experts. University had given them the right to do those things. There was that special school in the suburbs with its cold gymnasium, the remedial centers, and secure units.

The memory of those bleak days never left Cottle: it was a stain on his soul, a deep ache. He found it everywhere, that pain, it never left him.

"I'm quiet on a Tuesday. Never liked Tuesdays. Just a quirk of mine."

Sneck draped a smock over Cottle's shoulders and chest, fastening it at the back.

"Too tight?"

Cottle shook his head. Sneck picked up a pair of scissors from the shelf in front of the mirror.

"What will it be?" he asked. He didn't wait for an answer because he had one of his own. "A trim, I think. Short at the sides and back. Bit off the top. An inch or so. I can certainly do that."

Sneck began to snip.

"What do you do at home?" he asked. "Crosswords? Astronomy? Baking? I like to get to know a man before I start." Sneck was now at the back of the chair. Cottle could see him in the mirror and smell his cologne, rich and mossy. Sneck wriggled his fingers into Cottle's hair. He looked like he was mixing a salad. "Very thick. You're lucky."

"I watch television," said Cottle. He had no will to resist: might as well get it over. "But it's all rubbish, it's all made up, even the news."

"So why do you watch?" asked Sneck, pulling a comb through the dry grey strands.

"Can't think of anything else to do."

Sneck sprayed Cottle's hair with water.

"You've a fine head of hair."

"I don't feel too good," said Cottle. "I missed my bus ..."

"Too much hair, my friend. It weighs you down. It catches all the dirt and grime of the city. And all the words."

"Words?"

"I'll give you a nice trim. Nothing too outrageous. Nothing out of Enzo's book."

"You said something about words."

"Not me. You must be hearing things."

"My son heard voices. That's what they said. The doctors."

"Loneliness," said Sneck. "It's a terrible thing."

"I miss my son."

"I can imagine. A trim will do you the world of good. It's therapeutic."

"I want to go home. It's getting late. I've got a chop in the fridge."

Cottle pulled at the smock and tried again to unbuckle the belt. Sneck pressed down on his shoulders, forcing him back into the seat. Cottle had no power, no resolve. In the mirror he saw that Sneck wasn't Sneck at all. Sneck was Martin. There he was. His son. In his manly prime. Healthy and happy. And holding a pair of scissors. Martin with his future still ahead of him, safe and unsullied. There would be a wife, a child, a new family, Martin's family. It was just a matter of time, of getting through the days, the years. It happened to everyone.

"Martin," said Cottle. "I've missed you. There's not a day that ..."

Martin, with his lean face and blue eyes, stood behind his father, scissors poised. Cottle stared at him in the mirror. His beautiful boy. He had come good in the end. But he'd always been good. Cottle knew. That's what he'd told the doctors, told everyone – the teachers, the police, the neighbors. Cottle had believed. Cottle was loyal.

He twisted in his seat: he wanted to touch his son's face.

"Put the scissors down, Martin. Let's talk. Tell me what you've been doing. I want to hear everything."

When Cottle looked in the mirror again Martin was gone, replaced by Sneck, who was holding up a strand of hair with a comb: *Is this enough?*

Cottle frowned.

Sneck began snipping. "Tell me more about your son," he said.

"I've told you nothing."

"You said he heard voices."

"He passed away. But I think about him every day. I'm thinking of him right now. I saw him in the mirror. He was there. He was cutting my hair."

"Grief is a powerful emotion."

"It's not grief. It's something else. He's here. I know he is. That's why you called."

"You booked an appointment."

"I go to a bloke in Northenden."

"When did he die, your son? What was his name?"

"Martin. I dunno. Sixteen, seventeen years ago. Maybe more. Sometimes it feels like seventeen minutes. At other times it's like seventeen centuries ..."

"Time heals all wounds."

"That's not true. It makes things worse."

"No parent should see their child die."

"They put him in a cell. He shouldn't have been there. He needed help. Proper help. It was a bad place."

"Who put him there?"

"Police. Doctors. You know ..."

"Your son committed a crime?"

Cottle closed his eyes.

"It was you, Dad."

Cottle looked up. Martin was back in the mirror. His voice seemed to come from far away, from the street below.

"You were the voice."

"They put you in a bad place, the wrong place," said Cottle. "I told them. I warned them."

"You were the voice in my head. I did as I was told."

"No."

"You told me to kill myself."

"I'd never say that. I tried to help. I protected you from the doctors. They wouldn't listen."

"You were never there."

"I was always there for you, Martin. I remember hiding your pills, the pills that made you ill."

"You were always in the pub. I'd hear you crash in at night, shouting or weeping."

"That's not fair. That's not how it was."

"You told me to do things. It was your voice. I couldn't get away from it."

"No, no."

"Yes."

"I don't feel too good. I've had a funny pint. I did my best for you."

"Another excuse."

"Let's go home, Martin. Let's get out of here."

"I've not cut your hair yet."

Martin trailed the tip of scissors under Cottle's chin.

"I tried. I tried my best," said Cottle. "But there was nothing I could do, not against *them* – the doctors and lawyers, the police ... there was a whole army of them. They kept coming. There was only so much I could do."

"You should take pride in your appearance."

Martin pressed scissors into his father's neck, just below the larynx.

"Sometimes you don't know what to do for the best until it's too late..."

"You were the voice. You were always up here."

"No."

"I couldn't think."

"You went your own way, Martin, a bad way. You were weak, easily led. But I always loved you."

Martin jabbed the scissors into Cottle's throat. He did this several times, working the metal against skin and tendon until he had fashioned a gaping hole. It was hard work. But Martin did not slack. He stabbed Cottle in the eyes, in the heart, in the belly. Cottle was dead. Blood poured from his wounds. He had offered no resistance – indeed, he seemed to welcome the procedure – but the voices inside him remained alive. You could hear them. Little squeals and shrieks and puny cries of confusion.

Anderson entered the room. He unbuckled Cottle and lifted him out of the chair. There was no weight to the old man. Anderson breathed deeply with a connoisseur's greed. He liked the sound of the voices. He carried Cottle out of the room and closed the door.

Sneck, a cigarillo in his bloody fingers, looked at himself in the mirror.

"Time to shut up shop," he said.

Sneck turned off the lights. He thought of a fetus turning in a belly of blood. He thought of oil on the surface of a canal. He bounded down the stairs, eager to be out in the city, among the humans. He heard a voice from above, Anderson's presumably, shouting something violent, something urgent – something about money or blood or family, the usual shit, and Sneck began to take the steps two or three at a time, using the banister to lever himself through the gloom, past the windows covered in old papers and the portrait of Harris Sneck, down and down, until he reached the street. He saw a bus in the distance. Some of the shops were still open. The sky was dark, but the streets were full of people. They were rushing home from work. And as he joined the march of bodies, the jostling crowd, he looked from one face to the next, expecting to be denounced or questioned or hauled to the ground, to be punished for what he had done, but no one saw him, no one cared, and so he began to talk to the air because he knew that someone somewhere was listening.

Remembering Five Generations of Mayfly History, on the Sixth and Last Day

Marisca Pichette

T*UESDAY: AFTER MY therapy session, at 4:15pm, I'll kill myself.* I write it down in my planner so I don't forget. Gripping the pen hurts, and I see new bruises on my fingers. Probably from last night's fight.

I flip back to today's page. *Thursday*. All I've got written down is a note to throw out the milk, cause it's expired. I close the last planner I'll ever own and go into the kitchen. The milk doesn't smell bad, yet. I'll make muffins.

As I'm getting ingredients down from cabinets, I feel myself fracturing. My hands stop hurting and they look farther away as I measure out flour. By the time I'm adding the wet ingredients, the oven preheating at the other end of the kitchen, I'm not cooking at all.

I'm somewhere near the ceiling fan, watching her work.

She's skinny this morning, looking less than five days away from death. Some days she looks fat, disgusting, and slow. My therapist says that's dysmorphia. She—I, my body—only weighs 140 pounds. That's nowhere near overweight for someone who's 5'6".

Today, she looks no more than 90—bones poking through the sundress she put on to convince herself to be happy. I can see the bruises on her shoulder blades from where the asshole slammed her against the wall in the bar last night. Her breath still stinks of tequila and waffle fries.

What if things had gone differently, I wonder? What if he'd killed me—killed her—ground us into the pavement and wiped his feet on the grass after? That's a death I've often imagined, when the dissociation refuses to release me, and I'm trapped in a body covered in targets. But dying like that isn't the worst thing. Living through it, being alive and conscious and feeble...that's the true horror. Dying without release. Dying inside but outside enduring, scarred and bleeding and dripping everything done to me from every hole.

Up next to the fan, its blades covered in dust I've never wiped away, I stare at her. Last night didn't go the other way, and she's here. Not dead, carrying a handful of bruises and a thimbleful of regret.

I'm in control of those mistakes. It's been me, always, making choices to put her in impossible situations. I was trying to get her killed before I ever called myself suicidal. Is it me I hate, or her? Or both of us—the package we create, a mutilated mind wrapped up in a body riddled with faults.

I watch her like a pet I inherited without instructions, a plant I have no idea how to care for. She could break a glass now, cut herself and bleed out on the kitchen floor alone. I taste blood, the inside of her cheek I bit last night now rough and sore.

She could leave the gas on and collapse on the linoleum before the sun sets.

She could misjudge the scent of the milk and poison herself.

Are these fears, or options? I watch her cook, using my arms to carry the mixing bowl to the muffin tin. My feet, so far away, scuffing barefoot on the dirty floor. In this moment I hope she lives longer. I hope she gets past Tuesday, and the deadline I gave her. Gave me. I hope she eats all the muffins and becomes fat and healthy and soft.

It's me that should die. If there was a way to carve me from her pores, exfoliate me out of her life and moisturize something else into my place—a woman capable of love and commitment, a woman who knows how to cook and eat and hold down a job, a woman with ambition and an exercise regimen...

The oven bleeps; preheated. She oils the muffin tin, her hands moving in rhythmic circles. Hypnotized, I feel myself drifting closer, closer...

My hands hurt. I wince as I fill the tin with batter and put it in the oven. Am I solid again? Not really. I feel ready to float away at any moment. Being in full control is almost worse than watching. Now there's no one to blame for how I feel but me—whole and autonomous.

I set a timer and leave the kitchen, pulling out my phone as I sink onto the couch.

I have more exes than friends. I scroll past Alex the Bastard, Vivian the Slut, Corey the Drunk, Kayla the Ghost. I've texted and called almost all of them over the past week, collecting sexual favors like Halloween candy. It's funny, I broke all their hearts. I abused and manipulated and cajoled them into loving me. Then I threw out the catfish mask and if they didn't stray after seeing what I really am, I did, finding willing bodies to touch mine. Sometimes I was the one screwing everything up. Sometimes she was, while I sat on the corner of a stranger's bed, marveling at her ugliness.

How did I trick them into loving me? Me, fucked up mentally and only 140 pounds away from hell. That's less than a keg of beer.

Alcohol poisoning. That could end me if I'm not careful (if I try harder). I wonder how much of my weight I drank last night. My most recent ex—Caleb the Cheater—works at a bar that's a little too close to my apartment. He thinks I can't stay away from him. What I can't stay away from are the free drinks he gives me in the hope of getting head in return.

Last night no one got head. Some horny idiot grabbed my ass and Caleb lunged over the bar without asking me if I was okay (I'm never okay, and I'd already grabbed the asses of almost everyone around me, so whatever Caleb thought he was defending wasn't there anymore). Caleb broke Ass Boy's nose, I nearly broke my hand fighting Ass Boy's pal who was trying to haul Caleb off. The chaos that followed got the bar closed before the drag show. Pity.

As I scroll through my messages, planning my last five nights on earth, a text comes in from Caleb.

Are you okay? xx

Ha.

I delete it without replying. I think about texting Jay the Jerk but end up closing my messages and looking at my nudes instead. Not for the first time, I'm tempted to throw one up on my Instagram. So what if I get fired. I'm only going to work three more days anyway.

In the kitchen the oven starts beeping. I blink. 40 minutes past, just like that.

How do you measure a lifeless life?

Scattered around my apartment, plants are in various states of almost-dead. Weeks pass that feel like days. One cup of coffee lasts four hours, microwaved again and again.

"What is time?" I asked my therapist last week. Stephanie smiled at me.

"Time isn't any one thing. It's everything. It's what you do, how you feel, where you are and where you're going. We measure it, but lives can't be divided into hours and minutes. What do you remember: what time you ate breakfast, or how it tasted? Maybe you remember both, but the experience isn't relevant because of the time. It's relevant because of what you felt."

Bullshit. Pretty, but bullshit. Time is standard, and if you lose track, you're fucked.

After eating six mini muffins I log into my work email and quit my job. I post three nudes to Instagram, Facebook, and LinkedIn. My accounts get locked. I change out of my sundress and into an evening gown. The sun is still up, but what's time?

Time is what you make of it.

I leave my apartment carrying only a muffin. My bruises are fading, sunrise-purple on my knuckles. I walk down the stairs barefoot, my dress swishing behind me. I feel good—really good—for the first time in ages. I feel in my body, not drifting away, not tied to a screen that offers me nothing in return. I think I'll walk to the café on the corner and order a latte, pay for it with my muffin. Maybe I'll steal something too. Maybe I'll meet someone new, have joyful, lie-less sex. Maybe I'll never learn their name, nor them mine. Maybe I'll adopt a dog. Maybe I'll dig up a living flower and bring it home. Maybe I'll—

I stop in the lobby. It's dark outside. I look at the clock on the wall. Midnight.

What's time?

On Friday I wake up hungover and covered in crumbs. I put on lingerie and a sweatshirt. Dust Buster in one hand, I check my planner while cleaning up the mess around my bed. Today my past told me to make "some veggies" and submit a report for work. I switch off the Dust Buster and hunt around for a pen. All I find is a dying highlighter, but I pretend it's a Sharpie as I highlight the no-longer-relevant report deadline. I pull my hair back with my last scrunchie and go to the kitchen.

In the freezer I find one bag of cauliflower, banished here because I hate cauliflower. I stare at it. Someone liked it. Maybe Caleb, maybe Kayla. I rip the bag open and pour the white blocks into a saucepan.

My phone, when I finally find it between the sheets at the bottom of my bed, is dead. I stand at the counter while it charges, looking up recipes for cooking cauliflower.

My therapist calls it dissociation. I call it being already dead. While my body looks up recipes, I wander around my apartment. She hunts for spices, mechanical and ugly in her physicalness. Free of her weight, I leave.

Outside it's sunny. I walk along the sidewalk and go into Caleb's bar. It's closed right now, and he's probably home, waiting for me to text him back. He really shouldn't. Whatever happened to Dave? That's the last guy I remember him cheating on me with. Worse, Dave's gay, meaning revenge fucking the other guy wasn't an option.

Back in the apartment, she's found a recipe that she definitely won't follow. She starts grating coriander and cheese. I leave Caleb's bar and head to the river.

If I had her with me, I could throw us both in. Neither of us can swim. I stare at the current, dark and fast and cold. Kayakers go past, being healthy. She adds beer to the cauliflower pan.

Sometimes I feel just like her. Most of the time I can't decide if my body is part of me or not. I hate her and pity her. I hate me for what I've done to her. She used to be pretty. She used to be strong. I don't think I was ever either of those things. The same brain chemistry that has me imagining I'm standing here by the river while she's in the kitchen has sabotaged every relationship, told her she's not worth it. Not worth love, not worth life.

I step towards the water.

Before I can jump, imagine what the waves feel like when they close over me for the last time, I'm drifting back to the apartment. It's me putting too much cheese into the pan, boiling frozen cauliflower in PBR. It's me texting Caleb about whatever happened with Dave.

My hands hurt less today. I look outside, peeling cheese off soggy cauliflower and throwing the rest out. *Tonight*, not today. Breakfast became dinner. I wonder how late I slept. I unplug my phone and start shopping for houses I'll never buy. By the time I'm looking at furniture to go in my imaginary homes, it's 3am. I dump the rest of my meal and crawl into bed.

Saturday my planner tells me to call my mom. I don't.

Sunday it says to "do some exercise like Stephanie told you." I won't see Stephanie till our Tuesday session, and I don't really care if she's mad at me (she won't be; her job is to make me feel good), because I'll be dead before I see her again. So I don't exercise.

Monday would have been the one day a week I actually went into work instead of doing stuff remotely. Course, I quit. So I put on a crop top and a skirt I never wear and go outside, in my body this time.

I walk along the bike path by the river. No kayakers today. The water is moving slower than when I imagined it on Friday. I wonder if it would be strong enough to drown me. I guess it doesn't really matter. I can't swim, so I could drown in a glass of water if I wanted to.

Still, seeing it makes me nervous. I've always been afraid of water. Cold, dark. Heavy.

I've lost track of all the times I've nearly drowned. As a kid in camp, in hotel pools at family weddings, falling out of a canoe on the lake on the way to a friend's summer house.

Drowning seems easy. I've had lots of practice. Walking next to the river, I think about how all I need to do is slip, and that'll be that. I'll be dead.

But I won't be dead immediately. First, I'll be thrashing, my body trying to get air even if my mind is too tired. Then I'll be forced to breathe water, and it'll be so cold it burns. Then I'll sink, and my eyes will burn too. And then what will happen? Where will my body go?

Shit. Maybe it's better to take some pills or shoot myself. But I don't have a gun, and the only pills I have are ibuprofen. Don't those make your stomach bleed or something? Sounds fucking awful.

And what would happen if I almost died, but didn't? Rehab again, texts from well-meaning people I fucked over, questions from doctors.

On my way back to my apartment, I slip out of her. She's still skinny, still not eating enough. What has she eaten? I don't remember, watching her ass jiggle as she climbs the apartment building stairs. She didn't eat any cauliflower. Maybe some cheese, a few Oreos. Lukewarm PBR.

Can she starve to death? It wouldn't be immediate, or painless. But I'm not that afraid of pain. At least, not real pain. Not pain that tells you you're alive. What about pain that tells you you're dying? Does that hurt worse?

She walks into the apartment. I stay above, observing her like a Sim. I picture a green crystal floating over her head as she tries to cook and instead burns the apartment to nothing. She could fall out the window, down the stairs. She looks so fragile. If she forgets to eat again, will she die? Will I die?

I don't know how to take care of her—my little Sim-self. The only cheat I remember is MOTHERLODE and I know money doesn't fix people. Money doesn't make your brain work right or your relationships not fall apart. Money doesn't stop you from breaking hearts, getting broken.

I watch her sit on the couch, scrolling her phone as the sun crosses the sky. She doesn't really notice time passing, and it goes too fast. A day on the Sims lasts 24 minutes. What's 24 minutes? Mayflies, the shortest-lived animals, live for 24 hours. That's 60 Sim days.

If she was a mayfly, would she be happy? Would I know how to take care of her?

The apartment gets dark, and I stay by the ceiling, watching her, face illuminated by her phone screen. I don't know why I'm not going back. How long until I dis-dissociate? How long until I'm no longer a ghost, and she's no longer a body?

Will we die together or apart?

She goes to bed, and I drift with her, settling against the ceiling, watching her sleep. I know if she's asleep, I am too. I'm dreaming this, imagining the green light between us, sparkling crystal like a double-edged blade.

Through the night I'm desperately typing the only escape I know, hearing the keyboard in my mind, pressing the keys with imaginary fingers.

MOTHERLODE MOTHERLODE MOTHERLODE.

When she wakes up, I'm still here. Can this happen? Can I stay like this from waking to dreaming to waking again? I watch her open her planner and read what I wrote on Thursday.

After my therapy session, at 4:15pm, I'll kill myself.

She highlights it but might be crossing it off. Do I know how to do it? Does she? Maybe Stephanie will tell us. I've never gone to see her like this, broken apart. My Sim-self burns the last of my coffee and drinks it on an empty stomach. She'll have to shit if there's anything to shit after days without food.

Three mayfly life cycles without food.

180 Sim days without food.

I know that's not really true. She ate a little. I ate a little. I'm not going to starve soon. The idea of it taking a long time is worse. It's another form of commitment: starving yourself. I've never been good at keeping up with things. Suicide is a demanding hobby.

She looks even thinner today. Today—Tuesday. The last day.

She doesn't go to therapy. I look at the clock over the stove. 3:55pm. She microwaves her coffee for a fourth time, only to leave it next to her while she stares at her dying phone. She drinks a PBR. I try to go out the door, but I can't get away from her. For the first time, I can't imagine what's outside this apartment. I'm more trapped than I've ever been.

4:05. Ten minutes before the time I decided to die. What's the power of a decision? Stephanie says there's a lot. Layers and other bullshit. Maybe my decision to die will be strong enough to just make it happen. Maybe I'll watch her keel over, expire like a mayfly at midnight.

4:10. What if she does? What if she dies, and I don't? I know I'm not really outside of her. I know we're connected and it's just my stupid brain doing this. My brain that's in her stupid skull. If that brain dies, I should die too. I'll stop existing right when she stops. No mental illness can make you immortal.

4:11. What's time? Time is torture. Time is a prison sentence and all my life I've been angling for parole.

4:12. Shouldn't memories flash before my eyes? I stare at her. She doesn't know what time it is. She doesn't care what day it is. She's expecting to go on existing until the money runs out, until she's chucked onto the street and her only options are to jump in the river or crawl into bed with one of her exes. I close my eyes and for a moment I'm sitting on the couch with her, solid and whole and remembering all my life. I try to catch the good parts but instead I'm sinking and sinking and sinking, swallowing water flavored with salt, flavored with chlorine, flavored with boat fuel. I'm drowning and the only person who can pull me out won't stop looking at her phone.

4:13. Stephanie calls. I open my eyes and see me staring at the incoming call. She waits for it to time out, then returns to planning her future wedding despite knowing she's never going to marry. She hates men and she doesn't like women enough to stick around longer than a year or two. She's just a misanthropic bi imagining someone else's future, someone else's life. I watch her and the clock. She sips cold coffee.

4:14. A voicemail from Stephanie. Can I listen before I go? Will it change anything? I want her to play it, but she doesn't. Instead, she types in my name—our name—and hits *Call.*

4:15. The line rings.

And rings.

And rings.

In Caelo, in Terra

Aaron Worth

THE SETTING SUN was just beginning to darken the sidewalks of the boulevard that bore its name, and still Gus and his two best friends sat in their booth by the window, waiting for the bum to appear.

They had been at Sandy's for four hours at least, one of them hopping up to order another Coke or hot dog whenever the white-aproned owner behind the counter cast an impatient glower in their direction.

It was late July, and school had been out for some time. Two of the boys' fathers were in the war: Gus's was in the Pacific, Mike's was fighting the Nazis. Ben's dad, to his great shame (and the other boys' secret envy), had been declared medically unfit for duty, with an unglamorous diagnosis of chronic bronchitis.

Other than going to the movies, and playing flies and grounders, and following the press reports about the war (Gus had a map of the Pacific on his bedroom wall, covered with colored pushpins showing battles and other interesting events), there had been little excitement that summer.

But then, a couple of weeks ago, the strange vagrant had mysteriously appeared in town, with his Detroit Tigers baseball cap and dark sunglasses and erratic, shambling walk, pushing a shopping cart up and down the sidewalks of Hollywood. He had weird patterns of black dots tattooed all over his corpse-pale arms and neck and muttered to himself.

But the hilarious thing about the bum (all the kids thought) was the sign he had stuck on his cart. It was a ragged square of cardboard, on which had been scrawled in large, irregular letters: STAR MAPS.

There were lots of places you could buy maps to the homes of movie stars. Gus and his friends had even bought one themselves once, to see where their beloved Bogie lived.

So the idea that some tourist from Kansas or New York, in search of Lauren Bacall or Jimmy Stewart, would decide to get directions from that smelly, babbling derelict....

Well, it was just too funny for words.

A lot of kids, Gus's friends included, had yelled taunts at the bum when he first arrived in town. Ben, always looking for attention, had gotten a big laugh by approaching him with a one-dollar bill in his hand, demanding in a screechy voice to know where Lana Turner lived.

The bum had taken no notice of him. He just kept on making his crooked way up Sunset, pushing his cart, which was mounded high with mildewed army blankets.

In time, however, interest in the strange newcomer subsided. It was getting hotter, and it was more fun to escape to the cool of a movie theater, or the beach.

But then, yesterday, Ben had seen something which reawakened the three friends' interest in the stranger and caused them to stake out the booth at Sandy's which, they reckoned, afforded the best view of the street.

Now, however, as afternoon turned to evening, Mike was getting impatient.

"How long we gonna wait for this guy, anyway?"

Gus flicked a bit of crumpled napkin in Ben's direction. "Hey, you sure you didn't just see a coupla ordinary bums fighting over a bottle?"

Ben rolled his eyes in exasperation. "I told you guys a hundred times, it was *him*, definitely. I was going to the drug store to get Dad's prescription, and I see him stumbling up the sidewalk like usual. Then he goes into the alley. A minute later this other guy comes along, dressed real sharp.

Not a *bum*, that's for sure. He looked kinda like the guy in *Laura*: you know, Vincent Price. Except with a mustache."

"So, you go over to get an autograph," cracked Mike.

Ben ignored him. "So, I sneak over to see what's going on. And what do I see, but this guy, the Vincent Price guy, giving him a handful of dough, looking around all the time, and then the bum pulls out a map from his cart and gives it to him."

Mike pointed a chewed-up straw at Ben. "But how do you know it was a map? Why the big secret deal, just for some tourist map? You sure it wasn't, you know, *dope*?"

Ben threw up his hands. "Listen. It was a piece a friggin *paper*. The bum takes it out of his cart, all rolled up, and gives it to the guy. The guy opens it up, nods, and rolls it up again."

Gus frowned. "But you didn't actually see what was on it?"

"Well, no," Ben admitted. "I guess it coulda been something else." Then an idea seemed to strike him; his eyes lit up. "Hey! Dirty pictures, maybe?"

Mike snapped his fingers. He was suddenly interested again. "Not bad, kid! I bet that's it! Sure, I bet that filthy creep's got a box fulla girlie pictures in there, real hot ones! Or else maybe"—now his eyes were gleaming too—"maybe it *was* a map, but a *secret* map. Like to places in town where they show girls? Or else movies—you know, *blue* ones?"

"Or maybe," Gus put in, "a map telling where those girls live? You know, a map of the *blue movie stars*!"

At this last hypothesis Mike whistled softly, and each of them took a moment for private reflection. These were heady possibilities for three boys of fourteen and fifteen.

Then they ordered a fresh round of sodas and began to debate these and other theories, without coming to any clear consensus. But all agreed that *something* lay hidden beneath those blankets, something precious and forbidden, and they were determined to find out what.

But when another hour passed without any sign of the bum, Gus sighed, looking at the clock on the wall.

"Look, he's not coming today. And I got to get home. My mom's—"

"There he is!" cried Ben, jabbing a finger excitedly at the window. The three boys pressed their faces against the glass and saw him, not more than a couple of blocks away, coming up Sunset.

"OK," snapped Mike, like a C.O. in one of the war movies they loved. He took a last, gurgling pull at his Coke and slipped out of the booth. "I'll get into position. You two know what to do." And coolly he sauntered to the far end of the shop and vanished through the side door.

"Come *on*, Gus," hissed Ben, tugging at his sleeve. "Come on, or we'll miss him!" And the two boys scrambled out the front door and onto the sidewalk, where they adopted a slow, slouching stroll, a grotesque caricature of nonchalance: hands thrust into pockets, faces turned towards the cement.

Then, sneaking a look, Gus saw the man, not ten yards away now. He was walking towards them, with his usual Detroit Tigers cap, dark sunglasses, and tattoos like black freckles. He was murmuring something to himself, pushing his cart with one hand and scratching violently at his face with the other.

As the bum drew closer, Gus saw something he had, somehow, not noticed before. The man was missing three fingers: the pinky of his left hand, and the ring and index fingers of his right.

"OK, *now*," said Ben, giving Gus a sudden shove forward.

"Hey!" cried Gus, as he collided violently with the cart, eliciting a hoarse, surprised grunt from its owner.

"We're supposed to create a distraction, right?" tittered Ben, dodging around Gus and snatching the "STAR MAPS" sign from the cart. Then he danced nimbly away, brandishing the crude placard tauntingly, as the bum left his cart and shambled towards him, his mutilated hands outstretched.

Meanwhile, Mike had snuck up to the cart from the other side and was rummaging beneath the moldy blankets.

After a minute, he cried out in triumph, pulling something from the cart. "I got the dingus!" he yelled, waving a crumpled cylinder of brown paper in the air.

At this, the hobo abandoned his pursuit of the capering, elusive Ben, and raced clumsily towards Mike, shoving Gus aside with one four-fingered claw. As the bum rushed past, Gus's nostrils were filled with a smell that made his gorge rise.

The man, moving faster than Gus would have expected, seized Mike's shirt with both hands.

"Here," panted Mike, thrusting the paper at Gus, who took it, then watched in horror as the bum looked back over his shoulder to grin at him. The grin revealed a set of black teeth which had been sharpened to points, teeth which the man then sank deep into his friend's shoulder.

Mike screamed, then slapped frantically at the bum's head, as a bright blossom of blood began to spread slowly across his white T-shirt.

Under Mike's feeble assault, the bum's cap and sunglasses fell away, revealing filthy tangles of long gray hair, clinging to a red, scabrous scalp. The bum looked up and grinned again at Gus, his black shark's teeth now glistening wet. His eyes were pale, milky: the eyes of a thing that lived in caves or tunnels.

His heart pounding, Gus turned and ran, as fast as he could.

His panicked flight led him north of town, away from Sunset, away from the streets and stores he knew, away from all streets. At last, he found himself scrambling up a steep sandy hill, his heart still beating like a trip-hammer.

When he reached the top he stopped and bent over, fists pressed against knees, to catch his breath.

After a while he straightened again and looked around him. The sun had sunk into the Pacific, tingeing the western part of the sky faintly with blood. The sky above him was nearly black. Gus was standing atop a ridge of hills he did not know. To the south winked the lights of the city, while in front of him a dark canyon yawned. The sweet smell of sagebrush floated on the cool night air.

Then, almost as an afterthought, he realized that he still clutched their prize, and a sudden desire to see what was pictured or written there, while there was still light enough to see by, blotted out even the awful memory of the hobo's black teeth, wet with Mike's blood.

Gus knelt, carefully smoothed the paper out, and held it close to his face.

When he realized what it was he was looking at, Gus almost laughed.

STAR MAPS, the cardboard sign had promised. And that was just what Gus found himself squinting at, as he knelt on the sandy ground, sweat cooling on his skin....

The paper was thick and brown—butcher paper, maybe—and had been covered all over with tiny, six-pointed stars, carefully drawn in some sort of silvery ink. Strange symbols were scrawled in the margins, symbols like nothing Gus had ever seen before: maybe a bit like Chinese and Arabic letters, mixed together.

It was a map of the night sky.

Gus's father had taught him many of the constellations, when the two of them had gone for long night walks on the beach, especially in the weeks before he had gone off to war. This map was a pretty fair representation of the evening sky, seen from Southern California.

But, he realized with a frown, even though the *stars* were the same, the *constellations* were very, very different. Lines, thin as spiderwebs, had been traced in that same silvery ink, linking the familiar stars into new and strange configurations.

Gone were the familiar, comforting figures of the hunter, the bear, the watercarrier. In their places he now perceived alien forms, shapes which had no names, but which nonetheless tugged unpleasantly at dim regions of his memory...

Worse, the longer he looked at the map, the harder it became to make out the old constellations at all. Frowning, he tried to see Orion on the map and found that he could not; he could only recognize the new forms. It was as though the spidery, silvery lines were pulling his brain irresistibly into alignment with them....

Panic quickening his pulse, he threw the map away and looked up at the vast, black sky.

The stars were out now. And, for just a moment, Gus saw them as he was used to seeing them.

But then, as his stomach slowly and sickeningly turned over, the stars seemed to crawl and slither into their new positions, until the sky matched the map exactly.

Of course, they did not *actually* move. But the effect was much the same: it was like looking at an entirely different sky.

With every passing second, Gus could see more and more of the new constellations, and the shapes they hinted at were appalling, hateful....

Try as he might, he could no longer see even the Big Dipper, though he knew he was staring directly at the stars which made it up. But three of these—and not ones he had been accustomed to consider as adjacent—now made up their own, unspeakably hideous, constellation, whose secret name Gus now guessed, while the others had either faded to obscurity, or else been cannibalized by other constellations, transformed into part of a vertebra, a tentacle, a blemish...

Then Gus realized that it was quite useless to resist the influence of the map. It was far easier to allow it to *teach* you, to show you the shapes it wanted to show you. And realizing this, he soon abandoned his attempts to recover the old forms and gave himself up entirely to the contemplation of the new...

And so, as the hours of the night crept slowly past, Gus knelt in the cooling sand, his face tilted skyward, and stared, and stared, and stared.

When Gus Vadillo returned home at half past six the next morning, there was a police car in front of the house, and his mother, pale as a ghost, was making coffee for the two patrolmen who sat at the kitchen table.

Like a sleepwalker, he pushed open the screen door and shambled inside, and at the sound of the door banging shut his mother rushed into the front parlor and slapped him right across the face, hard, then began screaming at him in Spanish, while the policemen sipped awkwardly at their coffee. She cursed (which she seldom did) and threatened Gus with punishments such as he had never dreamed of, and she would have said much more, if it had not been for the sad, strange expression on his face as he looked up at her.

Finally, she ordered him to his bedroom, screaming after his slouching figure, "*Hablaremos de esto más tarde,* Agustín!" before bursting into tears.

But they did not talk about it later. For the next week, Gus hardly spoke at all, only mumbling vague replies to his mother's questions, until she began to think it might be a good idea to bring him to a doctor. That strange look never left his face, and his behavior was very unusual. No longer did he go out with his friends. One afternoon, Ben Seidel came over, anxious to see Gus, but he only murmured to his mother, without turning his head, "I can't, not *now*." (At least, that was what she *thought* he said—it was difficult to tell: he spoke so strangely since his return, in a kind of faint slurring murmur.)

On the night after his return, his mother found him standing in the backyard, his mouth open and his head back, staring up at the heavens. She brought him back in and scolded him. After that, he spent the nights sitting in a chair by his bedroom window, gazing at the starry sky. During the day he lay in bed sleeping, or staring at the ceiling, where he had arranged the pushpins from his map of the Pacific into odd patterns.

Then, on the seventh morning after his return, Gus's mother came into his room with his breakfast to find him sitting cross-legged on the floor, staring down at his hands. One hand held a small kitchen knife; the other was covered with blood. He had taken off the top of his left pinky finger, just above the first knuckle. It lay, in a spreading crimson pool, on the carpet. Mrs. Vadillo threw his bowl of CheeriOats in the air, turned, and ran screaming from the room.

Later that morning, Gus was sitting in the office of a Dr. Reed, a psychiatrist affiliated with the hospital where Gus had been treated for his injury.

At first Gus would do nothing but grunt or shrug noncommittally in response to Dr. Reed's questions. But Dr. Reed was patient and persistent, and by the time Gus's mother came to pick him up an hour later, he had told the psychiatrist a strange story about a map he had looked at, which had shown him things in the sky and taught him how to "see properly."

Dr. Reed nodded encouragingly and made a note. "Very good, son. What kinds of things?"

Gus looked sullenly at the carpeted floor. Then he said, irritably, "Just the things, you know, the things that are there. You can pretend. But you know. You know all about it!"

And, still looking at the carpet, the boy blurted out a litany of strange names: "Like the great jellyfish, you know, and the seven dead puppets...and the blind spider with the two names, and..."

Finally, Gus trailed off, and looked up at the psychiatrist, his terrified eyes filling with tears. "Don't—don't tell me you don't know all about them!" he yelled. "Don't you *dare*!"

Then he buried his face in his hands and sobbed. Dr. Reed made another note.

After a while Dr. Reed said, very gently: "Gus, can you tell me why you hurt yourself?"

The boy looked at him in confusion, then seemed to remember his bandaged hand for the first time. He held up both hands in front of his face and stared at them, disgust and horror twisting his mouth. "But doctor," he said in quiet reproach, as though stating something appallingly obvious, "just *look* at them!" And then he began to sob again, while the two hands fell into his lap, scratching and tearing at each other like wild animals...

The case frankly perplexed Dr. Reed. One evening he was in Pasadena, dining at the home of an old Stanford roommate. After his second Scotch, Dr. Reed told him the story. His friend, a well-known ethnographer, listened with great interest.

"Of course, you're right, Dick," he said after Dr. Reed had finished. "No doubt there are good Freudian reasons for the boy's condition. And being a good Freudian, you'll nose them out in time. But," he added with a chuckle, carefully stubbing out his cigarette-end in a chunky glass ashtray, "the curious thing is, it puts me in mind of a strange legend an Indian once told me. A very old Mohave—at least ninety, I should think. Of course, I can't remember the details. This was before the war—the last war, I mean."

Then he chuckled again, stirring absently at his unruly white hair with a tobacco-stained index finger, like someone gathering cotton candy onto a stick.

"But you know what an irredeemably *anal* type I am, as your beloved Freud would say! Just give me a minute, will you?"

He rose and left the room, only to return a few minutes later, holding a fresh cigarette in one hand, and an old, manila-colored notebook in the other.

The ethnographer sank back into his chair, blew dust off the notebook, and paged frowning through it for a minute. Then his face cleared.

"Ah," he said. "Here are the man's exact words, the *ipsissima verba*, at least as I Englished them at the time. But I flatter myself that it is a pretty competent translation." He cleared his throat and read:

"This story my grandfather told me, many years ago.

"In very old days, before the first men came to this land (he means the Mohaves, of course); nay, before these lands were desert, there was a city here, and the city was called XHOTOL. And when, after many ages, men did settle in these parts, still they did not venture near the city, for its inhabitants were not good to look on.

"Now, it was the case that Those-which-dwelt-within-XHOTOL...."

The ethnographer stopped, frowning again. "Now, that's a damned awkward, not to say ungrammatical, rendition. I wonder why I didn't simply say, 'The people of Xhotol'?" He stubbed out his cigarette, lit another, and continued:

"Now, it was the case that Those-which-dwelt-within-XHOTOL hated men exceedingly and were hated by them in turn....

"Now and again, some child or woman gathering herbs in the woods would happen upon a grotesque artifact of inscrutable purpose, or even (horrible to say) one of the dead of XHOTOL, and would never sleep easy again, being tormented by the memory.

"And so, one day, the chief men of all the tribes took counsel together and resolved that it was not meet that the city of XHOTOL should longer be suffered to stand, a blasphemy (as they said) in the eyes of gods and men; nay, an outrage against Nature herself.

"Accordingly, with the rising of the sun, a group of picked warriors set forth, well-armed, and entered into the city, and lay waste to it. And by the time the sun slept again in the West, there remained nothing living in the city, and its appalling dwellings were a smoking rubble. And no man who had entered XHOTOL that day could ever be prevailed upon to talk of what he had seen—or done—within those walls.

"Now, before the destruction of XHOTOL, one of the chiefs, a very wise man, had given commands that no plunder or spoil of any kind was to be taken from the city, but rather, that the things of that evil place should be left to rot beside their unspeakable makers.

"Notwithstanding this order, a few men, moved by curiosity or greed, did bring away with them objects which they found in the city, thinking perhaps to trade them, or to keep them as trophies of war.

"Among these were certain drawings of the night sky, which were not good for men to look upon; for those who did, came to perceive the heavens as had the unutterable dwellers-within-XHOTOL, and to discern strange and terrible patterns therein.

"Nor was this all. For in time, the awful shapes in the sky did begin as it were to instruct them, like a slow and patient whisperer, in how they were henceforth to construe the world around them; for very true are those words, which once I heard a priest utter: *As above, so below...*

"And so these men lost all sense of human proportion or relation, and came even to loathe their own forms, until at last they were unfit for any company but those who had also seen *the stars of XHOTOL.*

"Hearing of this spreading madness, the chiefs of all the tribes caused these pictures to be destroyed by fire, but some few did survive, and were copied in secret, in which manner they have survived the passage of long time..."

Here the ethnographer looked up from his notebook. "As I recall, I asked the man if he had ever seen one of these himself, at which he crossed himself fervently (he was as devoted a Roman Catholic as the pope himself could wish for) and said, 'Praise to Christ, no. But there are men who possess them, even today, passing them in secret from hand to hand, just as a plague-germ is passed...'"

Soon after that night, Agustín Vadillo ran away from home. His mother, frantic, had phoned Dr. Reed, who told her that the boy would probably come back on his own, in time. Privately he was not so sure.

However, Dr. Reed was friendly with several local policemen, whom he asked to keep a particular eye out for the Vadillo boy. One day he learned that a boy roughly answering Gus's description had been spotted the night before, in the company of a vagrant, underneath an overpass in Santa Monica....

But as the weeks passed, Dr. Reed's attention returned to his work, though he never quite forgot about the young man with the mutilated hand, who had told him so strange a tale.

Then, one day, a minor story buried deep in the evening paper caught his eye.

The item was jocularly titled "MOSES OF THE BOXCARS?" and told of a great exodus of vagrants from the city in the early hours of the morning, reported to the police by a bewildered truck driver. He had seen scores of them shambling alongside the railroad tracks, like a strange, straggling army, led by a gaunt, long-haired figure. It had been a moonless night, but the dazzling canopy of stars had illuminated the horde as it trudged north.

The writer, who had adopted a facetious tone for most of the story, ended in a more sober vein, noting that this "Moses of the boxcars" appeared to have had a teenaged boy with him (perhaps his son), seen pushing a shopping cart. This, he opined piously, was a sad commentary on the state of the nation.

Dr. Reed, whose bedroom windows commanded an enviable view of the Pacific, slept with the shades drawn that night, and for several nights after, until the waxing moon began to dim the burning intensity of the stars, those mocking, infinite stars that winked and leered at the ocean, in whose black, wrinkled surface they seemed to be multiplied without end.

The Conductor

Sarah Walker

THE NIGHT THAT Sterling first found them, they were on the side of a railroad car slowly creeping by the underpass. He'd been sitting with some other vagrants, drinking rotgut whiskey while they spun tales of their outlaw life. He knew those stories were a lie, but he also knew they hid a truth that they all tried to deny- their souls had been stolen by the gleaming dark gold liquid in the bottles that shone briefly in the dying summer sunset as they each took a swig.

Theirs was a truth that lied.

He'd had enough of their tales. He stood and staggered over when the train finally screeched to a stop while the tracks were changed. In the distance, a silhouetted shape of someone appeared and then vanished as they ran across the track back into the shadows. He wondered who they had been. And on the heels of that thought, *had any of them ever been anything at all?*

He smiled to himself and stopped, squinting at the strange graffiti trailing down the train car. It didn't look like it was intentional, at first. Then, slowly, he began to make something out, but try as he might, the images would not be deciphered. Confused, he tried to ask the others, who had been on the street longer than him, what the hell the drawings were meant to be. But like always, it came out all wrong,

"Wassss 'zat...?" He slurred his words, to the great amusement of Dirty Dave.

"And you said you could hold your weight? You're just a boy." Dave chuckled a scratchy laugh, then everyone else started laughing too.

Sterling hid his face in embarrassment, turning away from the drunken hilarity, ashamed and wanting to be any place but there.

Fortunately, drunks have short memories, so the conversation among the men in the shadows quickly moved to something else. Sterling walked closer to the stopped train car, taking it as a sign of fate that he had been forgotten for the moment.

The graffiti was unlike any he had seen in the past. Though just chicken scratches, it stood out from all the rest and as he stared, words began to become visible, and then a pattern developed. It was like one of those magic eye posters at the malls he'd seen when he was a child. He'd stare at the pixelated bits of nonsensical color, only to be surprised when an image of a sailboat would appear, or an eye, staring back at him.

This must be like that his gut told him. Something was there as he had first guessed. He forced his mind to focus, then remembered that to see the hidden image, you had to do the opposite. Letting his eyes rest, he zoned out; easy to do in his almost double vision drunken state. And as he had expected, letters began to manifest, and then a full sentence.

He is risen.

Sterling frowned. If it was just some dumbass Christians painting messages of their so called "Savior", why the hell had they gone and messed it up so badly? He cocked his head sideways and saw that he'd been wrong; the words weren't there at all. It was just a mess of squiggles and lines.

How the fuck did I manage to see words in all that scribbling?

But then they were there, again, and then they weren't. The more he gazed, the more the words shifted. Soon he was seeing more words, but this time they were saying something different, and ...

"Don't look at it."

The voice startled him from behind. He spun and saw DeAngelo, his dark face glistening with sweat in the humid heat, his breath smelling like wine and menthol cigarettes.

Sterling tried to sound sober.

"Why's ever not?" He didn't know why he'd worded it that way, but although it came out a little crooked, he had managed to hold his mud this time.

"Because it'll suck you in," DeAngelo whispered, voice lowered to almost inaudibility. "You'll disappear, following those words." His eyes had grown wide with anxiety, the pupils huge and black, dilated from whatever crap he'd taken that night. In them, Sterling saw his own reflection. "Don't disappear Sterling. I don't want to be alone again."

He touched Sterling's arm, and though Sterling wanted to pull away, worried that some of the less forward thinking of the group would see, DeAngelo's terrified face kept him from doing so.

"I won't disappear, DeAngelo," he said, to which his friend smiled weakly. Sterling added,

"Don't worry. Don't be so grim, man. Come on, I've got some wine. I'll share it with you. Just don't tell the others."

The stopped train car began to move again as they walked back toward the camp. Though Sterling had almost put it out of his mind, something made him turn for one last look. He saw the graffiti again, one word jumping out at him as the car passed by.

Come.

It tugged at him, like a command.

He woke with a headache to end all headaches, sleeping in an abandoned station wagon DeAngelo had found and claimed. It was a strange place, full of discarded children's clothing, but it made a passable bed for them.

He turned and realized that DeAngelo was gone. Sterling could have laughed, and then he cried. How stupid he'd been! Never should have fallen for the man, never should have trusted him! He wanted to believe DeAngelo would appear on the street, grin wide and friendly, two cups of coffee in his weather-beaten hands. But, after an hour of waiting, no such thing happened, and he knew the truth.

DeAngelo had disappeared on him, before he could do the same.

Maybe he was meant to be alone.

It didn't really matter, he told himself as he crawled out of the car. Another hidden emotion evaded his consciousness though, a strange knot of worry in his belly.

What if DeAngelo hadn't just left? What if something had happened to his one and only friend?

He pushed himself to remember more of the night before, when they had come back to the car, drinking sweet wine, and talking, but he had been so drunk.

He did have a vague memory of DeAngelo waking him later, the car humid with breath and sweat, DeAngelo's face hidden in shadow

"Sterling...wake up...I think they found us..." His voice had been whispering, low and barely audible.

He vaguely recalled turning away, grumbling for DeAngelo to go back to sleep.

Then, DeAngelo's voice, as loud as if his lips were pressed to Sterling's ear, blasting frantic, sharp words into his unconsciousness:

"*He is risen!*"

After that, nothing.

Sterling shook his head and pulled on his boots, sitting on the pavement in the already warm July day. He must have dreamed it; that would have been too weird. It was only a dream brought on by that graffiti. And DeAngelo had left him, just like the others.

"Yes. He just left." He said it aloud as if trying to convince himself, as if wanting it to be true. The alternative was too strange, and too frightening. The words flickered again in his mind briefly and he shook them off.

A bedraggled old woman walking a small dog saw him and quickly hurried the other way. He supposed he made a sorry sight, tumbling out of an abandoned car half-drunk still, his hair sticking up, his eyes gummy with sleep.

He turned the broken side mirror towards him, finger-combing his dark hair into a semblance of order. The cracked glass fractured his image into several. He wiped his face and straightened his clothes and then saw himself as he must have appeared to others - a 17-year-old boy with no one and nowhere to go.

He left Kansas City that night and wandered aimlessly, more lost over DeAngelo than he had first wanted to believe. He wept in despair alone on park benches, but finally the tears dried up and he turned cold, shutting himself down.

Then another message appeared to him.

Keep moving. Stay alone.

He listened to the message, without really knowing why. But the truth was there, swimming in the depths beneath the surface of his ignorance. He had nothing else to listen to or believe in.

He kept traveling across the countryside, making no friends in the towns he visited, only staying long enough to beg for food and drink. And the messages kept coming all summer, slowly at first, then more and more frequently as autumn approached. He followed them from train car to train car, not wanting to admit he must have lost his mind. But maybe even that was not real. Maybe truth wasn't true. Maybe it was more a matter of perception.

Another voice, deep in his mind suggested something that scared him at first, and then tantalized him with its mystery. Perhaps the messages were leading him somewhere.

That fall he used some money he'd spare changed to buy a notebook and began to record what the messages said. Once, as he sat copying them down, a thought occurred to him - did the messages write themselves?

No, that couldn't be right. Someone, or something, was writing them. But who?

He closed the notebook and put his broken-off pencil away, scared at what was happening to him but knowing he was in too deep. Like diving, he had gone so far below that he couldn't make it back to the top even if he tried because his air was almost gone. Better to stay below and see what the darkness held for him. He could sense something was there, close to him, waiting for him to see it. He could feel its great darkness beating in the depths.

More days rolled by, and fall fell into winter, he grew a beard, and his eyes grew sunken. When he saw his reflection in the plate-glass windows of department stores, he no longer recognized himself. He understood why people avoided him.

He looked like a lost soul; one being sucked into the oblivion of a collapsed star that poisoned the very air around him. No one wanted to be sucked into the gravity crushing void. So, they stayed away. Could he blame them?

The messages became even more frequent. He no longer had to search. He saw them everywhere now - in empty laundromats scratched into tabletops, in the flickering neon lights of a convenience store. They even might light up the darkened city block deep in the industrial district, and he would understand that they were talking to him, their occult Morse code a series of dots and dashes, light held for a moment before blinking into a black void, then back again, sequence after sequence, visible only to those who knew to watch.

There was soon too much to record in one notebook; he had filled it in tiny, cramped writing from cover to cover. He filled another, then another, and another.

One night a bum he didn't know grabbed his notebook from him and read aloud what he had written.

"*Tamam Shud*? What the hell does that mean? You some kind of foreigner?"

Sterling didn't reply but thought the man might be right. He was a foreigner now.

He soon gave up on writing them as the words began appearing in places where once had been only blank space, even in the white between words in books or the empty spots in ads on the subway. Sometimes, they would simply appear in the air front of him, floating like butterflies made of black ink, alive with a life force alien to humankind only to vanish when they touched his filthy skin, the letters sinking into him.

Eventually, he understood that the words humans used were merely an abstraction of the real message.

The truth could only be found where the words were not.

He destroyed his notebooks in a garbage can a few days later, pouring lighter fluid on them and watching them burn into ash beneath a starry night sky, the heat from the flames warming his face while his hands ached from the bitter cold. He stood there even after the fire was gone, letting the emptiness talk to him.

Stay moving. You're near.

At the railyard, he hopped the first train he could, staying on it in the corner of an empty car until he was caught. Though he'd known a cop would come, he also knew he was close to where the messages were leading him. So, he'd waited, and didn't have to wait long.

"Sir? Do you have any identification? Why are you here? You realize you are trespassing?" The cop approached him warily, as if he had the plague.

Maybe he *did* have a plague, maybe that was why he was being called to. He attempted to warn the officer, who turned to his partner - a mousy women who stood behind the larger man as they questioned him - and they exchanged a knowing look.

"Have you got anyone who can help you, sir?"

Sterling almost said yes, his friends had led him there, but the metal of train against track shrieked and he knew *they* were saying he needed to stay quiet.

He only shook his head. After checking his pack and jacket, and quickly patting him down, the cops conferred, and came to a decision.

"Just move along, ok? Stay out of the railyards, and we won't give you a ticket this time."

Sterling left the barbwired lot, emerging onto a street with a rainbow of cars traveling past. They smeared like an impressionist painting with their overwhelming numbers and speed. Scraggly palm trees danced in a gray smog. The sun, as red as a copper coin, sank slowly into a flat black line of ocean a world away in the distance.

He realized where he had ended up.

The land of dreams.

California.

At first, he walked around in a daze, the other people like black and white cutouts around him. He ignored them, until a man ran into him, said, "Watch the fuck out!" As Sterling tried to keep on walking, the man followed him, shouting, "What the fuck is wrong with you, man?" growing more and more agitated at Sterling's lack of response.

A realization came into Sterling's thoughts then. He wasn't the one on the outside; these people were. They spent their short lives running back and forth, buying, and selling, being sold, and bought, raging because they were fading, angry that they were slipping, falling into smoke...

He felt the angry man's fist as it connected with his face. Though he fell, it did not hurt. The violence only disrupted the empty space between them for a millisecond, causing ripples in the unknown dark matter holding the world together. Soon, the space would come back together. He understood it as if from a distance, and, just like that, the man's fist was gone.

He let himself lay there as the man spit on him, shouting more obscenities before finally walking away muttering that all the homeless bums were fucking crazy and why didn't someone put them out of their misery. He stayed there on the sidewalk while time passed next to a small cherry tree, and as the people went by, the tree's few spring blossoms fell onto his prone form, the slight wind from their movements shaking the blossoms free. Images came to him, of his mother screaming why couldn't he be normal, of his father telling him he was no longer their son if he was a faggot.

The memories came from another place, a place so far away now he could no longer know it and finally he understood. He stood up and started to laugh.

People really avoided him then, a crazy man walking the streets, always moving, grinning hopelessly at some secret joke only he understood.

More time passed, how long he did not know. He began to believe *they* had abandoned him, but even that seemed terribly funny.

Everything was nothing at all. He understood it now.

Then, to his surprise, he began to actually *hear* the messages instead of seeing them.

They began as a whisper, and slowly over the following days grew to many voices, finally coalescing into one. Like the cherry tree's flowers blooming in reverse, until he saw only the bud.

He is risen.

A scene appeared in his mind - a darkened concert hall. The ones who called to him were the attendees of an unknown performance, waiting for the Conductor to arrive. Though they owned the now audible sibilant voices, their faces invisible as they secretly mouthed the words to him, in his gut he knew that they spoke for someone else. Someone eternal, just beyond his fingertips as he groped in the dark room for the chain to turn on the light.

Yes, it was the Conductor he was hearing.

And then he knew. The Conductor was the lighthouse, a luminous dagger cutting through the hurricane of lies that is reality, slicing it open, exposing the beneath. Soon, they would take Sterling to him and show him too like they had been shown. Soon the dark would spill over

Soon, Sterling. Soon ...

He sat in an abandoned warehouse district, his legs hanging off the side of a loading dock near the dilapidated buildings, drinking. Since the scene in the opera house had appeared to him, the voices had fallen silent, but he knew the Conductor was coming soon. Without the Conductor, they had been like a poorly tuned radio that flickered in and out of existence, maddening to hear them only to lose them again. But he always felt them near, their broadcast like a flashlight trying to pierce a void of a black night sky.

He took another swig of the wine he'd managed to get with the last of the money that he'd begged in LA, the alcohol finally seeming to clear his thoughts. He knew he shouldn't drink so much, but he knew too much now. Heard too much. It had become tiresome and so he would drink until the Conductor and his orchestra came.

He panned his burning eyes over the cement lots covered in graffiti. Glittering bits of broken beer bottles sprinkled the whole place in stars as the sun set. Sterling tilted his head - if he looked at it just right, it was an ocean before him, and not just a glass-strewn empty lot.

He looked up and saw a murder of crows sitting nearby. They perched on a rusted chain link fence and eyed him with cool interest.

One suddenly flew towards Sterling, then changed direction without apparent reason, veering down behind some steel remnant of an ancient electrical box. He waited a moment, still watching, not knowing why he was waiting or what he was waiting for. When the crow reappeared, it was carrying something round and wet, glistening in its beak.

His turned his gaze to the crumpled shape that the crow had just flown away from. It looked like a discarded sleeping bag, or maybe a pile of clothing. Brown, soft, different from the angularity and clean angles of the inorganic. A gust of wind stirred the fabric, pulling it back some, revealing something darker, though still not identifiable.

Curiosity grabbing him, he rose on wobbling drunken legs. He was barely able to feel his feet though they were torn up from the gaping holes in his sneakers. It was probably just as well. The other birds didn't move, only watched him, waiting.

He looked back at the shape below. A sudden terrible thought flashed in his mind.

A body?

As he began to move towards it, he heard a whisper again.

The only way out is down.

As he reached it, he saw that, yes, it was a body.

Then the almost empty wine bottle crashed to the ground.

It was DeAngelo.

One of his eyes was gone. His clothes were in rags and covered in greenish algae like he had been dragged through a river.

He stared in disbelief, and then in horror as DeAngelo's dead remaining eye flickered open. Some part of him thought about running - this was too much to bear, too much for anyone to bear - but he didn't. He couldn't.

DeAngelo stood, and Sterling suddenly saw that they were not alone.

Behind DeAngelo were others. Hundreds, thousands. Sterling knew them. They were the lost, the ones who had crawled beneath. And he was now among them, the child who was lost from his home had been found.

He sobbed with madness, and then with relief. He let all the pain slide out, falling broken onto the pavement like the scattered glass, his weeping making the shards wet with tears.

DeAngelo reached out, and though his touch was moist and mushy, Sterling did not fight it. He gripped the dead man's hand tight instead. They began to walk together, the others following behind, into the burgeoning darkness toward an abandoned warehouse where a light so bright it hurt to look at it lit it up, spilling out through the cracks of its old, slated roof. It was brighter than the sun's now descending orb, brighter than the light of one million suns.

Like a dream, he heard an orchestra coming out, an unseen audience murmuring as musicians in the pit warmed up.

He let DeAngelo lead him inside where they joined the whispering audience, a sea of expectant faces staring at an empty stage surrounding him and trapping him. He looked around the strange music hall for some escape, understanding finally that something very wrong although he should have sooner, he knew. Something supernatural was happening to him, and something was coming for him. It had led him here as it had led the others. His eyes darted back and forth trying to find a crack to pull the misshapen reality away and bring back that flat predictable place he had just come from, but though he kept trying, looking, he knew that they would not allow it even if he did find that exit. Their bodies were too many and they would stop him, and the pull of the Conductor an inescapable force. D'Angelo gripped his hand tighter as if sensing Sterling's reluctance.

And then, it was too late.

The Conductor appeared, a magician conjured out of the air, he slipped sideways from invisibility into being seen. He did not look the way Sterling had expected and at first his mind would not accept it.

But what should one from there look like? a voice asked him hot against his ear.

And the orchestra began, their sound the cry of an abyss reaching out from the very molecules of air, from the spaces between the stars, from the spaces between the atomic particles. The emptiness that was the universe, the place we think is hollow. It was floating in front of him now and he heard himself screaming... or was it laughter? Had he ever seen anything so terribly... horribly... funny...

The emptiness began to bloom.

It was beautiful.

Tectonic: a Conversation with the Gore-ious Maureen Tellani

T.M. Morgan

Editor's Note: It is the ten-year anniversary of both this interview first appearing in Guise *as well as the disappearance of its contributor, Thomas Morgan. To read the wild theories about his case makes me at times bemused and at other times disturbed about the human condition.*

I did not change either Tom's or Ms. Tellani's words when I first published this piece in Guise Volume V, Issue II. *That edited version simply added some narrative based on Tom's taped notes. These are his words (and Ms. Tellani's). In the piece below, I have included his final recorded words for the first time. Despite what some of you cynics may believe, it is not to inflame curiosity for my own gain. I am a man of the utmost integrity. I simply feel it is important to share, as is my right. You will see that the tape is indeed disturbing and something that has weighed on me for many years. While we will never fully know Tom's state of mind, I found him to be thoughtful and inquisitive. He did, however, baffle me with his interest in the movie* Tectonic *and with Maureen Tellani. Much has been made of his intentions. I believe, however, that emotional issues were already present and contributed to this episode, as well as his disappearance. But I only knew the man casually though electronic communications, as he was a semi-regular contributor to* Guise. *Certainly, Thomas Morgan is not a pseudonym for myself; and I have heard that particular gossipy nuisance floated since the inclusion of his first article, "The Whims of Melancholy and Its Deathly Consequences: The Early Works of Thomas Ligotti." I will state once and for all that I am not the sort to mask my work behind a phantom name. Thomas Morgan did indeed disappear, as I have the police report to prove it. That is no fabrication either; it is as official as the lovely fragrance of nightshade. To suggest anything more would be…well, it's silly.*

Ms. Tellani also disappeared several years after this interview, though the exact timing is unknown as no one checked on her with any regularity. I had attempted on numerous occasions to contact her after Thomas' disappearance, to no avail. It was, shall we say, disappointing. At this point, we are only left with the interview and Thomas' tapes. (There is an Internet rumor that Miss Tellani recorded her own tapes of the interview that are much different. In fact, the rumors say that they discuss an entirely different movie, though it is also called Tectonic. To date, I have never seen evidence of these tapes, much less heard them. I find it all fanciful, like much that happens on the Internet. If they do pop up, I will investigate with full vigor.)

This won't quell the desire to attribute as le principal facteur of all this nonsense a supernatural anathema. (the famed Tectonic *curse) You are free to espouse your conspiracy theories about Ms. Tellani, the movie, Thomas, rogue tapes, and even me all you want. I can at least say, however, that I am done with it. Though it has brought* Guise *and myself much notoriety, the hassle of dealing with all of you is not worth the trouble. Voila!*

By the way (for you internet sleuths), on the matter of Ms. Tellani's neighbor, I did investigate his disappearance. Yes, he has not been seen since the timing of Tom's visit to speak with Ms. Tellani. I spoke, though, to his mother. She adamantly stated that Ms. Tellani had nothing to do with it. Her son, she said, suffered from drug addiction and "ran with a bad crowd." She suggested that Tom fabricated the controversial scene. (This is not true, as I have listened to the recording.) But believe what you will.

And now, without further ado, "Tectonic: A Conversation with the Gore-ious Maureen Tellani."

~ Gerald Riggers

Tectonic: A Conversation with the Gore-ious Maureen Tellani
By Thomas Morgan

In the 1983 film *Tectonic*, Maureen Tellani gave a performance so soul scathing she never acted in another film. Once production wrapped, she remained in Tulsa, Oklahoma, the location of her family farm. She has given only one interview since, a 1997 piece in Fangoria, "An Afternoon with Olivia."

The character Olivia Denholm, a young housewife suffering severe postpartum depression who discovers cracks running through the cement foundation of her home, caused an uproar in Reagan-esque America in the summer of 1983. The movie became a narrative in the run up to the 1984 presidential campaign, with Republicans proclaiming it was an example of the "degradation of our culture." And while it was not commercially successful (earning only $500,000, half of its rumored budget), its cult status has grown stronger over time.

Ask someone today about Olivia, and you will get comparisons to Ripley, Laurie Strode, and Carrie. Iconic. Relentless. And as an amalgamation of those three female icons implies, Olivia was not easily defined. By the end of the film, she brings such destruction that Roger Ebert called it "the most savage brutality ever put to film."

It is true the carnage of *Tectonic* shocked viewers. That it disturbed them more than the cannibal and rape/revenge exploitation movies of the 1970's might be because of the domestic placidity it came wrapped in. When the slaughter and gore arrive, it is only after the most mundane of setups. Pauline Kael wrote, "Imagine sitting down and enjoying *Ordinary People* for forty-five minutes, only to then watch Mary Tyler Moore's Beth Jarrett become Leatherface." A bit hyperbolic, but we get her point.

There is also the matter of the rumors and the deaths associated with the film. Many of the crew have disappeared under mysterious circumstances over the years. Suicides have been common. Some say the movie is cursed. Maureen herself has been implicated in theories that insinuate she is a deranged killer or something worse. Along with wanting to discuss these rumors with her, I have long been a fan of her performance in *Tectonic*.

So, in May of this year, I reached out to her, and we arranged a visit. The farmhouse looks both majestic and battle-worn, evoking a kind of grace, much like Maureen herself. Though the red hair she kept during her younger days has turned white and the lines have bunched around her eyes, upon first seeing her I was immediately brought back to the opening shot of the movie, a swooping dive from above the treetops that stops an inch from her troubled eyes as she stands absently in the front yard. (The scene is repeated at the movie's end; this opening is a flash forward. It is a little-known detail that, though these scenes look nearly identical, they are actually two different shots. I recognized this the first time I watched, so keenly had I paid attention to Maureen's eyes and saw how much emptier they are in the closing scene.) Those eyes still sparkle, though, hinting at—like her character from the movie—a depth that intrigues.

Once we settled down on her screened porch with some iced tea and her pack of Marlboro Lights, we began.

Thomas Morgan: Maureen, thank you so much for allowing me to visit today. I am honestly a little surprised. What made you agree?

Maureen Tellani: You're quite welcome, Tom. Maybe you caught me in a good mood. (laughs) It's been so long since I've thought about those days. But after we first communicated, I had the boy at the next farm over stream the movie for me. A lot of memories came flooding back. Some good memories, but a lot of terrible ones.

TM: Do you have issues with how the film has been regarded? In the Fangoria interview, you said you thought people missed the point of Olivia and had instead become obsessed with the gore.

MT: Olivia was a woman who couldn't stand the feel of her own skin. There was more self-hatred than people picked up on; or maybe I was too caught up in the script revision process and remember all the things she could have been, so mix that up with what she became.

TM: How so?

MT: The original scriptwriter June Artero doesn't get enough credit. Her first draft had a drastically different tone and third act. She intended for Olivia to obsess about the crevices that opened in her basement but not literally have monsters crawl from them. We instead watched Olivia's emotional state deteriorate. And when she turned on her family, the output was emotional not violent. Hers was not a gorefest but a crippling, emotional tragedy. A woman who lost everything, including her own identity.

TM: But once the script got handed over to R. Timothy DePaolo, everything changed? Didn't he want the name to be *Fun House*? And he also wanted to tell the story in reverse, right?

MT: Yes, that's all true. Tim wanted it all to be more ironic and meta—I think that's the term. He had this vision of an opening scene where Olivia drags that ax along the road at night, coming over the crest of a hill. She sees a two-bit carnival set up on a field below. The credits roll as the camera slides in close-ups along her body, so the audience can see that she's covered in blood and bone fragments and even has an eyeball settled into her cleavage. She slowly makes her way down that long slope to the carnival, its music and voices growing louder, a cacophony of madness. I'm sure you can picture how it was supposed to go. Then the opening credits end, a bruising security guard shows up, and Olivia plants her ax in his groin. Olivia screams maniacally, and we cut to white text on a black background: *30 minutes earlie*r. And so, it goes backward from there.

TM: Are you saying this scene was filmed? Does it still exist?

MT: Filmed? Yes. Sitting in a canister somewhere? Who knows. Bob [Tomlin, director] loved the idea of telling the story in reverse. We filmed everything so out of sequence because of it, to keep us all on edge from scene to scene. Plus, we were all using a lot of drugs. (laughs, lights cigarette) It wasn't until he got into editing that he saw what a mess the backward storytelling was. No pacing, all the violence upfront. Since then, a French director made a rather disturbing film told backward—

TM: — *Irréversible*. Gaspar Noé directed that.

MT: Yes, that's it. Well let's just say, Devil hold his soul, Bob wasn't up to the task. And once he'd cut the movie to be told going forward, the road and carnival scene didn't work.

TM: Do you think the weird pacing effects of the movie are because it was filmed with the intent to be told backward? Maybe that's why there's such strange disquiet in every scene.

MT: I've always thought that.

TM: You know, I have to bring up the tragedy that has followed this movie, which is part of the mystique. R. Timothy DePaolo committed suicide, as did cinematographer Bill Grazinsky, editor Holly Burgess, and eventually the actor who played your son, Joseph McCoy. Many of the other crew have simply vanished, Bob Tomlin being the most famous incident. None of those cases have been solved. Some say the movie is cursed. Some have even suggested you are involved.

MT: Yes, of course I'm aware they're all gone. And I know the rumors. I am the only one left. If you look at the end credits, every name on that list is now dead or missing. Susan Rockefeller, who played my daughter, vanished three years ago. She was only 32. Came to visit me a few times, and I could tell she was an addict. Heartbreaking to see. Sue was such a pretty and smart girl. People do so love a twisted story, don't they? And the movie being cursed? If anything is cursed, it's me, because I've had to watch them all die. I'm just like Olivia, I suppose.

TM: I'm sorry. I hope I didn't offend you.

MT: You just need to understand that I was changed in ways you cannot fathom making that horrible movie. Truth does that to a person.

TM: Truth? What do you mean?

MT: Did you know we filmed here, in this house?

TM: I didn't until I arrived here and instantly recognized it. For years I had read it was filmed at a house near Baltimore.

MT: (lights cigarette) Bob was looking to do the project there, as he was on the East Coast then. He had funding through these car dealer brothers. Something to do with John Waters, an acquaintance of his. I think John was going to be listed as co-producer, but that never happened. When the script required revision, June wasn't in a great emotional state, so Bob got Tim hitched on to do rewrites. But he demanded a higher salary. Cuts had to be made in other areas. So, the whole thing moved here, my home since I was born.

TM: I know your parents died in a car accident in the late 70s. I can't imagine how difficult that must have been.

MT: Yes and no. It gave me a certain amount of freedom. They didn't agree with my lifestyle. But I loved them dearly and missed them. It is one of many tragedies.

TM: I'm so sorry that happened to you. But you were talking about truth.

MT: Yes, truth. You see, I had to have June institutionalized at the Rosewood Center in Baltimore for the rest of the shoot, so I was all alone. It was the closest place when we were planning to shoot there. There seemed no reason to move her as, in her state, she refused to see me at the time anyway. I started to lose my mind without her. The shoot became grueling. One day we'd do a scene where I was cooking dinner. The next I'd be covered in blood and going insane. This house contains an evil that I can't describe. It's been ever present since my childhood. The whole sordid affair changed me, especially what happened to June.

TM: That all sounds horrible. I want to get back to this. But what about June?

MT: June was my everything. My life. Seeing what she was going through and what happened later, I realized that this is all a goddamn joke. (stands and faces out from the porch) Can you give me a minute? Can we change the subject from her?

TM: Of course. So, this house is haunted? It looks so peaceful.

MT: Haunted? No. Ghosts are nonsense. As if dead people linger on. This is evil, something as old as time. You don't believe me. That's okay, I wouldn't either.

TM: Maureen, I'm not sure if you're joking.

MT: (laughs) Maybe I am, Tom. The crew started to feel it. We spent a solid week down in that basement, sometimes sixteen-hour days. They built a false wall so the actors playing the zombies could crawl out. It's still there. There were nearly a dozen actors crammed into the space like clowns in a car. John [Butler, who played Klaus Schmidt, the Nazi general zombie] kept squawking that he was going to suffocate. He was the only levity because it was brutal. But no one laughed by the third day. The heat, the buckets of blood, the depravity, the aura of the place. That basement is dark, Tom, even with the lighting, corners where nothing exists except darkness. And do you know what's within darkness? Evil. That's what I'm talking about.

TM: This is unsettling, Maureen. Please, let's get back to—

MT: Tell me, what do you know about evil?

TM: Oh, god, I don't know. Evil is cruelty. It's Hitler and Manson. Ted Bundy. Not entities, not indescribable forces, but cruelty in people. How vicious we can be to one another.

MT: Funny that you only named men. But your answer is a cop out. Evil does, in fact, exist in the universe, an energy. It can sneak into our heads—yours and mine—and tell us, "Do what you want to do and fuck everyone else." They stain all your thoughts. The evil in this house fed off my depression, which is the purest form of selfishness: a mode of thought to excuse obsessing over our own lack of happiness. And that, Tom, is evil.

TM: We've gone off topic a bit. Can we talk about the production itself?

MT: Following your notes? Am I making you nervous? That's fine. The production was six weeks of hell. (lights another cigarette) Tim kept morphing the plot. Early on he retained much of June's finesse, but Bob's constant nudging, wanting more audacious thrills, had Tim rewriting scenes minutes before we shot them. Bob fancied Orson Welles, so had ideas of going experimental—guerrilla filmmaking. I think this was the first movie to feature Nazi zombies—

TM: The Nazi zombie subgenre emerged during World War Two. *King of the Zombies* came out in 1941.

MT: Is that right? But did it have a man's head poked up through a dinner table, his brain exposed, so Grandpa Nazi could take a bite of it, the same as if he'd bitten into a peach?

TM: *Cannibal Ferox*, which came out a few years before *Tectonic*, did something like that.

MT: Good for you, Tom. You're a cinephile whiz kid. Well, our brain eating scene was something else, and you know it. Intended as the big shock to kick off the tonal change in the movie, kind of like the gut buster thing in *Alien*, it cast me—Olivia into a tailspin.

TM: The brain eating scene is infamous now, though not as much as that disturbing, blood-soaked finale.

MT: The blood. Yes, I remember. Look, I need to take a break. This is giving me anxiety. Why don't I make some sandwiches for lunch? Later we can take a tour of the house.

TM: That sounds fine, I suppose.

[Tom's recorded notes: I am wandering the grounds while she prepares lunch. The surrounding woods are dense. The sound of cicadas buzzing in their droning rhythm is so loud it disturbs my thoughts. The next house over might be several miles away. I try to imagine the grueling shoot day after day, the drugs, the effects of the house, the slow decline into madness. It makes me wonder why Maureen still lives here. She's calling me in to the kitchen. I think I'll try a different tact, as I feel like this interview is springing off into tangents.}

TM: I want to apologize, Maureen. You're right, I am following my notes and not being a good listener.

MT: No need to apologize, Tom. And I'm ready to talk more about June now. (lights cigarette) This little break has been good. I find that time spent focusing the mind on menial tasks is more what our brains are meant to do than any amount of pondering or gabbing. So, June: she filled the empty space in the center of my heart. Sad, huh? (laughs) June drowned, and I was with her. By the time *Tectonic* premiered, neither of us were in a sound mental state. We were living here. June had constant night terrors. You know, those ones where you wake up and can't move and horrific devils are sitting on your chest, stealing your breath. And I felt my own mind collapsing too. This place was getting to us, getting its hooks in. I, of course, had more experience with it, so could ground myself. June, though…I shouldn't have brought her back here. I booked us for a month on the South Carolina shore.

TM: I didn't realize your relationship.

MT: June wrote that original script for me. She wanted to tell the story of a desperate woman who felt trapped, but not just in domesticity, not the standard "woman on the edge" story. Her idea was that the woman *becomes* the monster, devolves after an infestation of evil. But she wanted the story to empathize with the monster, too, for people to see how complete the corruption is.

TM: So, June wanted to explore the pathos of the monster? Are you familiar with John Gardner's *Grendel*? In that novel, he explores the nature of the self, of both good and evil, of the pathos of the monster. He said that he based the monster on John Paul Sartre, who, of course, maintained that our freedom is a curse. It sounds as if June was exploring similar themes, about how human choices can lead to evil and how 'the monster' is simply a being who has made such choices.

MT: Tom, with all due respect, I'm talking about June, not your collegiate philosophy class.
This was my life, the love of my life. Her script—

TM: I'm so sorry, I didn't mean—

MT: —her vision, was a thing of beauty. She is not here to answer for herself what philosophical motivations she might have had. I believe she simply loved me and, at the time, that love was tortuous. That was largely my fault, as I can be a…difficult person. And we changed her story, that vision, without her consent. Her dramatic if brutal tale about a struggling woman who goes down a dark path became something else entirely. Not subliminal but sickening. We took her insinuations and made them manifestly evil. It is a crime which will never be held just, how we did that to her. I can't imagine her shock watching it at the premier, though I did try to warn her.

TM: I can see how that must have been difficult.

MT: So, after the premiere, we're off to the beach. June and I had been lounging that day, soaking up the sun. She was beautiful, so gorgeous I ached for her and would watch her write for hours. I thought she was the happiest she'd been in a long time. I guess I was wrong. She waded into the water, a wide, ridiculous hat on her head. When I glanced up after a few minutes, the hat came rushing to the beach. June wasn't there. Just that hat flopping in the surf. I screamed so much my throat felt like I had swallowed razor blades. They searched for over an hour before anyone saw her body a hundred yards out. And that was it. I lost my only tether to being human that day.

TM: Maureen, I'm so sorry. I can't imagine losing someone you love like that.

MT: I finally understood what June was trying to say: the world beats you down and then leaves only emptiness, and that emptiness must be filled by something. Maybe it gets filled with love; maybe it gets filled with pure evil. But in its way—either way—that is a kind of purity.

TM: That makes sense somewhat. Are saying that after June drowned, the house filled you with evil? Are you evil, Maureen?

MT: We all stole from her, took advantage. And people like you ate up the final product. This isn't what she wrote, not what she created. That makes us all complicit.

TM: This sounds awfully close to a confession. Were you involved in any of the disappearances, Maureen? To get justice for June?

MT: (laughs) Do you have a minute? I want to show you something.

[Tom's recorded notes, made sometime after the interview concluded: Maureen led me into the dining room. There was a long table and chairs in the middle. I recognized it immediately from the movie.

Just like in that dinner scene, a silver domed platter rested on the table. In the film, the brother-in-law Jake—Charlie McGimmon, long-time B-movie actor—has been secured into the table, his head poked through, and his skull cap already sawed off, with the platter dome covering him. This is the scene similar to Cannibal Ferox.

When the family is brought into the room, Maureen, in a horrifying bit of acting, displays the fractures going on within her through subtle shifts in her expression. The zombie underlings place the family around the table, with Olivia and her husband Hank—an unrecognizable, young Clancy Bowen—on either side of Klaus. He gives his drooling speech about finally escaping their bunker. DePaolo never provided any exposition on how these Nazi undead became trapped in a Maryland bunker, but I've always thought it represented the vilest evil he could conjure in a manifest form. Then Klaus leans forward and yanks the cover up to reveal Jake. Amidst screams, he bites into the exposed brain repeatedly. Maureen's eyes hover in a state between devastation and fury. That's when the camera cuts to the ax that has been leaning by the fireplace the whole time.

Maureen directed me to the head of the table, where Klaus sat, then sat in the same chair she did in the movie, to my right, to the right of Klaus.]

MT: I set it up just for you. I kept all the props.

TM: It feels so strange. I feel like I should say the lines.

MT: Go ahead.

TM: (clearing my throat) Well, we're all here! Let's see what's for dinner. I bet it will be just delish!

MT: (lifts platter to reveal a man's head and exposed brain) Bon appétit!

TM: Jesus Christ, Maureen!

MT: (laughs hysterically) It's a prop! Oh, your expression!

TM: A prop? That's a sick joke. (I return to the kitchen)

MT: Oh please, Tom. I thought you would enjoy it. When you called to talk about the movie, I thought that was the joke. I thought, why would this young man want to write about *Tectonic* after all this time? So, I thought we'd have a bit of fun.

TM: (grabbing a cigarette from her pack) May I?

MT: Of course. May I? (I light one too)

TM: That head is so life-like. It's still moaning.

MT: A little air compressor inside. Nowadays they'd do something digital I suspect, but this was old school. That thing had us all giggling at first, until it wasn't funny anymore. The brain is Jell-O mixed with milk. I kept the mold. Please come back in.

MT: (she leads me to the table) Go on, take a bite.

TM: I don't think I can do it. That looks disgust—

MT: —Eat it! (she presses her hand forcefully on my neck and thrusts my face down) John, too, was so disgusted by it at first but eventually said he liked the taste. It was hilarious to watch him do it repeatedly, take after take. I think Bob was fucking with him.

TM: You can't just force me like that! This is assault, Maureen. I feel like I'm going to throw up.

MT: Oh, I'm sorry. I'm the one being too exuberant now. Talking about the movie, about June, it still—she was all I ever had. I can't—why don't we look around? You hold this while we take the tour. (she grabs a worn ax from its spot against the fireplace)

TM: I don't like this. The axe is heavy, not a prop.

MT: Well, technically it is a prop, but we used several. Obviously, I didn't swing that one at anybody. The foam one is around here somewhere, the one that I used in the scene I chopped my family up.

TM: Maureen, what are you doing?

MT: I want you to really experience *Tectonic*. Get an understanding of what evil feels like. In fact, let's check out the basement. That's where I—I mean Olivia—slaughtered her family.

[Tom's recorded notes, made sometime after the interview concluded: I nodded, though felt dizzy as we descended the basement stairs. The walls were not finished, ancient beams and nails showing. The steps leaned, feeling barely more than sticks under my feet. Once we reached the bottom, we stood on packed dirt. The single bulb she flipped on hung from exposed wires. A dark room—where Olivia

stacked the body parts—jutted away to our right. The boiler room, also pitch dark beyond the light's radiance, was at our left. The false wall with its cracks wide enough for scrawny actors to crawl through covered the wall at our backs, the one that ran under the stairs.]

MT: What do you think? As dread inspiring as you expected?

TM: It feels like a tomb.

MT: (laughs) Hmm. Now that I think about it, every other person who has stepped foot in this basement is dead. So, you're right. Can you feel it, Tom? The evil?

TM: There's something not right.

MT: (jams her index finger into my temple) Not right in there. Not right in the head, Tom. Not from ringing a bell, not from rotting in hell. Now go into that boiler room. That's where I hid when my family ran down the stairs. Go!

[Tom's recorded notes, made sometime after the interview concluded: As soon as I was in place, standing in darkness but looking out on Maureen, she snapped off the light. I immediately heard footsteps on the stairs. Just like in the movie, the entire scene was black, only sound hitting the ears. The soft thwap of a foot pressed into the dirt. There was a breath so close I could feel it.

I thought of the movie, when the lights flick on, and Olivia sprints across the basement. Blood sprays into the camera, the audience only able to hear her grunts and the screams of her family. The camera cuts to a shaft of light, and the ax swings directly at it. Tomlin quick cuts again, and we see the ax strike Hank center cranium. His head splits in a way that his eyes each glare off at a strange angle, yet he continues to wobble on unsteady legs. Here, Tomlin uses a split screen as seen from Hank's POV. Two Olivia's raise the ax up. Tomlin reverts to omniscient POV, and we watch in one, long, unflinching shot as she dismembers Hank in a crazed fury. The camera turns to Jenny, who stands in terror holding the baby. They are already covered in blood, the aftermath of Olivia butchering the zombie infestation. Klaus's head sits ridiculously at the bottom of the stairs, still undead, eyes rolling, mouth trying to laugh, but he's been chopped at the jaw line, so rests on his upper teeth. Tomlin pushes the movie full metal here, no restraint. We watch Olivia graphically chop up both Jenny and the baby. This is the scene that got the movie banned in several countries.]

TM: Maureen! This is enough.

MT: (her voice is distant and soft; I can't tell what direction it comes from) Why are you here, Tom? You've come here to dredge up my past, but why? Every night I think of her, dream of her, that instead she strode from the water, and we kissed and came home. Today, we'd be together, every breakfast a crescendo, every afternoon an interlude. You want to know if I killed them? That's your plan? And what if I did? What if we all deserve what's coming to us?

TM: Maureen, please. I'm sorry I've upset you. But people want to know about *Tectonic.* It is talked about more today than ever. Why wouldn't I want to talk to you? People want to know about you…about Maureen Tellani. I'm a huge fan; I told you that. Please, can we turn on the lights? I'm so sorry. I didn't know about June. I didn't know about any of this.

MT: You didn't answer my question, Tom. Do you want to know if I killed them all?

TM: I don't. It would be wrong to even ask.

MT: No one else came asking about Maureen Tellani or the movie. Just you. So, I'll ask again. What are you doing here? Come to taunt an old woman?

TM: Turn on the light. Please. This isn't funny.

[Tom's recorded notes, made sometime after the interview concluded: The light did come on. Maureen stood right where she had been before. She was crying. I looked at my hands and realized I'd squeezed the ax so hard my palms were bleeding. The axe dropped with an echoless thud. Her wrinkled hands covered her face. As I approach her, she used one of those hands to keep me at a distance.]

MT: It's time you left. I won't play our little game anymore.

TM: I—yes, of course.

MT: (she leads us up the stairs and onto the front porch; holds open the screen door) Please go.

TM: I'm sorry this didn't go as planned.

MT: It's my own fault for agreeing. I've put you in danger.

TM: Danger from what?

MT: From the evil in the world. It will come looking for you now because it's seen you. Don't get down. Don't question the meaning of life. Just cling on, and you'll be fine.

TM: Okay. Listen, Maureen, I was wondering: why do you stay here?

After all that's happened, this place must be full of sadness. Whether there's some evil here or not.

[Tom's recorded notes, made sometime after the interview concluded: She smiled, broad and beaming, her lips stretched as wide as they could go. It was the same disturbing, wonderful smile on Olivia's face at the beginning and end of the movie. This time, her eyes offered yet a different mixture of complexity. It was impossible to decipher exactly what they were trying to convey. Horror? Euphoria? Insanity? The only thing I could tell was that she seemed content with whatever that emotion is.]

MT: Why do I still live here? Because all my memories are here. Because everyone I ever loved is here. Because the evil of this place is no longer outside of me. It is me. And I can live with that. It no longer causes me any confusion. Because what rests here, what lingers in every board and nail, are the memories—the only things left—the fragments that are now my companions. Because, Tom, home is where the hearts are.

[Tom's last notes, recorded after the interview: It has been three days since I visited Maureen, and I can't get those last words out of my head: home is where the hearts are. I picture her with a mound of desiccated hearts she keeps as treasures.

I did some investigating on June Artero. Nothing in the way of biography. No mention of Tectonic. *She is mentioned in a 1985* South Carolina Gazette *article about her drowning. Just a name, a date, another casualty.*

I found one old picture of her online, and it has haunted me. Sometimes you look at an old picture and wonder what was happening behind the eyes. June's eyes convey even more complexity than Olivia's—or

Maureen's. It is as if she wants to tell us something.

This morning, I stood in the shower crying for an hour. No reason. Wave after wave of hopelessness. Is Tectonic *cursed? Is Maureen? Was she involved in all those deaths? It would seem silly to answer yes to such questions. But it's not that simple. We are all cursed. It just takes a thing to come along and remind us of that simple fact. Maureen is right that we are complicit, but not just in what happened to June. We glorify suffering, in movies like* Tectonic, *in life generally.*

If you don't hear from me again, don't come looking. I might just be another heart upon the mound.]

ART BY THIJS VAN EBBENHORST TENGBERGEN

From Darkness, to Darkness

Anzhelina Polonskaya
(translated by Andrew Wachtel)

O, how my vertebrae shift in my sleep,
like wolves,
victims of universal ennui that refuse to eat goats,

like a hunter, whose eye can make out nothing
but crimson in the shadowy snow.

This is existential fear. *From darkness, to darkness.*
Like snuff in your fingers, a begging bowl at your side.

The night feels pear-shaped in the mouth,
which spews words like *never return, not I.*

And as far as my motherland goes – a word cloud:
muteness, muted sound, mutedera, mutedgarden.

Your bowl's ready for a long journey;
you'll beg forever for them and yourself.

The Mark

C. O. Davidson

YOU SEE HER, one foot pointed out, like a Degas ballerina. She stands in line, waiting. You've just walked into the campus coffee shop, messenger bag weighted with ungraded freshman essays. And she stops you.

You know this feeling.

Jealousy, admiration, desire. To want. Not a sexual desire but a desire to be. You want to be her. Or at least get close enough to study her, deconstruct her, figure out this combination of beauty, style, and mystery. Is there a flaw? If you find it, will it make you feel less shitty about yourself? Your hair, a twisted bird's nest, your body, buried under a heap of puffy down, flannel, and denim, shuffling into line in old gray running shoes, you're invisible.

You take your place in line, two back from her. Her neck, a white line bisecting the edge of her swinging black-wing bob and the collar of her long black coat. Back straight, she's an exclamation point of poise, John Singer Sargent's *Madame X*, another woman you will never be.

Between you stand two girls. They could be your students, but you can't be sure, these girls with their expensive blonde highlights and coats of sorority-coded pastels, their legs Bahama-tan and bare, even on cold days like today. One nudges the other and stage-whispers, "You think she could get that thing on her face removed. Or at least cover it up."

Madame X pivots to face them. On her right cheek, a small port-wine stain, just below her eye, curved around her cheekbone as if to cup it. "And why would I cover my special charm?" She turns back to the counter and, in that voice of snow, orders a cappuccino.

"Bloody hand," the first blonde mumbles, as the other takes out her pink phone and disappears into it. Once at the counter, they order their pumpkin spice lattes and flock to a pastel-filled table of other blondes.

You order, the barista takes your name, and you wait for your flat white. Madame X now leans against the far end of the counter, her tall boots laced almost to her knees, they peek out of from the hem of her coat, they beckon you, and so you say, "I like your boots."

She sees you, and this seeing opens some locket inside you and more words pour out: "I have a pair, but they're short, only the eight-holes."

"The classics then."

"Gia!" the barista calls.

"That's me."

You step back to let her pass and collide with the news rack at the counter, spilling newspapers across the floor. "Shit!"

Shifting your bag, you bend to pick them up, and suddenly Gia kneels in front of you, her knee grazing yours as she gathers newspapers. You stand in synch, and together, you put the papers back on the rack. Gia slips one under her arm. A deft, sly move no one else notices.

"Those Docs of yours would look great with what you're wearing. A retro Seattle vibe," she says, and her birthmark, a red hand, pulls at you, but you stay, watch her walk past you, pick up her cappuccino, leave.

"Amy? Elmer?" The barista squints up at the writing on your flat white.

"Alyma," you whisper, not to the barista, but to Gia, now outside, walking past the frosted window to some place you could never find.

The red on your fingers is from your leaky pen, but you feel—in a moment of melodrama—it's your own blood.

This morning, a bright, cold Friday, when the rest of the world has promise, you're wedged into a corner table. You've been at the coffee shop for three hours and four cups, marking badly written, carelessly documented, poorly formatted, nearly plagiarized papers.

You look up, bleary-eyed, as Gia walks past.

You almost missed her. Hair now bleached and slicked back, she is no longer that black-winged girl, your Madame X. Now, she's a cool white bone wrapped in a long red coat, more Nagel than Sargent. Once in line, a man steps beside her and puts his arm around her waist. This man, gray hair, purposely tousled, cropped beard, he wears a tweed jacket, with actual goddamned patches on the elbows.

You know him.

Ford, the one holdout on your dissertation committee. He wrote "reductive" in the margins of all your chapters, trapping you in a revision loop until 2 AM, night after night. Five sleep-deprived weeks later, you had a revised manuscript reading Hawthorne stories, not as products of his life, but as "cultural products" of the mid-nineteenth century.

Ford accepted the premise.

But you could only see your work as a con, one that made sense in your head but not your heart.

After your defense, Dr. Fisher, a woman all wool sweaters and pearls, took you aside, and said your dissertation, this process, won't define you.

A kind lie.

Ford rests his hand on Gia's back, stroking the belt of her coat. When he orders, she slips away to a bulletin board near the bathrooms. She studies a bright red flyer, brushes the fringes at the bottom then tears one off and palms it into her pocket. She turns and winks at you. How long has she known you're here? Red lips, red coat, and on her cheek that red crescent: a triangulation of blood.

Ford crosses with her coffee, but she walks ahead, pulls him in her wake. She sits down, next to your table. You don't want him to see you, even though he never does. Adjunct teachers, after all, are invisible to tenured professors.

"Your thesis idea then?" Ford says to Gia. He leans forward.

Gia picks up her coffee. Her red lips blow across its surface. "*The Scarlet Letter*," she says. "Hester Prynne's sewing in the novel as Hawthorne's counter to nineteenth-century American capitalism."

"I love it."

She's his acolyte, then. Economic textual analyses and his hand on her back.

You look down at the essay you've been grading. In the margin where your pen rests, a red flower blooms. Your vision blurs. Feeling sick, you fumble the papers into your bag and leave.

Saturday morning, and you haven't slept well.

While getting dressed, you find a red slip of paper in a pocket of the jeans you picked off the floor. *Models! Arts Complex!* And a phone number. You finger it. It's from that flyer, the one hanging on the edge of the coffee shop bulletin board. Gia had torn one off. But when did you?

You rationalize a trip to campus. Don't you have a book you need from the library? You pull on a tank top and an oversized cable-knit sweater, but on impulse kick aside the gray running shoes and, from the back of the closet, drag out a cracked Sterilite bin. You dig through folded clothes that no longer fit to find your Doc Martens, leather stiff from a decade of no wear, but when laced, the boots remember the curves of your ankles.

You turn to your reflection, frizzy hair, long sweater, baggy jeans, all in the proximity of thirty-nine.

At least the boots will keep your feet warm, right?

You reach into your closet, hand hovering over that puffy coat. These boots deserve more. So you put on your navy pea coat, that coat for funerals and job interviews, your nice coat. But today you're wearing it for no reason. It's not like anyone will see you. There is no one to impress.

Outside the Continuing Ed classroom in the Arts Complex. You stare through the small window in the door. She sits in a chair in the middle of the room, her back to the door, her head turned in almost-profile, pale hair and shoulders stark against a black drape: *Gia.*

Adult learners, mostly retirees in Ann Taylor or L. L. Bean, sit in a semi-circle around her. Their sketchpads on easels, they draw, intent, only occasionally looking up. Walking into frame, the instructor, a pony-tailed silver fox dressed in jeans and a T-shirt of some obscure band. He strolls around the room, glancing at several students' work, then circles behind Gia, his hand brushing the back of her chair. Her birthmark, a crescent moon, disappears into the dawn spreading across her cheek.

The instructor glances at the door, and Gia turns to look, too, just as you duck out of view.

You rush out of the building.

In the lull before final exams, with all papers graded and returned, before the students' whinging begins, you find you have a rare free day. You could revise exam questions, but instead you drive to a favorite used bookstore just off campus. In anticipation of the Christmas break, you buy a stack of vintage paperbacks, Gothics with creased and faded covers of women in filmy dresses. They stumble over misty moors, away from houses with windows like eyes of lust and judgement.

Putting the bag of books in the trunk, so elated with the wanton freedom of the day, you almost miss her.

But all that red snags you.

Through the large window of a chic vintage clothing store, you see her, hair now dyed a bright crimson. She stands in front of a three-way mirror, pivoting back and forth in a short red dress, the skirt flaring, flashing strips of white between the hem and the tall red stockings that stop just above her knees.

You're pulled inside the store. A bell above the door announces your entrance to the two bohemian waifs behind the counter, a hipster and a goth, both beautiful. Their gazes slide back to their conversation. You flip through a rack of vintage T-shirts. Then sneak a look.

Gia stands at a nearby table, fingering necklaces hanging on the display. She lifts a locket, slips it over her head, and drops it inside her dress. She sees you. She smiles. Mouths, "Do you like it?" And turns in a slow spin, red flaring out like blood across a sheet.

You nod.

And suddenly she's next to you. She looks at your feet, then back to your face. "You wore your Docs."

"I figured they'd keep me warm today."

"Practical." After a beat she adds, "I have something to show you."

You follow her like the tide follows the moon, across the store to a rack of coats and jackets. Gia pushes several aside and pulls out a long red velvet coat, gold clockwork butterflies embroidered on the collar, around the cuffs, and along the belt and hem. "Isn't this the most beautiful thing you have ever seen?"

"Regal," you say.

Her eyes widen. "Exactly."

The fairy palm, stark on her cheek, it holds you.

"Take off your coat," she says. "And that sweater."

You hesitate, then take off the coat. She takes it and drapes it over a rack. Then she lifts your sweater over your head, and you're grateful for the tank underneath, pained that you haven't shaved under your arms in days. She drops your sweater on the floor. She holds the red velvet coat open, and, without hesitation, you slip your arms into it. The coat hangs on you in a straight and perfect line. Gia reaches around you, lifts the belt and snugs it around your waist. Encircling you with butterflies.

She smells like dusky spice.

"I knew it would be perfect for you," she says. You reach to smooth your fly-away hair, but she pushes your hands away. "No. Your hair's great. You only need one thing." She opens her purse, a perfect red envelope, hanging on thin strap from her shoulder, and with a flourish, she pulls out a lipstick and cups your chin. As she paints your lips, the birthmark—this crimson moon hanging above hills of snow—fills your vision. A charge runs through you. Arcs between you, an electric chain.

"There," she says, and releases you, as the last crimson tint of the birthmark—that sole token of human perfection—fades into the flush of her cheek. "Regal." A beat. "You'll wear it out of the store." She dons your pea coat, and you shudder, like she's stripped you of your dependable adult self, put her arm into your skin, into you. She is inside you now. You flush.

She calls to the girls behind the counter, "She'll take the coat," and heads for the door. But she hasn't paid for the red dress. Or the locket. Hidden beneath that blood red dress, against her white skin—

"Wait!" you cry.

She turns.

The price tag of the dress peaks out from the lapel of the pea coat.

You lean into her, your cheek brushing hers. The heat of her fills you. Pulls you into that light, no moon but a sun, the red star around which you now orbit.

You bite the plastic and slip the price tag into your pocket.

"There," you say. "Regal."

And inhale the parting breath of this perfect woman.

You sit in the center of the studio, surrounded by weekend artists. They're sketching you. Hair a bright red halo brushing your bare shoulders, breasts exposed, the black drape across your lap. You won't return as an adjunct in the spring. There's a new job available now. Ford's old position. His sudden death over the holidays. Asphyxiated. A case of torrid circumstances, involving a belt, long and red, from a coat. Tied around his throat. Little butterflies embroidered in gold along the tongue where it hangs beneath his chin.

At the end of class, the artists take their sketch pads from their easels.

Paper flutters like the wings of birds, and you can see yourself alive on all those pages, your face flashing again and again and again, each one some facet of yourself, a new you, seen through a stranger's eyes—but every one shining with the light of the bright red mark on your cheek.

You arch your back, a queen, a white bone wrapped in black velvet, a red sun setting on a plane of snow.

Winter at the Provincial Station

Anzhelina Polonskaya
(translated by Andrew Wachtel)

Wooden lips drink from your wound.
Winter at the provincial station,
as wintry as your feral and harried heart.
What of your wound? Wherever you go –
it's all around, wherever you go.

You've no place or date of birth.
No one's about to trim the lamp,
though for eyes scarred by light
any blindfold's a blessing.

An empty provincial station is any place you've left.
Someone approaches in a coat with a suitcase.
With every gesture, with his whole body it seems he's saying,
"I couldn't care less about you!
couldn't care less."

CONTRIBUTORS

Sophia N. Ashley (she/they) are writers of poetry. They have their works previously published in *Native Skin Magazine, The Capilano Review* & elsewhere. They won the International Human Right Arts Festival Award 2021

Barbara A. Barnett is a graduate of the Odyssey Writing Workshop, and her short fiction has appeared in publications such as *Beneath Ceaseless Skies, Lady Churchill's Rosebud Wristlet, Black Static*, and *Flash Fiction Online.*

David Bowman lives in Indiana. A software developer and illustrator, his art has been published by Undertow Press, Dread Stone Press, and Gibbon Moon Books.

John Brownlee is a professional non-fiction editor who most recently ran an in-house magazine for Amazon and lives in Massachusetts with his wife and three-year-old daughter. "The Bleating Belfry" is his first professional fiction appearance.

Venezia Castro is a Mexican writer of literary and speculative fiction in English and Spanish. She holds two Bachelor's degrees in Molecular Biology and Literature and is currently pursuing an MSc in Creative Writing at the University of Edinburgh. Her work has appeared in magazines in Mexico, Canada, and the United States. You can find her online at veneziacastro.uk.

C. O. Davidson's work has appeared in *Cemetery Gates, Georgia Gothic, Dark Moon Digest*, and Dark Ink's collection *Generation X-ed.* She has also co-edited *Monsters of Film, Fiction, and Fable*, a collection of scholarly essays. Davidson is a founding member of the Atlanta Chapter of the Horror Writers Association and a board member for Broadleaf Writers Association. You can find her on Twitter as @colearydavidson.

Originally from Liverpool, UK, **John Paul Davies** has had work published in *Rosebud, Apex, Banshee, Orbis, The Pedestal, Maine Review, Southword,*

Crannóg, The Manchester Review, and *Grain*. He was placed 2nd in the 2017 Waterford Poetry Prize, won the 2018 Letheon Prize, and was longlisted for the 2018 National Poetry Competition (UK).

Charlene Elsby has previously published *HEXIS,* with CLASH Books, and another two books, *Affect in October,* and *Alison*. She was recently a philosophy professor; her doctorate is from McMaster University in Hamilton, ON (Canada).

Sofia Ezdina is an emerging writer and queer woman from Russia. She befriends stray animals and whispers eerie things. Her works appeared in *Enchanted Conversation, Jalada Africa*, and *The Revelator*. One of her poems was also named as a runner-up for Barjeel Poetry Prize.

Amelia Gorman is a recent transplant to Eureka, California. She enjoys exploring the redwoods and coasts with her dogs and foster dogs. Some of her recent poetry has appeared in *Penumbric, Vastarien*, and *The Deadlands* and her first chapbook, *Field Guide to Invasive Species of Minnesota,* is available from Interstellar Flight Press. Her fiction appears in the *Nightscript* series, *Nox Pareidolia* from Nightscape Press, and *She Walks in Shadows* from Innsmouth Free Press.

Stephen Hargadon's work has appeared regularly in *Black Static* magazine (TTA Press). His stories have also featured in *Structo, Confingo, Crimewave, Popshot,* and in Dan Coxon's anthology of weird fiction, *Tales from the Shadow Booth*. He has received an honorable mention in Ellen Datlow's annual survey of horror fiction. He was shortlisted in 2017 and 2019 for the Anthony Burgess / Observer prize for arts journalism; a runner-up in the 2016 Irish Post short story competition; and second in the 2018 Dinesh Allirjah prize for short fiction, run by Comma Press. Please check out stephenhargadon.co.uk for reviews of his work.

Aleco Julius is a literature teacher and essayist living in Chicago. He has designed curricula for public schools and has designed courses in literature. This includes "Fear of the Unknown," a seminar for the Newberry Library which focuses on Edgar Allan Poe, H.P. Lovecraft, and Thomas Ligotti. He also recently presented on "The Medieval University Library" at a summer seminar at Cambridge University. He has recently been published in *Hellebore* zine, Anathema Publishing's *Pillars: Seeds of Ares,* and the Holland Files International *Swamp Thing* zine, *Cold Signal Magazine, Fantomes* zine, and *Pillars: A Wayfarer's Hearth* (Anathema). He is on Instagram as @dagger_of_the_mind and Twitter as @DaggerMind, where he shares his book collection, as well as his taste for funeral doom, drone, and dungeon synth.

Agwam Kessington (he/him) is a budding writer and poet whose works are forthcoming in *Mermaid Monthly, Celestite Poetry, Revolutionary Review, Cicada Lament, Paredolia Literary*, and elsewhere. His twitter handle is @TheAgwam.

Alina Măciucă lives and dreams in downtown Bucharest, Romania. Her work has been published in *Space&Time* Magazine and *The Sirens Call eZine*. In her spare time, she is most likely immersed in a book or video game. If not, she can be found roaming the streets and gazing at the beautifully decaying buildings in her hometown, which she sometimes captures in highly imperfect photos.

Romana Lockwood is a lady, and ladies do not reveal their age. Her many incarnations have included nurse in a devastating war, typist, war correspondent, television news anchor, housewife, waitress, and columnist. Her column "In My Eyes," which ran from 19__ to 20__ was, in the eyes of many, a serious contender for the Pulitzer Prize, or at the very least the Horace Greeley or the Breindel awards. Her first marriage was to Ernest James Hayden, a shoe salesman, who passed in 19__ from a failure of the heart, the variety that physicians refer to as "massive." Of her second marriage she does not speak. She rejects in toto the Abrahamic religions. She takes daily walks, her coffee black, her cats calico, and her tea sweet.

Erik McHatton's passion for horror literature began in grade school and can be credited to an early fascination with the "Terrific Triples" horror collections of Helen Hoke. He began writing fiction seriously in 2019 and has since been published several times in print and online publications. He hopes to follow in the footsteps of authors like Ligotti, CAS, Bloch,

Jackson, Barker, and Cushing. He lives in Kentucky with his beautiful wife and kids, along with dear friends and family.

Scott McNee is a PhD and tutor at the University of Strathclyde. His short fiction and poetry have been published in *Tether's End, Kalopsia, Gutter, Quotidian* and *The Grind.*

T.M. Morgan has been published in *Vastarien, Lamplight, Penumbric,* and *Mythaxis*, and in the anthology *Tales From Omnipark*. He has upcoming work in *Pseudopod, Sley House, The Wicked Library,* an *Apokrapha* (*Lamplight*) radio play, and in the anthology *Vinyl Cuts*. He is the editor of DreadImaginings.com. You can read more about him at thetmmorgan.wordpress.com.

Michelle Muenzler's poetry is in magazines such as *Liminality, Polu Texni,* and *Dreams & Nightmares.*

Shawn Phelps made his first fiction sale to S.T Joshi, and his short story, "Quiet," appeared in *Penumbra* in August 2022. He has an MA in Anthropology from The University of Chicago. After leading three expeditions to remote areas of the Amazon, Phelps was elected to The Explorer's Club. He currently works as an outreach RN in Vancouver's Downtown Eastside neighborhood.

Marisca Pichette is a queer creator of monsters and magic. Her work has appeared and is forthcoming *in Strange Horizons, Fireside Magazine, Fusion Fragment, Apparition Lit, Uncharted Magazine, Grimdark Magazine, PseudoPod*, and *PodCastle*, among others. She lives in Western Massachusetts, surrounded by bones and whispering trees.

Anzhelina Polonskaya was born in Malakhovka, a small town near Moscow. Since 1998, she has been a member of the Moscow Union of Writers and in 2003, Polonskaya became a member of the Russian PEN-centre. In 2004 an English version of her book, entitled *A Voice*, appeared in the acclaimed "Writings from an Unbound Europe" series at Northwestern University Press. This book was shortlisted for the 2005 Corneliu M Popescu Prize for European Poetry in Translation. Between 2006 and the present

Polonskaya has had the opportunity to participate in a number of prestigious writing residencies, including those of the Cove Park Scottish Arts Council, the Hawthornden International Retreat for Writers, the MacDowell Colony, the Rockefeller Foundation Bellagio Center, and the Villa Sträuli in Zurich. Polonskaya has published translations in many of the leading world poetry journals, including *The American Poetry Review, AGNI, Ploughshares* and *The Kenyon Review*. In October 2011 the "Oratorio-Requiem" Kursk, whose libretto consists of ten of Polonskaya's poems had its acclaimed debut at the Melbourne Arts Festival. In 2013 the bilingual edition Paul Klee's Boat was published by Zephyr Press and shortlisted for the 2014 US PEN Award for Poetry in Translation. Zephyr Press published a second collection of Polonskaya's work entitled *To the Ashes* in 2019. Her work has also been translated into German, Dutch, Slovenian, Latvian, and Spanish.

Steve Rasnic Tem's short fiction has been compared to the work of Franz Kafka, Dino Buzzati, Ray Bradbury, and Raymond Carver, but to quote Joe R. Lansdale: "Steve Rasnic Tem is a school of writing unto himself." His 200 plus published pieces have garnered him a British Fantasy Award, a World Fantasy Award, and a nomination for the Bram Stoker Awards.

David Rees-Thomas is originally from Wales, and now live in Japan. He has previously published in *Shimmer* magazine and has assisted as a first reader for *F&SF*, and, currently, *Nightmare Magazine*.

Dyani Sabin is a queer, female of speculative fiction, poetry, and science journalism. She has a Master's in science journalism from New York University and an MFA in Popular Fiction from the University of Southern Maine's Stonecoast Program. Her work has been published in *Strange Horizons*, as well as *National Geographic, The Washington Post, and Popular Science.*

Matt Sadowski studied creative writing at Columbia College Chicago and currently works as a writer and editor for a newspaper in Beijing.

Thijs van Ebbenhorst Tengbergen has sold artwork to *Daily Science Fiction*, Nightland website, *Plasma Frequency Magazine, Future fire, Postscripts* *to Darkness, James Ward Kirk Fiction, IFWG publishing, SQ magazine, Albedo one, Pulp literature magazine, Top publishing, Perihelion sf, Deep Magic, Factor Four, Write ahead, Amazing stories*, and the *Spatterlight* e-books of Jack Vance.

Brian Thummler is an old man who does as he pleases, but mostly found crawling through the wooded ravines of western Pennsylvania looking for the hideous and the gruesome.

LC von Hessen is a writer of horror, weird fiction, and various unpleasantness, as well as a noise musician, multidisciplinary artist/performer, and former Morbid Anatomy Museum docent. Their work has appeared in such publications as *The Book of Queer Saints, Your Body is Not Your Body, Stories of the Eye, It Was All a Dream: An Anthology of Bad Horror Tropes Done Right*, multiple volumes of *Nightscript* and *Vastarien*, and the short ebook collection *Spiritus Ex Machina*. An ex-Midwesterner, von Hessen lives in Brooklyn with a talkative orange cat.

Sarah Walker is a teacher, artist, and writer living in the Pacific Northwest. Her work and art have been published by *Lovecraft Ezine, Test Patterns*, Silent Motorist Media, Planet X Publishing, *Antimony and Old Lace*, Shoggoth.net, *Audient Void*, Oxygenman Books, and more. She has stories appearing in the upcoming tribute to Joseph Pulver, *Nightmare in Yellow*, and in *Vastarien* as well as by other publishers soon to be announced. She has also assisted editing, writing, and illustrating the anthology of Folk Horror titled *A Walk in a Darker Wood* with veteran writers Gordon White and Duane Pesice. She is at work getting her first novella published.

Shaoni C. White's poetry and short fiction has appeared or is forthcoming from *PodCastle, Uncanny Magazine*, and *Fantasy Magazine*.

Charles Wilkinson's publications include *The Pain Tree and Other Stories* (London Magazine Editions, 2000). His stories have appeared in *Best Short Stories 1990* (Heinemann), *Best English Short Stories 2* (W.W. Norton, USA), *Best British Short Stories 2015* (Salt), *Confingo, London Magazine* and in genre magazines/ anthologies such as *Black Static, The Dark Lane Anthology, Supernatural Tales, Theaker's Quarterly Fiction, Phantom Drift* (USA), *Bourbon*

Penn (USA), *Shadows & Tall Trees* (Canada), *Nightscript* (USA) and *Best Weird Fiction 2015* (Undertow Books, Canada). His anthologies of strange tales and weird fiction, *A Twist in the Eye* (2016), *Splendid in Ash* (2018) and *Mills of Silence* (2021) appeared from Egaeus Press. A full-length collection of his poetry came out from Eyewear in 2019, and Eibonvale Press published his chapbook of weird stories, *The January Estate*, in 2020. He lives in Wales. More information can be found at his website charleswilkinson-author.com.

Sara Wilson is a graduate of Vancouver Island University, with a BA majoring in Creative Writing. My poetry has appeared in various publications in print and online including in *Dinosaur Porn, The Dalhousie Review, CV2, Nod, Existere, Qwerty, Ottawa Arts Review*, and *Event*. Wilson is a Red Seal Sheet Metal Journeyman, a terrible birdwatcher, and, while once a novice cellist, has recently embraced the ukulele to appease her inner bard.

Aaron Worth is an Associate Professor of Rhetoric at Boston University who has previously edited *The Great God Pan and Other Horror Stories* (2019) by Arthur Machen and *Green Tea and Other Weird Tales* (2020) by Sheridan Le Fanu for Oxford World's Classics. His own horror fiction has appeared in publications including *Cemetery Dance Magazine* and *Vastarien*.

GRIMSCRIBE PRESS

www.ingramcontent.com/pod-product-compliance
Lightning Source LLC
LaVergne TN
LVHW011948060526
838201LV00061B/4255
9798218109561